HOPE AND DREAD IN MONTANA LITERATURE

Western Literature Series

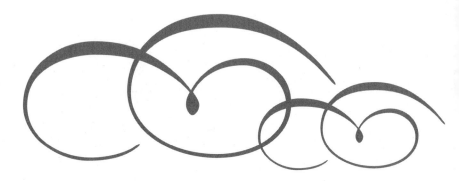

Hope and Dread in

UNIVERSITY OF NEVADA PR

Montana Literature

KEN EGAN JR.

RENO & LAS VEGAS

Western Literature Series

University of Nevada Press, Reno, Nevada 89557 USA
Copyright © 2003 by University of Nevada Press
All rights reserved
Manufactured in the United States of America
Design by Kaelin Chappell

Library of Congress Cataloging-in-Publication Data
Egan, Ken, 1956–
Hope and dread in Montana literature / Ken Egan, Jr.
p. cm. — (Western literature series)
Includes bibliographical references and index.
ISBN 0-87417-508-9 (alk. paper)
1. American literature—Montana—History and criticism.
2. Frontier and pioneer life in literature.
3. Montana—Intellectual life. 4. Montana—In literature.
I. Title. II. Series.
PS283.M9E37 2003
810.9'9786—dc21
2002011992

First Printing
12 11 10 09 08 07 06 05 04 03
5 4 3 2 1

Portions of this book have previously appeared in *Fifty Years
after The Big Sky: New Perspectives on the Fiction and Films of
A. B. Guthrie Jr.*, ed. William E. Farr and William W. Bevis
(Helena: Montana Historical Society Press, 2001), 9–19, and
Western Futures: Perspectives on the Humanities at the Millennium,
ed. Stephen Tchudi (Reno: Nevada Humanities
Committee, 2000), 17–30. I thank the editors of both
volumes for granting permission to reprint those materials.

For Tess and Ken Egan Sr.

and

Millie and Mark Dutton Jr.,
who taught us to love the place

*For all its aura of beginnings, the
American West is haunted by endings.
The West throughout the nation's history
has offered the gleaming dawn of a new
national day, yet it also holds the sunset
glow of terminus, and elegiac reflections
upon endings in western life are
inseparable from mythic visions of
progress to come. . . . [O]ur nagging
knowledge of the shrinking wilderness,
the dwindling buffalo, the played-out
mine, the vanished Indian, the last
gunfighter, and the closed frontier itself
without question tempers our vision
of western promise. That knowledge,
however, is not necessarily bad. To the
mythic West at large it supplies a healthy
realism to counter our naive yearning for
the freedom that the West traditionally
offers, and sparks a dialectic that can,
at last, transcend the frontier's closing and
lead to a comprehensive vision embracing
the nation, the region, and the people.*

—FRED ERISMAN,
"Coming of Age in Montana"

Contents

Acknowledgments

WRITING A BOOK IS NECESSARILY A COMMUNAL ACTIVITY, NOT ONLY because composing presumes an ultimate reader but because all writers need thoughtful, caring respondents to improve the prose. I have been unusually fortunate in my reviewers of this project.

Bruce Wendt, western historian, high school teacher extraordinaire, and enthusiastic supporter of academic enterprises, deserves first and deepest thanks. He encouraged this project from the start and literally went to great lengths on road trips to help me work out key ideas. He is true West. Danell Jones, talented writer and editor, was the first reader of the manuscript and helped me refine voice and political themes. Tim Lehman brought a gifted historian's eye to the text and asked me to reconsider discussions of Native American and politically engaged writers. Bernard Rose, approaching the manuscript as "an intelligent lay reader," raised vital questions about the overall argument and my use of personal anecdotes. David Strong first recognized the germ of a book in an article on A. B. Guthrie Jr.; Jay Cassel steered me clear of interpretive shoals early in the drafting process. I also thank Susan DeCamp for offering helpful leads on extremist movements in the West.

O. Alan Weltzien, showing extraordinary generosity in reading the manuscript over a Christmas break, provided astute, detailed comments. I thank him particularly for helping me foreground the dialectic between hope and dread as a theme in the book. Richard W. Etulain was crucial to the evolution of this project. He read the manuscript twice, thoroughly, urging me to polish phrasing, interpretation, and logical consistency. He improved this book in ways too many to count. James H. Maguire challenged me to reconsider my claims from the ground up, a process that resulted (I hope) in a sharper, more consistent, more credible analysis. Gerry Anders brought a meticulous eye and ear to the task of copyediting the manuscript.

Trudy McMurrin, acquisitions editor at the University of Nevada Press, took this project under her wing and saw it through to acceptance with enthusiasm, humor, and professionalism. Her assistant, Monica Miceli, was unfailingly good-natured and efficient in dealing with the unavoidable mechanics of bringing a manuscript to publication. The staff in Central Operations at my former institution, Rocky Mountain College, was vital to this project as well. Leon Bruner and his assistants cheerfully took care of the reproduction, mailing, and tracking of manuscripts.

This book emerged from deeply personal sources, and so finally I must turn to my family when tallying thanks. I extend love and appreciation to my wife, Terry, and my sons, Devin and Brian, for their patience, curiosity, and teasing humor during the long evolution of the project. I have dedicated this book to my parents and parents-in-law because they showed me, through words and actions, what matters most in the course of living.

Introduction

DURING THE SPRING OF 1996, MONTANA SEEMED ON THE VERGE OF apocalypse. On an isolated ranch in the state's north-central plains, self-described "Freemen" proclaimed themselves citizens of "Justus Township," an independent, utopian homestead. Images of Waco circulated in the popular media and in the minds of those living in the society the extremists had rejected. Fire and destruction seemed imminent, inevitable. Daily reports from "the compound" hinted at weapons stored, violence planned, martyrdom looming. It became a kind of deathwatch, made all the more surreal by national reporters' attempts to provide "local color" about a region they could neither like nor begin to understand. What made the standoff even more latent with tragedy was the event of exactly one year before, the bombing in Oklahoma City. It was as though some terrible earthquake had sent shockwaves through the western United States, and the aftershocks were surging on the high plains.

Montanans could hardly avoid the implications of the bombing in Oklahoma, since that event had brought to the surface an apparently home-grown manifestation of conspiracy theorizing and threatened violence: the Militia of Montana. Led by the voluble, strangely personable John Trochmann, the Militia had gained national notoriety on its own terms, even getting a full spread in *The New Yorker.* Preaching the need to return to Constitutional purity and local governance, the Militia promised to lead Americans back to their patriotic roots, complete with local militias that would circumvent the corrupt National Guard and the forces of one-world government. Barely concealed behind these patriotic cries in the dark was a politics of hate advocating the necessary segregation of the races. Even more disturbing, the amiable Trochmann hinted at a looming apocalypse, a dire end time, that would result in the triumph or defeat of the white patriots. His publications (and now Web page) urged acquiring the skills and equipment for surviving a terrible cataclysm, a battle to the end for the soul of the nation, of the world.

As if locals had not suffered enough revelatory shocks, on April 3, 1996, Theodore Kaczynski, every American's vision of the madman of the mountains, was arrested in Lincoln, a true mountain community that seemed at a far remove from either Justus Township or the Militia headquarters in northwestern Montana. The madness had now blanketed the state, confirming the nation's worst fears about the effects of isolation and exposure to the natural elements in the remote West. It made sense, it seemed, that the Unabomber would be discovered in this parodic land of the brave and home of the free. Preaching the need to destroy a decadent, dehumanizing, ecologically destructive technological culture, Kaczynski urged that we assault the monster by any means necessary, including violence. In a discourse ranging from the sublime to the ridiculous, he suggested that only retreat to a Walden-like simplicity could save us from our worst rationalist selves.

Not only had the strangeness covered the state geographically, but it had also demonstrated striking ideological patterns. In all three events, troubled citizens espoused a sense of the end time approaching, a cataclysm on the horizon. All three agents of virtue demanded the turn from a corrupt, overregulated, outsized, materialistic national culture toward a localized utopian enclave, a space apart, a community (or cabin) of saints. And all three explicitly or implicitly advocated violence as the necessary means to that end. In fact, since all three voices prophesied apocalypse now, all three urged preparation for a time of tribulation, a time of trial by literal fire, a time of necessary conflict between the light and the dark, the virtuous and the evil, the white and the black. As such, these movements correspond to a pattern of rural radicalism analyzed with skill and bite by Catherine McNicol Stock: "Far from centers of political and economic power, engaged in the difficult labors of agriculture and extractive industry, increasingly unable to participate in aspects of American culture available to city dwellers, rural Americans have often turned to collective protest to make themselves heard. And because they have also shared a culture of hardship, self-defense, and intolerance, that protest has more often than not manifested itself through acts or threats of violence."[1]

Montanans have been eager to distance themselves from this madness, rightly insisting that many of the extremists come from outside the state and bear little or no relationship to its culture and history. Yet things are not quite that simple. While it would be unfair to assert that the extremists represent all citizens, there are distinctive habits of the heart that inform both the fringes and the center of Montana culture. The sense of lacerating manipulation by outside forces, quest for a world apart, and attraction to violence as a solution are elements of our collective soul. Rather than easily dismissing these militant individuals as entirely other, we might consider the recent eruption of extremism an opportunity to examine these tendencies of the regional character. We might, in other words, treat the madmen as distant mirrors of inclinations within the region's psyches, its communities. This study offers an analysis of those embedded inclinations, using literature of the place to gain insight into forces of fear and expectation, dread and hope that have circulated since Montana's founding as a territory.

Events contemporary and historical hint at sources of unease in the region. In 1989, Montana, Wyoming, Idaho, and Washington celebrated the hundredth anniversary of statehood, a jubilee that produced a sobering, even depressing sense of failure. National publications highlighted the isolation, backwardness, and poverty of the high plains and northern Rockies: "for the ranchers, farmers, miners and millworkers of this Centennial West, the commemoration is pocked by scarcity and stillborn dreams. The region most emblematic of the nation's grandeur and strength is, today, the region most exploited and ignored."[2] This skepticism was fueled in part by the work of Frank and Deborah Popper, scholars at Rutgers University who advocated returning the Great Plains to a "buffalo commons" in light of the evident failure of settlement in this region. Ironically, the end of the cold war fed into a sense of paranoia already inspired by these home-grown critiques. Unable to break the psychosis of fear in which

most of us were immersed for nearly fifty years, many westerners res-
urrected and reinforced their earlier distrust of impersonal, oppressive, "evil" empires such as the United Nations, the Trilateral Commission, and the federal government itself. The debacle of Ruby
Ridge, in this very region, further stoked the fires of fear by demonstrating federal power brought with full force against a contemporary
"homesteader." Finally, the approach of the millennium, replete with
a sense of end time, of passing from one epoch to the next, of entering
into some decisive moment of change, added fuel to the fire.[3]

History lends some credence to Montanans' fears of marginality,
insignificance, and domination. After an era of tentative contact
between fur trappers and Native Americans, gold mining became the
spur for territorial identity, exploding in 1862 with finds in south-
central Montana. At that moment, armed conflict between whites and
Indians became inevitable; at that moment, the history of depredation
toward native peoples and places accelerated. A series of Indian Wars
followed, eventually resulting in the creation of seven reservations in
what was soon to be the state of Montana. With the apparent removal
of natives from the range (only apparent, as we will see in part I) and
with the mindless slaughter of the buffalo, that range became the
available site for the cowboy legend. The era of the open range that
lasted so briefly—little more than a decade—would become in many
ways the defining story of the high plains, displacing more substantive,
more representative stories.

The devastating winter of 1886–87 demonstrated the impractical-
ity of allowing cattle to range over an open terrain without sufficient
feed. Ranchers scaled back their dreams of a cattle El Dorado, and
settlers increasingly turned toward homesteading and extractive
industries such as silver and copper mining. Trails were plowed under
and swept away by farmers and massive mining operations. These
activities dominated early-twentieth-century Montana economics and
politics, resulting in sometimes-radical labor movements, boom-and-
bust cycles, industry-dominated newspapers, and increasing pressure
on the ecology. The Great Depression only exacerbated these trends,
though large infusions of federal cash softened the blow to the economy. Post–World War II Montana has resembled much of the West in

its increasing participation in a global economy, cultivation of tourism, and interest in education and high-tech industries. Montana citizens have also carried on a love-hate affair with the federal government, by turns accepting largesse such as highway and urban renewal funds and attacking attempts to raise grazing fees on Bureau of Land Management land. The installation of ballistic missiles on the plains has intensified a sense of living in the eye of a hurricane, a gathering storm of violence.[4]

This Montana chronicle shows the remarkable brevity of that history, a concision with profound consequences for our sense of ourselves. Such a young culture necessarily has fresh memories; it is impossible to repress or evade a past so pressing, so present. This is quite literally true of Montanans living today. I brag that I am a third-generation Montanan, since I can trace my roots back to 1913, the year my grandmother arrived as a homesteader in the northeastern part of the state. My wife and I have attended high school and college, raised our children, and worked most of our adult lives here. And though our careers have called us away, Montana remains home. While this personal connection hardly grants me an aboriginal pride of place, it reminds me that my family has witnessed most of this state's existence. That means the history of political strife, economic struggle, and environmental degradation resides in the collective memory of my relatives.

All this suggests that history is alive, is real, is realized in this place, and that the complex, often tragic events live with us. That's why we cannot so simply laugh at the Freemen, the Militia of Montana, and the Unabomber. Our short chronicle tells us that the intense dreaming, sense of failure, violence, racism, pride, struggle for control of place, ambiguous relationship with the federal government, and sense of impending doom are woven into our political unconscious. Rather than simply dismiss our fringe elements, we should try to make sense of our relationship with them, and then, in a necessary act of cultural maturity, consider alternative ways of responding to our crises.

But we must begin by recognizing that the extremists present our fears in caricature, exaggerating our worst tendencies to the point of parody. Militants inhabit a melodramatic conception of the world that simplifies the past and forecloses serious options for overcoming difficulties. In the apocalyptic imaginings of the Militia, for instance, the federal government equates with Satan, converting a human institution into a metaphysical nightmare. In such a Manichean vision, citizens are left with two options: submission or armed rebellion. Montana literature has presented a far more complex, far more open-ended sense of our dilemmas. Alternating between tragedy and comedy, creating a dialectic between dread and hope, writing of the region allows us to examine our worst fears and most promising prospects. Acknowledging the difficult history of the state, Montana writing provides context and nuance for the citizen.

Part I of this book presents a prehistory for Montana literature. "Worlds Transformed" shows how a collection of fantastic dreams necessarily inspired their antithesis, catastrophic dread. Reading the Montana past through the eyes of traders, cowboys, female settlers, and especially American Indians, we see how diverse peoples carried their vivid fantasies of economic, religious, and cultural success to these tough places, only to see those visions thwarted. With astonishing quickness, the hope becomes the dread, the dream the nightmare, the belief the despair. But those same stories often carry the germ of another narrative possibility. Side by side with tales of woe move tales of endurance and even recovery. Thus, writing from the state is dialectical to the core, representing competing responses to common concerns that hint at a vital, sustaining synthesis.

Part II demonstrates the tragic tradition in Montana culture. The dread of earlier writers transmuted into the stuff of much of our best literature, informing the texts of A. B. Guthrie Jr., D'Arcy McNickle, Richard Hugo, and others. Because of the lingering fantasy of paradise lost, because of persisting economic struggles and political immaturity, because of cold-war militarism, Montanans continue to clutch close to their ideological hearts the mantra of despair. The result has been a series of western tragedies. Tragedy portrays the lone, yearning self confronting the forces of destruction. Aristotle famously claimed that the form evokes both pity and terror—both empathy and horror—in the reader. Since modern tragedy typically focuses on an everyman rather than a great man, our responses veer toward sympathy rather than sublimity or awe. Willy Loman's demise in *Death of a Salesman* tallies the cost of seeking happiness within "the American dream." The character's restless pursuit of pleasure and recognition leads to suicide. The audience experiences a sickness of the soul rather than a sublime ecstasy. The tragic characters of our time tend to represent us as victims of fate, of oppressive forces beyond our control. Aristotle invoked the term *catastrophe* to name the final outcome, the terrible climax to the protagonist's tortured story. At the risk of courting redundancy, I will often use the phrase *catastrophic tragedy* in this study. This term should remind the reader of the inevitable climax of tragedy, and also link these dire plots to a more pervasive cultural tradition of waiting for the fall, for the moment of deepest hurt, for the vision of personal or communal cataclysm. In the face of catastrophe, we typically throw up our arms in despair and supplication.[5]

As the introduction to Part II makes plain, tragedy has become the default mode for an age riven by violence and displacement. Montana writers have transplanted the form in the West, showing how yearning characters are time and again struck down by specific agents of ill in the region. These tragedies perform a crucial cultural function by summoning visions of anxiety and dread in the face of personal and collective failure. Hugo's engaging poems, for instance, demonstrate the Medusa-like effect of cultural memory on our visions of ourselves.

These catastrophic tragedies, however, exist in vital dialectic with an alternative tradition of pragmatic comedy. Given the hard weather, geographic isolation, and economic underdevelopment, Montanans have had to find provisional solutions to their immediate difficulties. Visitors to the region often comment on the apparent stoicism of the locals. At first glance the outsider might assume a lack of intelligence, an insular stupidity, if you will. Probe the surface, however, and you often find shrewd, clever, funny, mildly ironic, but rarely cynical folks. By turns stubborn and welcoming, these dwellers on the plains and inhabitants of the mountains can disarm with their charm and frustrate with their determined convictions. These character traits have evolved as a necessary adaptation to external conditions. The very circumstances that have encouraged dread and distrust have also nurtured the traits we admire most in citizens of Montana. We discover as much by paying close attention to many of the state's significant recent writers, including James Welch, Mary Clearman Blew, William Kittredge, and especially Ivan Doig. Openly asserting the need for "new stories," rejecting the glamorous allure of what Doig has called "Wisterns," peeling back the layers of memory to uncover the exemplary conduct of locals, these writers provide a vocabulary for action, a language for choosing to dwell rather than mindlessly rebel.

Part III, then, focuses on writings that dramatize tough, resilient, provisional hope in the region. We can counterbalance Montana tragedies with pragmatic comedies. Though we typically use *comic* to suggest humor or ease, the term has a much more complex meaning. Think here of classic texts such as Shakespeare's *Twelfth Night* or Jane Austen's *Pride and Prejudice* or more recent narratives such as Willa Cather's *My Ántonia* or Toni Morrison's *Song of Solomon*. Comedy tells the story of how an alienated self is reintegrated into society, finding a place, a purpose for being. Such a tale begins in pain, doubt, and confusion, and leads toward salve, hope, and order. If tragedy shows us humanity stripped of dignity and control, comedy reveals a protagonist who grows in stature and knowledge. But that growth is always offset by a lingering modesty, a perspective on one's limitations, one's follies. An element of the tragic always hovers in the margins of a comic tale. This narrative form thus demonstrates humility and perspective, a knowledge that solutions are often provisional and incomplete. We seek answers but do not expect their easy arrival.[6] By modifying *comedy* with *pragmatic*, I mean to suggest that comic stories in Montana engage the concrete dilemmas of making a go here, such as struggles over native rights, land use, and economic development.

Catastrophic tragedies and pragmatic comedies should be seen as dialectical depictions of Montana's struggles. They stimulate contrasting but complementary reader responses: dread and hope. We need a balance of awe and anticipation, passivity and activity to achieve aesthetic, psychological, and political synthesis. If catastrophic tragedies fully disclose the potential harm we might suffer, pragmatic comedies represent the actions we might take against our sea of misfortunes. Giving undue weight to either element of our cultural history could distort and even destabilize us. Full allegiance to the tragic mode could inspire a self-pitying conspiracy mentality related to our fringe elements; all-out commitment to the comic mode could encourage an inflated sense of our power and possibilities. An unbalanced commitment to either mode, then, could return us to the melodramatic sensibility of the extremists, either under- or overstating our capacity for insight and change. Above all, the synthesis of tragedy and comedy allows us a rounded, fully human response to the real issues that confront Montanans in particular and westerners in general.

What lessons can we draw from these sophisticated tragedies and comedies? In contrast to the self-pity of our extremists, we experience endurance, a hanging on, a tough hope. In contrast to a self-indulgent paranoid politics, we observe a strong sense of the concrete history of this place, including both human depredation and dwelling. In contrast to violent melodrama, we witness thinking-through, dialogue, and provisional solutions. These complex stories are not for the faint of heart, but they can sustain us emotionally, spiritually, and politically long after the extremists' naive accounts have merged into the background noise of contemporary anxiety.

HOPE AND DREAD
IN MONTANA LITERATURE

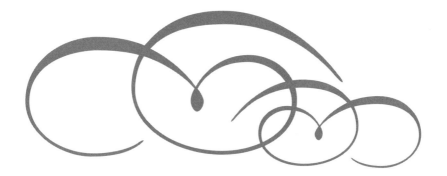

PART I

Worlds Transformed
1862-1940

The foolish In-who-lise and Squaw Kid,
instead of keeping their eyes and ears open,
kept on dreaming and like all sweet
dreams that are too good to be true,
theirs had a cruel and rude awakening.

—ANDREW GARCIA,
Tough Trip through Paradise

THE FIRST EIGHTY YEARS OF MONTANA'S OFFICIAL EXISTENCE witnessed a series of disappointments, most profoundly the defeat of tribal cultures, the closing of the open range, and the failure of the homesteading boom. Montana writers registered these calamities in autobiographies and fictions that enunciate the trauma of failed dreams. Above all, writers record the blending of dread and hope, terror and success, in their texts. "Teddy Blue" Abbott, for instance, writes the most heartfelt elegy for the cowboy way, showing in graphic detail how his kind were displaced by farmers and fences. Yet Abbott also demonstrates remarkable adaptability, turning from pure elegy to an almost uplifting account of how he came to terms with the new order, married the daughter of Granville Stuart (charismatic rancher and vigilante), took up ranching and farming, and lived to a respectable old age. Even Native American taletellers uncover possibility in the nightmare of buffalo extermination, forced life on the reservation, and boarding-school displacements. Perhaps the very act of sharing the stories marks survival in the face of virtual apocalypse.

As we trace the origins of Montana identity, then, we must of necessity listen to storytelling traditions in dialogue. Undergirding these diverse voices, though, are harsh truths of changes to the land. Butte will forever provide the paradigm of exploitation because it embodies the exuberance, excesses, and exhaustion of a mining boom. If you stop by for a visit, it's a surprisingly sober, even "classical," town. The elegant nineteenth-century downtown, the enduring Victorian mansions, the glimpses of mountain glory to the south, all reflect a town long past its prime, and probably just as glad of it. But, of course, there is also the forbidding open pit, now filling with poisonous water, remnant of the final phase of extracting copper from the place. Those landmarks also hint at the turmoil that created this now apparently stable place. That story has often been told and does not require extensive retelling here. Suffice it to say that first silver, then copper were discovered in "the richest hill on earth," three powerful men competed for financial control of that wealth, miners poured into the city and created one of the most colorful communities ever in the American West, a smelter at nearby Anaconda denuded the hills of their trees and infected the water system with arsenic and other chemicals. When Anaconda Copper Company gave up its Montana holdings in the early 1980s, Butte truly seemed on the verge of total collapse, like that silver mill Hugo describes so powerfully in "Degrees of Gray in Philipsburg." Yet the community has demonstrated the power of the "New West" paradigm, bringing in high-tech industries and taking advantage of tourism and history to sustain a living wage.

In short, Butte provides the ultimate example of processes that striate Montana history: beginning with that dream of El Dorado, advancing to a state of entropy and collapse, and recovering with surprising gusto.[1] Many other, far quieter stories of the same stripe have recurred on the plains and in the mountains of the state. Ranchers, homesteaders, and, above all, Native Americans can tell related tales. No more poignant account has been provided than that by the tribes that resided in and competed for Montana land: the Blackfeet, Crow, Assiniboine, Sioux, Gros Ventre, Cheyenne, Shoshone, Salish, Kalispel, Kootenai, and Metis. They too had their dreams and dreads, and have had to come to terms with the loss of their vision of paradise. But surely by now we can move beyond that Rousseauan image of the noble savage living in an ideal state of nature. By now we can admit that life for the aboriginal peoples was by turns tough and rewarding. William E. Farr has put it best in his account of Blackfeet medicine bundles: "To face their uncertain and hostile world of endemic intertribal wars, of constant danger, of incomprehensible sickness and misery, the Blackfeet cried out for pity, pleading for help and supernatural intervention."[2] There's no point in reverting to some fantasy of a high plains paradise. Instead, "Montana" Indians ran the gamut of human emotions as they tried to defend, then hold on to, their way of life.

Chapter 1

VANISHING AMERICANS

CHARLIE RUSSELL SAID OF THE INDIANS, "THEY'VE BEEN LIVING in heaven for a thousand years, and we took it way from 'em for forty dollars a month."[1] There is not much doubt about the second half of that assertion, but it is difficult to credit the first. As contemporary Montanans struggle with a localized legacy of conquest, we often revert to this way of figuring things.[2] And since Russell is our official artist and storyteller, there's no gainsaying his reading of the event. But that claim does a disservice to Indians and whites alike by over-stating what was lost and understating what might still be gained. If Pretty-shield is to be believed, her Crow people lived in a state of pro-visional grace but were hardly free from accident, folly, and the terror of encountering their traditional enemies. If we grant the human complexity of the native experience, we can overcome a desire to romanticize their past, a move that often disarms us for future action. After all, if we have lost heaven, how can we possibly move forward to make a better life? It is precisely this mawkish treatment of various "losers" in western history that leads to our current crises of faith.

There is no better place to begin to piece together the imperialist process in Montana than with "Yellowstone Kelly," fabled hunter, trapper, and scout, a mediocre writer but an observant participant in the transformation of the place. His grave provides one of the landmarks in my hometown of Billings, so he is very much present in his absence in the region. Kelly's memoirs trace the changes from 1867 to 1880. He's a curiously nonideological writer, or at least reveals no explicit ideology. His comments on Indians, for example, range from the comical to the admiring to the empirical to the demeaning. Perhaps his editor deleted the heavy-handed pro-American sentiments, or perhaps Kelly left it up to Nelson Miles, famed Indian fighter, to do the hard lifting in his tendentious foreword to Kelly's book: "The nomadic Indians in time had to give place to the home-builders, who developed the vast treasures of agricultural and mineral wealth that have made our republic prosperous and great."[3] In any case, Kelly expresses neither an intense civilizing impulse nor a strongly utopian desire for roaming eastern Montana. His motivation was far simpler, and intensely American: he just wanted to keep moving. A young man who entered the Civil War as it came to a close, he typified the nineteenth-century American male, bound by codes of masculinity that emphasized physical courage, chivalry toward women, and a refusal to be fenced in.[4] Whatever the admirable aspects of these traits, they also mark a thoughtless pursuit of the right stuff that left destruction in the self's wake.

When Kelly reached the confluence of the Missouri and the Yellowstone in the late 1860s, he came upon a land remarkably pristine despite the history of fur trapping, gold mining, and territorial formation. Over and over again he bears witness to the vast herds of buffalo, abundant antelope, teeming deer and elk, aggressive wolves, and peevish bears. He enters into cycles of hunting and rest seemingly indigenous to the place, noting ideal sites for killing buffalo, for lodging, and for keeping company with whites and Indians. He cannot resist narrating in detail his various hunts and the means by which he gutted and skinned his kills. Though he avoids the overheated rhetoric of Russell, the place must have seemed paradise to the American male in his early twenties in the 1860s.

But Kelly also marks the subtle and intensifying interactions among whites and Indians in this contested space. He traces the important trade centering on furs of all types, including those of wolves and buffalo. He takes us from isolated fort to isolated fort, showing how tribes carried on complex commercial transactions with the white encroachers while playing politics to gain protection from dreaded enemy tribes. It's important to remember (especially as we look ahead to James Welch's *Fools Crow*) that Indians avidly participated in these initial exchanges of goods and services. Hardly foolish innocents, purely powerless and acted upon, the natives more than held their own in economic and military terms on the high plains of the West.

The young American demonstrates these cross-cultural exchanges best when describing his many personal negotiations with Indians of various tribes. By turns comical and frightening, these encounters reveal the humanity and inscrutability of Indians for even an experienced frontiersman such as Kelly. He tells of tobacco offered, pipes shared, food and lodging proffered, hunting trips jointly pursued. He comments on the genteel manners of Crow warriors, the hospitality of Blackfeet, the mourning of Cheyenne women upon being separated from their people. He returns often to his encounters with Sioux war parties, leading on occasion to violence, and on more occasions to cautious negotiation and careful partings. We have to credit Kelly here: he does not overstate his command of Indian languages, or lapse often into the formulaic anti-Indian rhetoric of savagery, or indulge the Cooperian clichés about noble savages. He seems genuinely interested in recording the events as best he can remember them, downplaying the heroic or the dehumanizing. But there's no mistaking that finally, ultimately, these native peoples are precivilized and Other for the memoirist.

Perhaps that is why Kelly, for all his expressed fondness for the wonder world of territorial Montana, could not resist participating in

that world's undoing. Most famously, he served—in the year following the Custer defeat—as Miles's chief scout, helping to rout the
Sioux, Cheyenne, and Nez Perce in a series of conflicts he renders
with violent realism. Since he is a reticent storyteller, it is difficult to
know, in depth, his motives for serving in this capacity. We might
speculate that his frequent conflicts with the Sioux made him a willing participant in their displacement. Or perhaps he was flattered by
Miles's regard. Or perhaps, as with his other actions, he was simply
indulging a young man's desire to be up and doing. Or perhaps we
cannot overestimate American pride in the aftermath of the Civil War,
a desire to extend and solidify the nation.

Kelly participated in the transformation of the place in a still more
comprehensive sense. We witness his aiding a supply train serving the
gold-mining region of south-central and southwestern Montana; we
watch as he helps a steamboat captain trying to navigate his way up
the Yellowstone River; we observe his work as a wolfer, methodically
poisoning with strychnine what he himself describes as beautiful
creatures. In this sense especially, in his pursuit of a quick, convenient
economic payoff, Kelly represents many who journeyed here: "On
the third morning Jean Erwin and I made the round of our baits and
piled up many wolves. At the place where I had had an attentive audience while cutting up the body of the cow, we found twenty-two large
wolves around the bait, though some had got several hundred yards
away before succumbing to the effects of the powerful poison. From
the wolfer's point of view they were beauties" (130). Still later in his
recounting of his frontier days, Kelly focuses on what was typically
referred to as the civilizing function of the scout, evoking images of
emerging farms and settled communities: "The great blank spaces on
the map of this extensive region had now been filled with trails and
wagon routes; hunters, stockmen, and prospective settlers roamed at
will looking for locations" (240).

At a few points in his narrative, Kelly bemoans the loss of the pristine Montana he had first encountered as a young man: "The beautiful land is still there, but it is now fenced in and the romance and the
wild life are gone forever" (147). Casting our eyes back, we can see
such moments as the ultimate western irony: Americans often dam-

age the places they remember with awe, even love. Who else could Kelly blame than himself for the lost romance and wild life? Who, after all, aggressively helped the U.S. military force native peoples onto reservations? Who helped navigate the rivers, map the terrain, and trap out the wildlife? But I do not believe for a moment that Kelly is being sly or disingenuous when he mourns the world he lost. Just blind—terribly and completely blind. That is, after all, the nature of tragedy.

Enter Andrew Garcia to continue the story. It is difficult to imagine two more dissimilar storytellers than Kelly and Garcia. If the former is reserved, graphically specific, and rarely comic, Garcia is Montana's ultimate clown or jester, the raconteur with a bite. *Tough Trip through Paradise* provides a western picaresque, with Garcia the twenty-three-year-old "Squaw Kid" as the starring picaro. For all its textual oddity, *Tough Trip* manages to capture the carnival quality of territorial Montana while registering with unusual frankness the price paid for change by all parties involved. Garcia's role as rogue and roustabout served him perfectly as the means for witnessing horse thieves, buffalo hunters, trappers, Crows, Piegans, Nez Perce, and even, occasionally, solid citizens trying to homestead on this neutral territory. Garcia casts himself as the passive naif, neither good nor bad, drifting in and out of relationships with this assorted cast of characters.

Readers are often led to wonder how much Garcia embellished his account, especially in his hilarious dialogue between the Squaw Kid and various native females contending for his favors.[5] He narrates these adventures in a voice that combines frontier lingo, Mark Twain, 1920s jazz speak, antiwestern satire, and hellfire-and-brimstone preaching. Garcia's narrative embodies in particular two strands of Montana writing: a deflating, satirical, realistic voice that repeatedly undercuts highfalutin' legends of the West; and an almost prophetic vision of a world destroyed, in part through the writer's own transgressions. In a telling moment early in the narrative, Garcia describes how his father had stopped him on the streets of El Paso to say he'd rather see his son dead than turn out bad. The terror of that moment lingers over the memoir as Garcia uncomfortably weighs his own guilt and innocence in the bizarre and ultimately tragic proceedings.

Garcia picks up the story of Montana's transformation in 1878, following the major events transcribed in Kelly's more sober book. Having helped the military himself as herder and packer, Garcia decides to strike out on his own as a businessman: he purchases the goods needed to make a killing as beaver trapper and tradesman on the Musselshell River in central Montana (a key location for many of Kelly's adventures, including the wolfing episode). At least three realities immediately strike the reader about this vocational choice: there are still enough wild animals in Montana in 1878 to make trapping a paying proposition; the Indians, supposedly tamed in the clashes of the previous year, are still active, wandering almost at will to pursue buffalo or fights with other tribes; and Garcia is the biggest fool imaginable to take up with Beaver Tom, as demonstrated in this hilarious episode:

> When I was riding into the camp they had moved three or four miles up on the Big Timber to a nice secluded spot and, while still some distance away, I could hear a carnival going on in our camp. . . . With all kinds of ki-yi's they encouraged the senior member of the Beaver Tom Trapping and Trading Company, Tom, who was now branching out and was drunk as a fiddler's bitch. He had a young Crow squaw of magnificent girth and beauty. . . . This Amazonian prairie Juno went under the poetical and soul-stirring nom de plume of Leather Belly. . . . Both of them were trying to dance together some kind of a grizzly-bear tango.[6]

Garcia's wildly playful language perfectly mirrors the chaos of the scene. As it turns out, Beaver Tom and the narrator have taken up with a gang of horse thieves who lubricate their Indian trade with whiskey. Garcia has just come upon the result of those transactions: a free-for-all cross-cultural party. This moment typifies the first half of *Tough Trip*, which recounts a series of comic encounters with Native Americans, particularly women, on the still-wild frontier of the northern plains. As the narrator wryly remarks at one point, perhaps with an obscene pun in mind, "Some squaw killer you are, little boy; you are surely wasting your time as a trapper and one-hoss trader. It's a missionary you ought to be" (140–41).

Garcia occupies an intermediate position in the difficult race relations on the Montana frontier. He comments often on his Spanish Catholic upbringing on the Rio Grande, suggesting his own otherness in relationship to many of the white journeymen who surround him. His ne'er-do-well partner Beaver Tom refers to him as a "damn half-breed, American greaser" (91). Garcia even suggests that his dark skin establishes a rapport with those "copper-colored Junos." This in-between status allows Garcia both an inside and an outside view of what's occurring on the high plains during this transitional period. No doubt the fact that he wrote as an aging man, casting a backward glance, contributed to this double vision as well. Surely remarking upon his own behavior in his early years in Montana, Garcia observes that "[m]ost of the trappers and hunters took along very little, if any, grub with them as they killed what they ate. Most of them were as destructive and wasteful as a pair of cougars and did not think anything of shooting a fine big elk or buffalo just to take enough for a meal and leave the rest to spoil" (55). Garcia also "confesses" to his role in the Indian Wars, especially during the Nez Perce travail: "I knew better than to tell [In-who-lise] I was at the Bear Paws the day Chief Joseph had surrendered. I had been with them when they went as prisoners to Fort Keough and had helped to drive their large band of horses along with them. . . . I had seen her people driven on flatboats in the cold like cattle to be floated down the Yellowstone" (127). Having just met the Nez Perce woman who will become his wife, Garcia conceals his role in helping defeat her people. That concealment has at least a triple significance: the writer is of course ashamed, but he is also manipulative and, to a degree, not entirely embarrassed by his work for the military. After all, he expresses fondness toward the soldiers he has worked with, and he continues to refer to Indians of various tribes as thieves, liars, and murderers. After White Grass, a Blackfeet chief, narrates his own raids on Hispanic settlements in Texas, Garcia remarks, "As I sat by the fire with this bunch of cutthroats, I could not help but think what my people would think if they could only see me sitting there as one of this savage band. . . . Every one of them either had a father or brother, or perhaps a mother or sister, who was butchered by the merciless red hands I was with. It was no wonder that they thought a good Injun was a dead one" (167). In such moments Garcia stands very close to Yellowstone Kelly, the scout for Miles who also narrated the American victory at the Bears Paw Mountains.

In other ways, however, Garcia's first encounter with In-who-lise marks the narrator's major turn, his almost complete reversal of perspective. As Garcia draws closer to the Nez Perce woman, as she tells her story from the native point of view, and as the couple journeys back over the ground of retreat that blended victory and defeat, the Squaw Kid becomes increasingly bound up in the Indian perspective. *Tough Trip* revises the white telling of events on the Montana frontier not only with broad humor and cultural confusion, but by moving closer to the actual of the Indian battles that raged in the '60s and '70s. That is why Garcia's visit to the Big Hole Valley provides one of the emotional climaxes of the memoir: "This ghastly display of Indian dead made me doubtful for the first time in my life if there is a Jesus or a God. And to make matters worse, my wife, since the time when we came to this cursed place, has been crying and calling to her dead sister's spirit in Nez Perce Injun" (276). The second half of the narrative, and especially the final section, take on a dark cast, almost Gothic in atmosphere and meaning. Garcia emphasizes the rapport between his Catholic upbringing and the spiritual beliefs of the Native Americans. He sincerely believes that he has been accosted by the evil spirits lingering over the Big Hole battlefield.

In a sense we might think of these ghostly visitations as the return of the repressed, the vengeance of those who have been defeated in a vicious betrayal by the white settlers in the Bitterroot Valley. As Rosemary Jackson has observed, fantasy often projects the unsaid and unseen of culture, revealing the violent subtext (or political unconscious) of a society.[7] If the winners always write the history, the losers must rely upon the haunting ghosts of suppression and treachery to carry their message. In a fantastic encounter with a grizzly bear, a form of evil spirit for the narrator, Garcia comes face-to-face with his own sins of defeating and exiling the Nez Perce people. In a book with surprisingly intense metaphysical dread, this passage through the Big Hole reads like a judgment upon the usurpation of Montana by greedy interlopers.

But since Garcia is a complex, in-between figure, he by no means comes to a simple resolution of the moral dilemmas faced by whites and Indians in this shape-shifting terrain. Just as the reader seems to regain equilibrium following this dreadful episode, Garcia once again reverses perspective by telling of aboriginal atrocities toward miners. In one sense, the episode of renegade violence toward the gold-seekers reinforces the aura of paradise usurped, of native ground put to an obtrusive, even destructive, use by American emigrants. *Tough Trip* supplies one of the most graphic, revealing descriptions of the placer miner at work, and through quiet understatement suggests just how intrusive the gold rush must have been for the place and the peoples:

> I could now see up and down this gulch the worked-over bars of wash or tailings, and knew that this was a placer mining camp. Both men stood to one side at a spring of clear water, one of them was washing a pan of dirt, as the other stood looking on waiting to see the prospect the other got. They had a full head of water running through ground sluice and string of sluice boxes. There was a line of galvanized hydraulic pipe that came from a penstock on a small ridge higher up than their diggins and across the cut and diggins from me. (313–14)

The young Garcia responds with anger, even hatred, toward these invaders, in part because of In-who-lise's suffering, in part because of the maltreatment of these ideal hunting grounds. He even goes so far as to rush at the two unsuspecting miners, convincing them that a real Injun threatens their lives.

But just when we think all the ideological weight of the episode falls on the native side, Garcia realizes that he misses the company of whites (his wife refuses to speak English with him, though she is able to do so), and he even feels a kind of comic pity for the miners who are frightened witless by his appearance. More than that, Garcia narrates in grim detail the slaughter of several miners by Indians who have broken loose from the Nez Perce retreat and are returning to Idaho to reoccupy home ground. In the lengthy (even tedious) description of one native's calculated play with his white victims, Garcia accentuates the stereotypically cunning, cruel side of the Indian character. Even more poignantly, the narrative recounts the senseless death of In-who-lise at the hands of Blackfeet raiders, a death made only more terrible by the realization that Garcia's wife had been rendered completely, utterly homeless by the Nez Perce defeat. The native woman had crossed over into a kind of tribeless state, wandering with her husband toward the buffalo grounds east of the Continental Divide, with few hostile intentions toward other tribes.

Tough Trip through Paradise often brings to mind what Patricia Limerick has playfully called her "jerk rule": in every culture, at least 10 percent of the population will qualify as jerks. We see plenty of skulduggery, trickery, and savagery on the Montana territorial frontier, qualities limited to no single race. "Breeds," Spanish Americans, Mexicans, white Americans, and Native Americans all take turns playing the jerk. Despite his at times overbearing religious overtones, Garcia does not seem to arrive at any single major meaning for this chaos. He appears to remain the picaro to the end, the Squaw Kid without a clue, the cipher who cannot decipher the events sweeping him up like a tornado. In part because of this perhaps calculated innocence, Garcia manages to evoke the terrible price paid by peoples and place in the contest for control of the space called "Montana." Since he does not impose an obvious moral on the bizarre, disjointed events recorded in his account, Garcia comes across as ultimately credible, even revelatory, despite the apparent tall-tale qualities of the book made out of his jumbled manuscript.

But what did this time of change, of exhausted hope, of played-out options look like from the native perspective? As a middle-class, white academic, composing in an air-conditioned study in the Yellowstone River Valley that was once crisscrossed by various tribes as they followed migrating buffalo herds, I am in the peculiar position of attempting to assess the experience of peoples who suffered worlds ending. As Two Leggings, the Crow warrior and pipeholder, tells it, "Spring season finally came and camp moved toward Elk River near the mouth of Arrow Creek, stopping just east of the present Billings

Fairgrounds and on top of the rimrocks. The Elk River Valley was below us and in those days seemed covered with buffalo."[8] Hovering over any analysis of Indian tellings of this terrible time must be the massacre at Wounded Knee, the symbolic and virtual end of native dreams of resurgence, rebirth, reclamation. The Ghost Dance movement marked yet another millennial moment in western history, an instant of deep belief in the possibility of end time, redemption, and paradise regained. But like many western American dreams of paradise found, the Ghost Dance episode resulted in cataclysm, the collapse of the hope, the death of the believers, the massacre of innocents: "a people's dream . . . died in bloody snow."[9] There's nothing academic about that atrocity. I also must rely upon secondhand retellings of native experiences, translated, expurgated, certainly in some cases reorganized. Yet these events are so central to the cultural memory of this place, so essential to western self-understanding, so profoundly connected to the legacy of pain in the region, that I would ignore the Indian experience at the peril of accuracy and decency.

Black Elk offers the most memorable catastrophic telling of the Plains Indians' betrayal. His collaborative effort with John G. Neihardt discloses the piety, the orderliness, and the "worldhood" of native cultures. In an inspired commentary, Kenneth Lincoln observes that "Black Elk envisions a world of interconnected, renewing life forms in overlapping images, from grandfathers who turn into horses that turn into elk, buffalo, and eagle." Put even more strongly, "Black Elk's vision . . . places the tribe within all the ecological beauty, continuity, and organic order alive in the earth household."[10] The reader is struck by the medicine man's sincere connection to a sacred order that erupts time and again into his seemingly pedestrian life. As he matures, these intense visions emerge at any given moment, revealing dangerous enemies or needed game. While Black Elk often refers to the "queerness" of his much-loved cousin Crazy Horse, uncanniness hovers over the taleteller's experiences as well. It is this convincing, poetic spirituality, blended with the crude violence of frontier warfare, that sets this testimony apart from other native texts available to the contemporary reader. And there's no mistaking that violence: in recounting his part in the Battle of the Little Bighorn, Black Elk describes beginning to scalp a dying soldier with a dull knife, only to be forced to finish him off with a pistol when the still-living soldier grinds his teeth.

Black Elk would remind us that he and his people were fighting for a land and a way of life they had been promised in perpetuity. He would emphasize that the Wasichu (whites) attacked their native ground, not vice versa. He would say along with Crazy Horse that he only wanted to be left alone. And since Neihardt presents Black Elk's astonishing dream vision at the beginning of the story, the reader realizes that the white invasion is an assault on the very order of things, the heart of beauty and truth, as well as on a people tied to the place through hunting, making war, dwelling, and worshiping. After Crazy Horse's murder on the reservation, it is difficult to know where the story can go. Didn't the world of the Oglala Sioux effectively end at that moment? Yet the book is only half completed, and there is far more that Black Elk wishes to share. His people do not have the Crow option of seeking favors from the invaders they had helped. Quite the contrary, the Sioux are recognized as among the most recalcitrant, violent resisters to the expansion of the United States.

And in fact, Black Elk's story becomes the essential apocalyptic tale, the paradigm of woe. The Sioux youth attempts various remedies for the catastrophe of the chief's death and the people's incarceration: living with Sitting Bull in "Grandmother's Land" (Canada); enacting rituals based on his great vision; serving as a healer for his people; playing a part in Buffalo Bill's Wild West show in order to gain knowledge about the Wasichu ways; and most hauntingly, participating in the Ghost Dance ceremony, then witnessing the massacre at Wounded Knee. Coursing through all these futile attempts is the vision itself, reminding Black Elk of his duty to a divine order. The Ghost Dance especially renews the teller's hopes for his starving people (starving because the federal government had failed to deliver on its promise of rations): "Because of my vision and the power they knew I had, I was asked to lead the dance next morning. We all stood in a straight line, facing the west, and I prayed: 'Father, Great Spirit, behold me! The nation that I have is in despair. The new earth you promised you have shown me. Let my nation also behold it'" (207).

The dream of a new earth seemed so real, so realizable. Black Elk believed that his people (and all Indian people) would leave the dire black road, the path of darkness and confusion and pain, and walk again the glorious red road of life. The buffalo would come again, the Wasichu would disappear, the sacred tree of life would revive. Yet the story must end with the grotesque, savage murders of women, children, and warriors at Wounded Knee. The visionary is left to lament, "A people's dream died there. It was a beautiful dream" (230).

To turn from Sioux to Crow memoirs is to experience the gap between those who firmly resisted and those who attempted to accommodate the invading Americans. Since several important Crow narratives have come down to us through the work of Frank Linderman and others, these stories provide an especially informative entrée into Indian culture of the region. Of the Crow memoirs available to us, none is so affecting in its concreteness and clarity as Pretty-shield's humorous, humane, and ultimately elegiac recounting of her tribal life. Time and again the reader is startled by intimate details of the Plains Indians' experience: a young girl's ball made of the skin of a buffalo heart; the uses of bitterroot in Crow culinary practices; wild rides on foolish horses caught up in buffalo stampedes; friends senselessly killed by horses or bears; the chickadee's changeable number of tongues; and marriage and birthing rituals. Pretty-shield's marvelous stories of human dealings with spirits—especially the stories of Red-woman and the Little People[11]—demonstrate a vital religious as well as physical connection to the environment. In Linderman's seemingly heavy-handed presentation of these memories, the gap between past happiness and present decadence could not be greater. Pretty-shield often returns to the aimlessness, formlessness, and anomie of her grandchildren's lives. By contrast, the dedicated grandmother can say she lived through happy times before the elimination of the buffalo and the closing in of a grim reservation existence.

Pretty-shield evokes a devout sense of place, of belonging, of dwelling. There is nothing sham or romantic about her relationship to the mountains, valleys, and plains of "Crow country." She is essentially at home in this world. That belonging is marked by the details of daily existence listed above, by her relating of Crow history, by her

connection with various "People" or spirits, especially her own medicine, the ant-people. That sense of place is also revealed by her fondness for moving, for taking down the village and relocating in the
mountains or plains or nearer the buffalo. Through her narrative the
reader can grasp the appeal of the wide-open plains for the soul that
loves to cross terrain, to inhabit a novel space, to see new vistas. (In
this sense, Pretty-shield has much in common with Kelly and Garcia.)
It was in part this liberty of movement, of change, of revisiting familiar and cherished locations that Plains Indians surrendered when they
took up reservation life. This relationship with a knowable but varie-
gated place allows her a sureness of identity, an emplacement in
sacred time and space, that eludes her grandchildren. It is precisely
that possibility of dwelling that calls to us as we come to terms with a
tradition of disappointment, even failure.

Fitting with the theme of realism that courses through this study,
however, Pretty-shield resists converting her youth into a romantic
idyll. If she can claim happiness for her childhood, she cannot assert
painlessness or steady pleasure or stability. She comments on war's
effects in a way that undermines a simplistic treatment of Indian battles as somehow morally superior to modern mechanized conflicts:

> We women did not like war, and yet we could not help it, because
> our men loved war. Always there was some man missing, and
> always some woman was having to go and live with her relatives,
> because women are not hunters. And then there were the orphans
> that war made. They had to be cared for by somebody. You see
> that when we women lost our men we lost our own, and our chil-
> dren's, living. I am glad that war has gone forever. It was no
> good—*no good!* (168–69)

This disdain is only made the more compelling by specific instances
of wounded and dying Crows. In a startling example, Pretty-shield
describes the final moments of a warrior wounded in the lung: "When
he smoked, taking four deep draughts, I saw the tobacco smoke come
out of the hole in his breast. Then he laid down, drew the end of the
robe over his face, and went away forever. He was a good, brave man.
We mourned for him" (207).

Yet Two Leggings and Plenty-coups make it plain that warfare was the very reason for being for Indian males. Commentators on reservation life often noted that the end of manhood as defined through warfare and horse stealing proved catastrophic to Indian cultures. Two Leggings's startlingly vivid descriptions of conflicts with the Piegan, Sioux, and Salish show how central honor realized through counting coup and defeating enemies must have been. Once again I am struck by the graphic violence, the intense physicality of the narration. Killings are awkward, protracted, and intentionally humiliating. Two Leggings often stops to scalp an enemy while that warrior is in his death throes. The narrator himself often verges on death, though he reiterates that dying is inevitable for all natural beings and so he will take the crossing-over when it comes.

But Two Leggings also adds a surprisingly comic twist to many of these incidents, demonstrating that famous Indian humor, mainly at his own expense. Wittingly or not, these stories carry an unexpected antiheroic tenor. Repeatedly we see mistakes, missteps, and miscalculations by the Crow warriors. It is as though the Crow remembrancer is determined to undermine any naive sense that Indians were somehow innately superior beings in the Cooper mode. As we shall see shortly, in this sense Two Leggings's humor is of a piece with his deep piety, his belief that he lives within a sacred order that demands obedience and humility. The examples of humor taken at the narrator's expense are many. He falls off a crumbling bank as he prepares to attack an enemy; an enraged buffalo bull, having hooked his belt, all but drowns him in its fury; he loses his horse in the middle of a terrified buffalo herd and is forced to hoof it home; a raiding party gets caught in a snowstorm unprepared. Best of all, the narrator's adult name results from his desperate measures during that terrible winter storm:

> I was only wearing a torn pair of buckskin leggings and as we started out my legs grew numb. I took the red blanket from around my shoulders and cut it into leggings. The buffalo hide we had brought was frozen stiff and I cut off its long hair. Pulling the extra leggings over my old pair I tied them at the ankles and stuffed hair in between. . . . When [Bushy Head] called me Lots

> Of Leggings the others laughed, telling me to eat or I would have
> only extra leggings for my meal. (118)

These mishaps mark an immature, ambitious, energetic, even rebellious character who must, over and over again, receive his comeup-
pance.

And that observation leads to a crucial distinction between the restless masculinities of Kelly and Two Leggings. The American hunter,
trapper, and scout strikes the reader as a youth on the make, adrift,
seeking the next adventure, operating outside any clear value structure or norms. He is every bit the nineteenth-century American male
produced by an expanding, industrializing, aggressive capitalist culture. Two Leggings, by contrast, undergoes a complex initiation into
the mores of his culture, learning over time to tame his anarchic personal drives, to conform to the demands of sacred vision and practice.
The Crow warrior's story is very much a bildungsroman, a novel of
development and education, a narrative with an overriding purpose
and end. In contrast to the picaresque qualities of Garcia's tale, this
narrative (surely shaped by the editorial work of William Wildschut
and Peter Nabokov) shows how the orphaned male, desperate to
achieve a name, a status in the culture, sets about realizing his dream
in the wrong way: selfishly participating in, and even leading, raiding
parties without the sanction of the tribe's elders. While these raids
often net scalps, they also result in near death, starvation, and humiliation for Two Leggings. The narrator makes it clear that he has not
achieved the necessary medicine, the needed supernatural assistance,
to succeed in any meaningful way. While he often attempts to realize a
vision through fasting and self-mutilation, the clear, powerful sacred
contact will not come.

Yet despite these repeated half successes, Two Leggings in his
restlessness and ambition continues to pursue honor through selfish
violence. It is only when his best friend dies in a superficially effective
attack that the Crow teller realizes, painfully and personally, the errors
of his ways: "My dream had come true, but our homecoming was sad.
Crooked Arm's dream had also come true. Young Mountain's death
was a great sorrow for me. I could not be content with our success and

made up my mind to take revenge" (126). Two Leggings learns that he must align personal ambition with the sacred order as defined by the Great Above Person and articulated through the insights of the great medicine men: "And it happened as Sees The Living Bull said. The events he foretold always came true. He had given me his medicine and now he gave me his dreams and visions which brought me many victories as the summers and winters passed" (166). Yet Two Leggings continues to struggle with his duty to the tribe, indulging in personal rivalry with the head of another warrior society, effectively humiliating that rival in front of his family. Humility comes hard to the ambitious orphan, and time and again, it seems, he must be reminded of the limits imposed by honor, decency, and duty. The narrator realizes his error (while still gloating over his subsequent superiority to the warrior), claiming "[a]fter that I decided to obey our tribal rules" (176).

Those read like the words of an aging man looking back on his splendid youth, and they are in part that. But they are also the words of a more profound elegy, an elegy for the very order of living and believing that the warrior has shared through his personal growing-up tale. Two Leggings's story moves toward a painful (though not unexpected) anticlimax: "Nothing happened after that. We just lived. There were no more war parties, no capturing of horses from the Piegans and the Sioux, no buffalo to hunt. There is nothing more to tell" (197). The final "chapters" of the narrative are half formulated, incomplete, almost stammering in their delivery. When Two Leggings turns to the Crow "collaboration" with the invading Americans, he seems to lose his way, his confidence. He asserts that the Crows helped the invading nation only because they wanted to be left alone, yet his pointed anecdotes of victories over various enemies suggest otherwise. When he announces the white betrayal—the taking of large tracts of Crow land and the devastation of the buffalo herds—the storyteller cannot bring himself to scrutinize his own participation in this debacle. It is as though the Crows have been unwitting participants in their own undoing, yet the very narrative suggests otherwise. After all, Two Leggings served as scout for the military seeking to defeat the Sioux and Cheyenne after the Battle of the Little Bighorn. Perhaps in his desire to preserve what he had strived so mightily to achieve, Two Leggings betrayed the land and spirits that nurtured him. He cannot return to the connection, the relationship with the place he had so thoroughly loved:

> Shortly after our close escape, camp moved to the Arrowhead Mountains, stopping near Hits With The Arrows. Grass season had passed and leaf-falling season was nearly over. The mountains gave us wood and sheltered us from the cold eastern winds. There was plenty of game and we faced Arrow Creek, which gave us all the water we needed. Our camp site was so good that everyone was glad to hear we would stay for the snow season. (115)

Plenty-coups's famous autobiography is both more mundane and more apocalyptic than Two Leggings's. The two qualities are interrelated: because the Crow chief receives his powerful medicine dream so young (he is only nine years old), his life lacks the compelling drama of the lesser pipeholder's. Plenty-coups's various raids seem impressive but pro forma, the inevitable triumphs of a man predestined to succeed. His famous vision foreshadows the decimation of the buffalo and the transplantation of cattle to the high plains. It also determines Plenty-coups's future approach to the white invaders: accommodate them so as to preserve what he can of the Crow heartland. Here especially the reader senses the problem of translation, for one can't help wondering what, in his heart, the Crow storyteller made of his decision in light of white mistreatment of his tribe. After all, by the time Plenty-coups sat down to narrate his life experiences to Linderman, Crow lands had been steadily reduced by white settlers. Yet there's a curiously upbeat tone to the memoir, as though the chief (or transcriber) were putting the best possible spin on the Crow interaction with the Americans. That tone is taken to almost absurd lengths when Plenty-coups explains that he will set aside his homestead as a park because he admires George Washington (and Mount Vernon) so much. No wonder one of my Crow students referred to the famous chief as an "apple" (red on the outside, white on the inside).

But perhaps this assessment is altogether too harsh, given Plenty-coups's canny observations about white behavior both as soldiers and frontiersmen. The account of Crook's unnecessary defeat at the Battle

of the Rosebud eight days before Little Bighorn reveals an unpercep-
tive and unreceptive white commander who cannot recognize that he
has placed his troops in a compromised location. Perhaps the Crow
chief overplays his own prescience, but Plenty-coups makes it clear
that he and other "wolves" (native scouts) warned the general of
impending disaster. This account also not-so-subtly foreshadows the
catastrophic misplays by Custer in a nearby watershed. Even more
memorable is Plenty-coups's tale of pursuing stolen horses with four
whites who are ill equipped to pursue the Pecunie (Pikuni) thieves.
After narrating several of his successful raids on various enemies, rendered with only slightly less gore than in Two Leggings's narration, the
Crow chief makes plain the sheer incompetence or unsuitability of
these white men for high plains tracking and fighting. The narrative
thus slyly suggests how poorly adapted these settlers are to the region:
"with all his wonderful powers, the white man is not wise. He is smart,
but not wise, and fools only himself."[12]

And after all, Plenty-coups does describe the stupor, the sadness
that results from the reservation condition. As he bemoans late in his
autobiography, "Those were happy days. . . . Our bodies were strong
and our minds healthy because there was always something for both
to do. When the buffalo went away we became a changed people"
(252). We may be observing here that ultimate western irony from a
reverse angle: Plenty-coups cannot fully disclose (or realize) that his
charmed life has been hemmed in by history, the history of American
victory over tribal cultures. The chief had placed his bet on accom-
modation, and what did he have to show for it? His vision had foretold
the Four Winds of apocalypse sweeping away all peoples save those of
the Chickadee, Plenty-coups's own people. Perhaps that's why he
insists upon the comparison to Washington, and the heavy-handed
defense of Crow policy toward the white usurpers. To argue otherwise
would be to confront his own life's final defeat, and his possible complicity in his tribe's failure.

But then, couldn't we just as easily argue for the Crow warrior's
clever pragmatism, his willingness to sacrifice an overt moral victory for
a more difficult, seemingly dishonorable partial triumph? Plenty-coups
emphasizes at the end that he hopes the Bighorn and Pryor Mountains

will remain a place apart for his people, and this precise dream has been imperfectly realized. We cannot avoid the terrible misdeeds of white Americans on the northern plains during the latter stages of the nineteenth century, nor the continued neglect of Native Americans in contemporary political culture. As with all the tales of woe written upon this terrain, the story of Indian displacement, bordering on genocide, must be seen as a tragedy of our collective history, but one we must take stock of and somehow move beyond. Indigenous peoples' worlds were not entirely vaporized by the savagery of the American invasion of their native grounds. And so Indians must weigh the losses and gains of Plenty-coups's variety of compromise, his possible snatching of diluted hope out of absolute despair.

And that is the tenor of Mourning Dove's difficult, amusing, but telling novel *Cogewea, The Half-Blood* (1927). Despite the textual and editorial problems attending this novel, it moves the historical memory beyond horrific loss toward something like possibility.[13] Set in northwestern Montana on the Flathead Indian Reservation, *Cogewea* captures perfectly the liminal condition of the original American (as Mourning Dove often referred to native peoples). The half-breed of the title symbolizes the in-between position of the reservation Indians, drawn to the approval and sophistication of the whites but at the same time longing to preserve the old ways of their people. The conflicted love plot brings out these implications: Cogewea is simultaneously courted by two males, the pure white easterner Densmore and the half-breed westerner Jim. The white-educated female lead is almost inexplicably drawn to the forked-tongued Densmore, preferring his unexpected endorsement to Jim's earnest but familiar love. As Cogewea tells the westerner more than once, he is more like a brother than a lover to her.

If the narrative stopped here with an almost silly cowboy romance cut in the mold of such popular Westerns as *Riders of the Purple Sage*, we would pay little attention to one of the first novels published by an Indian woman. Instead, the narrative opens a space for the grandmother Stemteema to tell a series of stories, allegories of white betrayal of native peoples.[14] The reader learns of the first two vexed visits by whites to the Okanogan people and of an Okanogan woman's capture by Blackfeet after she flees her abusive white husband. The grandmother reminds Cogewea that her own white father had abandoned his family to pursue gold in Alaska. To intensify Densmore's links to the absconding father, the narrative informs us that the white interloper desires wealth through the half-breed cowgirl, returning us to the gold madness that led to such catastrophe for the Sioux. While the novel does not make fully credible Cogewea's attraction to the scheming white male, as a template of Indian-white misunderstanding and betrayal, the writer and her editor, Lucullus Virgil McWhorter, could hardly have done better. As if to underscore this political argument, the narrative devotes a chapter to courtship "on the old buffalo grounds." In a kind of submerged murmur, Cogewea describes how "the Four Riders of the Apocalypse passed through the valleys, over the plains and mountain ranges of our former possessions."[15] Yet in the same scene, the protagonist refers to this transformed place as "my Eden" (143). The novel represents the catastrophe of treaty negotiations and neglect in a melodramatic love triangle but will not settle for the cataclysmic denouement.

The half-breed woman, who often returns to the thought that she prefers her Indian heritage, makes the right choice in the end: used and put aside by the duplicitous white man, she turns toward the far more compatible Jim. At the same time, Cogewea's younger sister marries a distinguished Frenchman, Eugene LeFleur, who embodies ultimate European manners. The novel's ideological implications could not be plainer. They show that an independent, spirited, well-educated Indian woman can find happiness even in the murky environment of early-twentieth-century reservation culture. As Jim puts it upon at last winning Cogewea's hand, "'S'pose we remain together in that there corral you spoke of as bein' built 'round us by the Shoyah-pee?" (283). Though tempted by the white culture she had imbibed at Carlisle, a culture that had rewarded her as a "good" Indian woman, Cogewea remains true to her grandmother's teachings. She also remains true to her "Eden," rejecting the false allure of the East in favor of the openness and familiarity of the reservation lands. Her sister Mary's experience suggests that white/Indian marriages can work, but only when the male is willing to set aside his patriarchal, imperialist attitudes and enter into the spirit of the half-breed's world. That spirit includes humor as much as hard work, the playful give-and-take among equals that signals affection and humility. Louis Owens observes that the novel achieves "the illumination of the kind of teasing humor that permeates American Indian communities and is universally ignored in writing about Indians."[16] If humor often functions to disarm power and level social hierarchies, the novel's playfulness goes beyond levity toward something like a radical political gesture.

In sum, *Cogewea* demonstrates why Mourning Dove opened her autobiography with these words: "There are two things I am most grateful for in my life. The first is that I was born a descendant of the genuine Americans, the Indians; the second, that my birth happened in the year 1888. In that year the Indians of my tribe, the Colvile (Swhy-ayl-puh), were well into the cycle of history involving their readjustment in living conditions."[17] The novel reinforces the writer's commitment to her Indian heritage, while tracing the difficult negotiations with the modern and the alien. In the end, as Owens asserts, "the dilemma of the mixed blood poised between red and white worlds remains unsolved."[18] Surely the ending feels forced, even incredible, as Cogewea inherits a fortune from her unfaithful father. Yet native storytellers have come a long way from the devastation of Black Elk's memories (though, technically, Black Elk's story appeared in 1932, after *Cogewea* finally saw print). No doubt, as Mourning Dove herself suggests in her autobiography, generational change makes all the difference. Since she had no firsthand recollection of the hunting and gathering culture that sustained her elders, the aspiring Indian writer was not transfixed by a lost world. If nothing else, *Cogewea* argues that Indian peoples can stand firm, refuse further temptation, embrace the stories of the elders, and cherish their "Edens" wherever they may find them.

Cogewea reminds us as well that individual indigenous people have the difficult task of living after the aboriginal dream dies. During a conference dedicated to the Columbian Quincentenary, an event emphasizing the elegiac, tragic themes so painfully revealed in Black Elk's story, an American Indian colleague reminded me, "I'm still here." We often run the risk of lapsing into an emotional attachment to past woe, leaving us blind to the present realities. Gerard Baker, a man of native descent who served as director of the Little Bighorn Battlefield, once remarked on how few visitors to that famous historical site realize that many of his people still live in desperate poverty on reservations. But where can contemporaries turn for plausible solutions to the nightmare enunciated in the Sioux healer's narrative? It is important to hold on to the specificity, spirituality, and humor written into the accounts of Pretty-shield, Two Leggings, and Mourning Dove. Recovering their submerged traditions through community colleges and rituals, arguing for what is most precious in their places, resisting quick payoffs or short-term fixes, the tribes of the West might just endure and flourish in new ways. Certainly writers such as James Welch will suggest as much.

Chapter 2

DON'T FENCE ME IN

KELLY, GARCIA, BLACK ELK, PRETTY-SHIELD, TWO LEGGINGS, Plenty-coups, and Mourning Dove narrate western catastrophes from white, in-between, and native perspectives. Their memoirs provide multiple points of view on the remarkable, tragic changes to whole cultures in the diverse geographies of Montana during the transitional period between the first gold rush and the final resolution of reservation boundaries. They simultaneously describe alterations to the land and life forms, showing indirectly but surely the despoliation of the place by white invaders. Whether we think of Kelly's casual description of poisoning wolves or Garcia's detailed account of placer mining or the native tellers' disclosure of wholesale slaughter of the buffalo, we come to realize that nothing could really be the same for the various ecologies of Montana.

It is common to hear in Montana these days that ranchers now are what Indians once were. This is a shorthand way of saying that those who run livestock in the valleys and plains of the region participate in a self-contained, vital, but threatened subculture, one deserving respect and protection. On one level these notions seem insensitive to the plight of native peoples in the region: How could ranchers, typically members of the dominant culture and recipients of various government subsidies, compare their situation with that of Indians savagely suppressed, their cultures shocked and all but wiped out? But if we return briefly to the narratives already discussed, we can see a crossing over, a merging of cultural practices, on the part of both whites and Indians. Kelly demonstrates how members of various tribes participated in the sophisticated trading networks of the Missouri and Yellowstone River regions, acquiring guns, utensils, fabrics, and sometimes whiskey in exchange for pelts. Garcia shows how a marginalized member of the dominant culture can absorb characteristics of native peoples. And Cogewea is, after all, a cowgirl of real verve and talent, one who relishes her home on the range. One could argue for the influence of place upon individuals from whatever cultural group as those individuals adopt the necessary means for survival offered up by the natural and social structures inhabiting the region. Perhaps, after all, ranchers might demonstrate values and behaviors surprisingly reminiscent of native peoples: "we were just white Indians anyway," Teddy Blue Abbott claimed (16).

In any case, we have to wonder why ranchers would make such a claim about themselves. Surely the persistently volatile futures markets, cattle prices, capital expenditures, subsidy structures, and fees on federally owned land would compel anyone to dis-ease, even dread. We are also confronting another deep-seated belief structure or archetype in western society: the cowboy myth. There is no evading the stubborn appeal of this regional story for people living on the plains. As Jim Robbins points out in an acerbic assessment of the current crisis in ranching culture, "The cowboys aren't resigned to becoming ghostriders just yet. They represent a still-powerful political force on the national and state levels, and are fighting range cuts. This assault is not only a strike against cattle, but an attack on the whole cowboy myth, the image of cattlemen as rugged individualists who go one-on-one with the elements and make their own way in the world. No one believes more devoutly in the Cowboy Way than cattlemen. They hate being called welfare ranchers."[1] Ranchers would immediately point out that Robbins slights many admirable qualities in their way of life, including a commitment to community and the land they work. He is surely accurate, however, about the enduring appeal of legends emerging from the open-range era of cattle ranching in Montana. It is not altogether surprising, then, when a thoughtful writer such as Ivan Doig remarks that "you bet, I'm writing against the cowboy myth. The West was settled by a hell of a lot of people, different kinds of people—miners, homesteaders, schoolteachers, merchants, sheep ranchers, Chinese laundrymen—and the guy out herding cows was pretty minimal among them in most cases. So I find it bizarre that the cowboy is the emblematic Western figure that so much potboiling fiction has made him."[2]

Narratives by Abbott, Nannie Alderson, and B. M. Bower exist in an uneasy relationship with the Western as first popularized by Owen Wister in *The Virginian* (1902) and as encoded in the cultural unconscious by countless films and television programs. On the one hand, these writers consistently cut against the grain of cheap sentimentalization found in the popular form. Abbott especially relishes mocking the conventions of the romanticized cowboy. (In this regard, he holds a great deal in common with Garcia, who often pauses in his memoir to mock "eastern" accounts of home on the range.) On the other hand, no other writers have so precisely articulated the elegiac sense of a way of life passing as the open-range era came to an end. Abbott put it best and most simply: "the cowpuncher of the eighties . . . was in his glory. . . . In character [his] like never was or will be again" (7–8). The narratives we examine in the next several pages provided the pretext for the form that would circulate through *Stagecoach, High Noon, Bonanza,* and even, perversely, *Unforgiven.* The popular Western represents the region's history in near-epic terms, converting the cowboy into a knight of the plains, a figure of decency, courage, and chivalry. There is a utopian quality to these tales, a vision of paradise past, a sense that in the magical terrain of John Ford's films, men were men, good men who embodied the virtues of the nation. In our own time, apparently, we can only sense the gap between that glamorized fantasy and our present failings. And so the Western, for all its explicit hopefulness, supplies another source of unhappiness, of tragic sensibility in the region. No story has so movingly, even pitiably, communicated belief in a vanishing wonder world as the tale of the open-range cowboy.

Abbott provides the best place to begin to make sense of this devotion to cowboy life, for he memorably wrote, "I believe I would know an old cowboy in hell with his hide burnt off" (230). No book in all of Montana writing is more fun to read than *We Pointed Them North*. Blue consistently portrays himself as full of a kind of manic energy, expressing itself in practical jokes, songs, and frolics with willing women. It is easy to see what drew Abbott to Charlie Russell, another full-blown character blessed with an abundance of silliness and humor. A contemporary reader can readily imagine these fellows killing time during deadly dull winters or oppressively hot cattle drives with their tall tales and schemes. Blue also stresses the openness, the freedom, the sense of arriving in a "new" country (ironic since he also expresses deep sympathy for the Indians the cattle herds had displaced). The open-range cowboy life that flourished for little more than a decade continues to call to the aging rancher, reminding him of youth and happiness lost. In this sense, Blue can claim brotherhood with Indian remembrancers such as Plenty-coups: "But all those river towns except Fort Benton have practically disappeared today. There isn't any reason for them any more, now that the steamboats, and the buffalo, and the bull teams, and the army posts, and the Indians, too, are all a thing of the past" (122).

Still, for all their hilarity and nostalgia, Abbott's recollections often pierce the veil of mythology surrounding the open-range era. The storyteller frequently pauses to debunk popular legends of cowboy life, legends most clearly represented in Wister's novel and film Westerns. The reader cannot avoid the amount of sheer physical labor, the sleeplessness, the constant danger of thunderstorms and badger holes, the risk to life and limb posed by a runaway herd. Hand in hand with that hard work is the physical suffering. Blue's memoir describes a litany of injuries, at times bordering on the disabling. The aging cowboy makes it clear that he still suffers from the falls and injuries to his hands that claimed him during his youth in the 1870s and '80s. This attention to cowboys' ailments climaxes with the harrowing account of a young man's death by tuberculosis in a hotel room in Miles City: "I went back where he was, and he wanted to know if I would lay down beside him and let him rest his head on my shoulder. In a few minutes he mumbled something about Ethel, his sister I think, and then he was gone" (82). Along with the death of a beloved brother at an early age, this loss tempers Blue's frolicsome mood throughout the autobiography.

Abbott also exposes two features of the cowboy way that are still very much with us: racism and vigilantism. Here especially can we trace a clear genealogical line from the Montana past to the present militancy. Blue demonstrates the fusion of nostalgia for a lost life with implied distrust of "others" and a willingness to employ violence to protect one's way of life. While he has nothing but good to say about indigenous peoples, especially the Northern Cheyenne, the memoirist frequently refers to "niggers" in an unselfconscious way. Abbott often mentions that southerners dominated the Texas–Montana cattle drives, and those immigrants carried a combined hatred for "Abolitionists" and paternalism toward African Americans onto the Montana cattle range.

Vigilantism is one of the central themes of the book, no doubt because the storyteller feels compelled to defend the conduct of Granville Stuart, his father-in-law and most famous of Montana vigilantes. Blue argues that "frontier justice" had to prevail in an isolated place where decent people had no backing for their lawful stands. (Abbott heaps scorn on the military forces on the plains, hinting that these soldiers were of little or no use in contending with violence against settlers.) The narrative describes in detail the planning for hanging the rustlers during 1884. This is one of the few episodes when Blue lapses into an almost defensive tone; the reader senses that he's been challenged more than once about the conduct of the "Stuart Stranglers." If we doubt the importance of vigilantism in the settlement and mythology of the West, we need only recall Thomas J. Dimsdale's gory but fascinating *Vigilantes of Montana*, recounting the destruction of the Plummer gang in the goldfields during the 1860s. The historian Richard Maxwell Brown has shown that violence in general, and vigilante justice in particular, were defining features of the emerging West. If Blue seems to soft-sell the ferociousness of the Stuart gang, Brown seems almost clinically harsh in his assessment. Noting that Stuart could claim "over a hundred fatalities to his credit," Brown further asserts that "[b]y the time Stuart's Stranglers disbanded in 1884, the Montana-Dakota range country was conquered territory in the Western Civil War of Incorporation."[3] For this historian, the vigilante movement was more than the attempt to protect private property (horses and cattle). Instead, Stuart's actions were part of a larger attempt by powerful landholders to squeeze out troublesome renegades (hence the term *incorporation*).

But Brown traces other sources of western violence beyond the overtly economic. His summary of ideological causes suggests why violence remains a weapon of choice for contemporary antigovernment radicals: "the doctrine of no duty to retreat; the imperative of personal self-redress; the homestead ethic; the ethic of individual enterprise; the Code of the West; and the ideology of vigilantism."[4] And although Blue argues against the strong presence of gunplay in the Montana of his era, surely we can recognize a genetic link between these norms and those exerting a force in the western United States today. The homestead ethic seems especially relevant to our current traumas, for "[t]his grass-roots doctrine had three key beliefs: the right to have and to hold a family-size farm, the homestead; the right to enjoy a homestead unencumbered by a ruinous economic burden such as an onerous mortgage or oppressive taxes; and the right peacefully to occupy the homestead without fear of violence (such as that by Indians or outlaws) to person or property."[5] Living out an extreme version of the homestead ethic, contemporary antigovernment activists would see violence not just as an option but as a duty.

Of course, for much of *We Pointed Them North*, Abbott berates the homesteaders who huddled around water sources and blocked the herds moving through on their way to the rangelands. At times the book reads much like a nonfictional *Shane*, but told from the point of view of the Riker gang. Yet, in a surprising reversal (no one has ever accused him of ideological consistency), Abbott notes, "Cowboys as a rule were good to the settlers. I have been on both sides of the fence and know both sides, and they are both good if you are honest about it" (208). I take that as the example par excellence of the pragmatic spirit in Montana writing. Having devoted so much space to an amusing, even loving, recollection of his cowboy high jinks, Blue now turns to affirm his settled ways. This easy balancing act, praising both the herdsman and the farmer, obscures real conflicts over water and land, conflicts with tough real-world consequences. Yet Blue's willingness to adapt, his *choice* of hard work and steady acquisition of wealth, mark him as a resilient westerner who acts outside the bounds of fixed, destructive ideologies. Perhaps this is the legacy of the cowboy life that Abbott and later writers such as William Kittredge best embody, the tradition of attending to the here and now, the real, the immediate. Following cattle rumps for thousands of miles, in all kinds of conditions, will no doubt have that effect on you: you don't fall into the trap of easy philosophizing or abstract analysis!

In this sense, then, Blue's connection to the Freemen and Militia of Montana must seem tenuous at best. While the unconscious racism and stern defense of Stuart's tactics suggest otherwise, this refusal to fall into rigid political or cultural stances separates the cowpuncher from the current pack of dissenters. We could add Blue's strong antireligious attitudes. As he writes with obvious commitment, "Ninety per cent of them [cowpunchers] was infidels. The life they led had a lot to do with that. After you come in contact with nature, you get all that stuff knocked out of you—praying to God for aid, divine Providence, and so on—because it don't work. You could pray all you damn pleased, but it wouldn't get you water where there wasn't water. Talk about trusting in Providence, hell, if I'd trusted in Providence I'd have starved to death" (28–29). Blue later explains that he was saved as well by the love of a good woman (to invoke the relevant cliché), rather than by religious conviction itself.

But what did the cattle culture look like from the point of view of that silent partner? The scholar Julia Watson reminds us:

> Regarding that myth of masculinity as *the* voice of Montana auto-biography makes it difficult to hear the differing voices and values

that many women bring to writing their lives: an emphasis on family and domestic life, on the importance of small communities, on survival rather than conquest, on generational networks, and on pleasure in place. And it obscures the myth's underside, violent male enforcement enacted on women and indigenous peoples in the name of maintaining rugged individualism.[6]

Watson rightly provokes our thinking about certain moments in *We Pointed Them North* that suggest a classic patronizing attitude toward female partners: "Those Indian women made wonderful wives. The greatest attraction in a woman, to an Indian, was obedience" (149). A virtual contemporary of Abbott's, and twice mentioned in his memoirs, Nannie Alderson brings out the hard work, loneliness, and borderline madness attending the ranching life for women. Alderson composes in the autobiographical mode to narrate her dream's chance-ridden death. As she explains in a poignant aside (poignant because of both her nostalgia and her sense of gender difference), "Raising cattle never was like working on a farm. It was always uncertain and exciting—you had plenty of money or you were broke—and then, too, work on horseback, while dangerous and often very hard, wasn't drudgery. There was more freedom to it. Even we women felt that, though the freedom wasn't ours."[7]

But Alderson is far from bitter about her treatment by the cowboys who surrounded her. On the contrary, she speculates as to "whether the splendid comradely attitude of American men toward women did not originate in just such conditions as those of my early days in Montana" (76). She later asserts that "[h]alf the charm of the country for me was its broad-mindedness. I loved it from the first" (109). Alderson goes out of her way to praise cowboys for their true chivalry, resourcefulness, and courage. She is often amused and impressed by the culinary and domestic skills of these men of the range, abilities they demonstrate time and again by helping her out as a young ranch wife. She asserts that she would have failed miserably as a frontier woman if not for the kindness of strangers. Yet cowboys could also prove exasperating, and all too human. In one of the heartbreaking sequences in *A Bride Goes West*, Hal, an otherwise friendly and useful fellow, almost kills a Cheyenne on a bet that he could shoot the

Indian's hat without harming the man. The result is the burning down of the Aldersons' first (and most beloved) home, a consequence that seems to leave little impression on the thoughtless cowboy. Yet Hal is the exception that proves the rule. Walt Alderson, for instance, is the very model of modern rancher, kind, brave, and thoughtful. As recreated in this nostalgic casting back, Walt is both every bit the man and the loving husband and father.

For all her claims for the virtues of the ranch life in the late 1800s, however, Alderson is equally blunt about the incredible hard work and the sheer loneliness, especially after the children are born. Here in particular we get a glimpse of the gender differences that Watson would call to our attention. The solitude, the constant demand to keep up the place, and the lack of financial success wear down the originally resolute settler: "There was an old and rather brutal saying out west, to the effect that this was a great country for men and horses, but hell on women and cattle. Without going into the latter part of that statement, I should like to amend the first part. It was a great country for men and children" (221). Though this memorable paragraph precedes a charming account of her four children's fortunate lives, the opening epigram is suggestive, bordering on frank. After the Aldersons lose their first home to the fire and try to make a go of it on the more isolated Muddy Creek, Nannie becomes more and more worn down by childbirth, work, and crippling fear. Hers is an unusually blunt account of the dream's slow death. Her husband must be away to work roundup, care for the livestock, and tend to business; the country slowly changes as cowboys are replaced by hired help of variable quality. Women live at a far remove from each other, and so there is little chance for sympathy or advice.

Several years ago, the scholar William Bevis caused quite a furor when he suggested that Nannie Alderson may have suffered a nervous breakdown. So many readers seem invested in the legend of settlement, especially the myths of cattle kingdoms and the cowboy way, that this suggestion bordered on the sacrilegious. But really the madness question is a nonissue, since Alderson "confesses" at several points that the strain of her tough, economically marginal, dangerous life got to her. As she writes in a gently self-mocking tone, "Perhaps it was being alone so much that made things work on my imagination. Were other women on lonely ranches as foolish as I? I know that the worst ordeals I suffered were nearly all in my own head" (213). This is surely a sentiment one will not encounter in Teddy Blue Abbott's account of the ranching life. But in case we are tempted to see Nannie as aberrant, apart, strange, and even hapless, we might turn to one of the toughest of all settlement characters to witness a similar crisis. In *All But the Waltz,* Mary Clearman Blew reserves special praise for her grandmother Mary, a tough woman who managed to piece together a decent living through teaching after her husband's homestead failed. Yet at one point this stoical, no-nonsense, resilient woman lapsed into hallucinations every bit as vivid as Alderson's: "she began to see shapes on the other side of the spring, the shapes of women, beckoning to her. A few years later she told an aunt that they looked like the shapes of her dead mother and her dead sister. She decided she was losing her mind. . . . So she began to go for her water at noon, in the full sun. She never saw the shapes again."[8] Gwendolen Haste also evokes this drift into psychosis on the high plains in her terrifyingly understated poem "The Ranch in the Coulee." Having described the ranch wife's mounting loneliness and fear, the persona concludes: "The winter was the worst. When snow would fall / He found it hard to quiet her at all."[9]

In several senses, Alderson confirms Abbott's account of the ranching life, including the transition from open to fenced range. She also emphasizes the role of southerners in settling the high plains, the sense of freedom available to young cowboys, and a deep love for the place, especially the Tongue River Valley. Yet her relationship with Indians is far more troubled and confusing than Blue's romanticized approach. Alderson frequently returns to the Cheyenne chief Black Wolf, the partial cause of her home's razing. He visits the Aldersons on several occasions after the fire, as though all should be square between him and the white settlers. Nannie rightly asserts that she could only guess at his motives, his world view. She also mentions a series of misunderstandings between white settlers and reservation Indians, confusion that almost leads to widespread mayhem. Once again we are reminded that the period between the Indian Wars and the start of the twentieth century was a deeply unsettled time on the plains, far from the static order we seem to glimpse in history books. In this sense, Alderson's world is closer to Andrew Garcia's than to Abbott's. And to complicate this account of Indian-white relationships even further, Alderson particularly esteems Little Wolf, the great Cheyenne chief who befriends her husband and children. In a truly touching scene, the Indian chief weeps upon learning of her husband's untimely death.

And that death of course ends Nannie's original vision of "making a killing" on the Montana plains. Any final illusion of prosperity, or even realizing a decent living, is gone: "after my husband's death, I was no longer a bride who went west, nor a woman who was helping to open up a new country; I was merely an overworked mother of four, trying to make ends meet under conditions which were none too easy" (263). Yet Alderson's memoir does not conclude with Walt's death. The autobiographer instead attaches an additional chapter detailing her efforts to get by, as well as her children's ultimate successes and failures. Ominously, she tells of yet another financial failure in 1919, one that catches both her and her son. Yet she stoically remarks, "When you have lived without money as much as I had, it loses a great deal of its power to hurt you" (273). A bittersweet moral, to be sure, but Alderson avoids the obvious self-pity and stresses instead the determined hanging on. I might almost assert that the writer is a living embodiment of Frederick Jackson Turner's influential (and now contested) thesis about how the frontier transformed migrants by encouraging independence and resourcefulness. While that seems too extravagant a lesson to extract from this amusing and pained memoir, it would be unfair to Alderson to view her text as pure catastrophe, a kind of cry in the wilderness, a story of unrelieved woe. *A Bride Goes West*, like Garcia's and Abbott's texts, incorporates both a haunting sense of loss and a pragmatic will to survive that will circulate in later writings.

Another female writer is less circumspect about the catastrophes of ranching in pioneer Montana. In a remarkable novel about the ranch-woman's disappointing life, *Lonesome Land* (1912), B. M. Bower diagnoses the disappointments of the eastern woman who becomes attached to an abusive mate. Valeria Peyson arrives in Hope, Montana, a town reminiscent of Bower's own Big Sandy, enthusiastic about her impending marriage to the authentic cowboy Manley Fleetwood. This is a brilliantly antiromantic novel that combines a somewhat melodramatic plot with shrewd, even painfully honest landscape descriptions. In truth, Bower borrows heavily from *The Virginian*, but she employs the cowboy romance as the means for exposing women's suffering, much as Mourning Dove and her editor made use of the same form to expose white injustice. Manley (the name suggests his masculine strengths and failings) turns out to be a Trampas-like cattle rustler, mainly because he is too lazy and too much a drunkard to work his own place. Kent Burnett is the Virginian type, kind, smart, down-to-earth, and gallant in a cowboyish fashion. He becomes Val's pal and, it's implied, will ultimately join her in the East, following her return, perhaps to establish a long-term relationship.

The plot is fairly straightforward: Val arrives while Man is sleeping off one of his drinking binges. Kent sobers him up and gets him through the marriage ceremony. The newlyweds journey to the rather pathetic Cold Spring Ranch, Man's place, where Val must face the grim realities of life on the northern plains:

> Val stood just inside the gate and tried to adjust all this to her mental picture. There was the front yard, for instance. A few straggling vines against the porch, and a sickly cluster or two of blossoms— those were the sweet peas, surely. . . . For the rest, there were weeds against the fence, sun-ripened grass trodden flat, yellow, gravelly patches where nothing grew—and a glaring, burning sun beating down upon it all.[10]

The shaky husband tries to keep his word to remain sober, but he falls off the wagon repeatedly. A dramatic prairie fire brings out Kent's gallantry and Man's failings, for while the husband gets drunk in town out of despair for his wife, Kent comes to the rescue. Driven deeper into the trough of self-loathing, Man turns to rustling to make up for losses incurred in the fire.

Val takes up writing to support herself and her hapless husband. Meanwhile, trying to save Man from prosecution, the protagonist releases one of the calves clearly belonging to another rancher. Enraged by this interference, Man almost strangles her to death. This is the decisive moment in their relationship: Val vows to return east and divorce the failed cowboy. Meanwhile, the somewhat villainous Fred De Garmo, policing the rustlers for the local ranchers, figures out that Man is in fact stealing cattle, but when he attempts to arrest the failed husband, he's shot down. What ensues is the classic Western chase, with Man racing to his ranch, grabbing Kent's horse, and attempting to cross the river, only to be shot by the sheriff. In the end, Val is left with this half-bitter compensation: "She was not the prim, perfectly well-bred young woman he had met at the train. Lonesome Land was doing its work. She was beginning to think as an individual—as a woman; not merely as a member of conventional society" (210).

In a curious sense, then, this hard-hitting novel also seems to affirm Turner's argument for the constructive effects of the frontier on the American self. Unfortunately for that theory, Val retreats to her eastern home with her newfound wisdom, suggesting disillusionment toward her westering experience. The dream of a cowboy paradise has gone bust, another hope wasted to dust. *Lonesome Land* projects the most complete rejection of the ranching myth, yet this novel's critique is of a piece with the gritty antiromantic narratives by the "stickers" Abbott and Alderson. The fantasy of a break from a familiar, prosaic life meets unexpected economic, ecological, and psychological constraints. The cowboy legend remains, however, the most stubborn, most enduring of American myths. Montana narratives suggest a truth similar to that Joan Acocella uncovered in Willa Cather's plains fiction: "The dream is still there; we just can't have it."[11] Perhaps because it is the most distinctive of American stories, or because it appeals to a national obsession with freedom, or because it taps into an archetypal romance story, the cowboy legend refuses to die. I admit with some embarrassment that I used to break into "Home on the Range" or "Don't Fence Me In" when driving through the rangelands of south-central Montana. But circumstances often do fence in the idealistic or dreamy immigrants who fantasize of their homes on the range. In this way, the Montana ranching story foreshadows the arrival and withdrawal of many homesteaders during the notorious boom of the early twentieth century.

Oh the Indians an' the cowboys
They used to live in peace,
'Til the goddamned dryland farmers
Come adriftin' from the east.

—SPIKE VAN CLEVE,
40 Years' Gatherin's

Chapter 3

A HANDFUL OF DUST

THE ATTEMPT TO ESTABLISH AN AGRICULTURAL EMPIRE ON THE
high plains of Montana provides another unforgettable account of
transformations to people and place in the region. Yet the homesteaders of the early twentieth century are among Montana's most belittled
immigrants. As Spike Van Cleve's hard-bitten verse makes clear,
ranching culture often treats the dryland farmers as despoilers of a
grand life on the northern tier. Nevertheless, the tale of this vast
migration and its aftermath forms a core story in this region's cultural
archive. And once again we hear linked accounts of dreams deferred
and hopes partially realized.

The homestead boom was once again brought into the foreground
with the publication of Jonathan Raban's widely praised *Bad Land: An
American Romance.* Raban treats the land rush as sheer madness, thus

reinforcing a grim reading of the boom. Tracking in particular the experiences of immigrants from England, the British expatriate shows that a combination of railroad promotional materials and urban desperation led to the transplantation of ill-suited farmers to the unforgiving high plains. In this sense *Bad Land* is a retelling (in splendid prose) of Joseph Kinsey Howard's *Montana: High, Wide, and Handsome*. There is, of course, plenty of historical support for Raban's catastrophic theory of the settlement story: "During the period 1919–25, roughly two million acres passed out of production and eleven thousand farms, about 20 percent of the state's total, were vacated. Twenty thousand mortgages were foreclosed, and half of Montana farmers lost their land."[1]

Yet when I toured eastern Montana shortly after the publication of Raban's acerbic account, I stopped in Terry to visit the Evelyn Cameron studio so admired by the writer. I asked the hostess what she made of the book (Raban had spent much time researching in Terry). Her reply: "He's a nice man, but he made those of us who stayed here seem crazy." That's a refrain you'll hear among many eastern Montanans, one they've had occasion to hone in the past decade as their way of life has seemed under increasing scrutiny, even suspicion. The controversy over the "buffalo commons" provoked a special fury among residents. Frank and Deborah Popper have argued that white settlement of the Great Plains has been an ecological and economic disaster. Citing statistics demonstrating the outflow of population from rural areas in the region, they assert that encouraging homesteading on the plains has proven a long-term mistake. They urge returning large portions of the area to a prairie preserve that could both restore environmental integrity and provide a meaningful economic alternative to agriculture. Needless to say, this argument has drawn a strong reaction in Montana and elsewhere.[2] To suggest that America and the world could do without the region's beef and wheat seems shortsighted and insulting to folks who occupy the land.

But my own grandmother's homesteading story makes me wonder if Raban hasn't uncovered at least a partial truth. In a charming, at times didactic unpublished memoir, Grandmother tells of moving to northeastern Montana in 1913 to join her family in a homesteading adventure. She describes her love of the place, her sense of opening possibilities, her independence. She also narrates amusing tales of learning to shoot a gun (apparently a common practice for single women living in isolation on the plains), her courting by lonely settlers, and her trips cross-country in an unforgiving wagon. But my grandmother's dream of a long-term family farm on the northern plains went for naught. Her cash-poor husband sold the land in the late 1920s to purchase a hotel. Grandmother never forgot or forgave that decision. A seemingly unsentimental woman, she turned emotional when discussing the land that was sacrificed to financial necessity.

And what of the land itself? A friend and I tracked down the deed to the property at the Daniels County Courthouse in Scobey, then drove south of Flaxville to find the 320 acres. We were immediately struck by an obvious reality: my grandmother's land had been absorbed into a massive wheat-farming operation. Although we knew we were within a few miles of her place, we couldn't stand with confidence on the exact spot. So Grandmother's story suggests that homesteader dreams really did seem to fall apart on average, a story repeated by writers such as Mary Clearman Blew and Ivan Doig; yet we've also seen a process of consolidation, a gathering up of homestead parcels, to create more efficient units of production. Grandmother's tale of disappointment also points toward another realization: she never regretted the settlement experience itself. Though I have a hunch she was born tough, her three years on the plains added a layer of endurance, a coating of sureness, that served her well in her future, complex life, both before and after her husband's death.

Other homestead tales confirm the blend of pleasure and pain found in Grandmother's story. Percy Wollaston and Pearl Price Robertson provide gritty inside accounts of the experience of trying to make a go on the desiccated high plains.[3] Both writers bring out the incredible hardship of the settlement process, including the constant threat to health. Wollaston, for instance, describes the devastation wrought by the great influenza epidemic of 1917, a catastrophe he rightly believes we can hardly imagine today. In fact, much of the trauma recounted seems alien, almost medieval to a reader sitting, say, in a comfortable suburban home in a Montana city approaching a population of 100,000. The isolation, lack of rain, howling winds, terrifying hailstorms, failed crops, and sheer despair seem at a far remove from the amenities of "big-city life." But another theme also flows through these two stories, a belief that contemporary westerners would do well to take to heart: the importance of community, of neighborliness, of common decency. As Robertson tells it, "The settlers of our prairie were of many kinds and classes and had hailed from many different states, both east and west, but we were all one great brotherhood. If a man had a homestead alongside the others, he was accepted by all the others without question. We helped one another; what one had, he shared with the next."[4] While writers such as Raban and Howard accentuate the apocalyptic mood of the homesteading collapse, and while these firsthand witnesses in part affirm that attitude, this countertheme of community-building and care suggests once again an alternative reading of our past, a reading that can serve us in the present time.

Wollaston offers a quirky, detailed, often hilarious impression of the agrarian boom in Montana. He can certainly sound the despairing note, the familiar refrain of woe: "So many high hopes and dreams ended in tragedy and the sites of the homesteads have vanished like the tepee rings of the Indians."[5] It is precisely this note of regret that Raban responded to (he had a hand in getting *Homesteading* into print). Yet Wollaston is just as convincing on the vividness and credibility of the dream: "This was the land of opportunity. Some of the early ranchers had come into the country with nothing but the shirt on their back and wound up owning big ranches. If some had been successful here, others could too, only it would be done by stable farming this time and not the risky type of ranching where a bad winter could wipe out a whole herd" (74). There's nothing condescending about this statement; Wollaston allows us to inhabit, though only briefly, the optimism, even idealism, that brought the homesteaders to Montana. Robertson likewise makes that belief, that ideal, palpable, describing her fantasy home, complete with husband, children, and garden, the Jeffersonian homestead made real. She discloses how the Montana land boom seemed the means to that end, the actualization of desire. And she writes convincingly that for all the pain, the failure brought by drought and low prices and grasshoppers, "We have no regrets; life is fuller and sweeter through lessons learned in privation, and around our homestead days some of life's fondest memories still cling" (542). Based on my grandmother's and Wollaston's tellings, this is an attitude that must have extended to many settlers who, ultimately, left the place.[6]

One reason for that fondness, that nostalgic haze, is the youthful exuberance of the homesteaders. Wollaston narrates several bizarre, downright laughable episodes among the settlers. He has a field day telling of a neighbor's decision to buy a pet monkey for his children. Unfortunately, the restless creature had a habit of hopping onto the backs of steers, riding bareback, as it were, and in general causing mayhem in the neighborhood. Our last glimpse of the creature is as a pile of bones beneath a sagebrush, a victim of exposure after he had stampeded a herd by playing the rodeo hand once too often. Wollaston also evokes the unusual intimacy of the frontier kid with the wild life of the region, giving an entirely different twist to the wolfing legacy than that glimpsed in Yellowstone Kelly's memoirs. Wollaston takes the reader through his futile attempts to trap coyotes, a failure that leads to deep respect for the intelligence and resilience of wild creatures. On a more macabre note, he tells with almost shocking understatement of a shotgun suicide by a complete stranger in the immaculate home of Wollaston's neighbor. In the climactic moment, that neighbor finds the victim's eyeball in his bed.

Make no mistake about it, Wollaston saw his family's attempted settlement in Montana as both understandable and finally untenable. In a refreshing reversal of perspective, he mocks the cowboy culture that showed such scorn for the immigrant farmers: "I have always wondered where the glamour of cowboy life actually came from. It was really about as glamorous as ditch digging and about equally renumerative [sic]" (66). This devastating remark takes on added bite since Wollaston's own father worked a ranch and the young Percy spent time with local cowhands. But Wollaston also expresses deep admiration for the ranching outfits that "stuck," the ones that took into account the actualities of climate and landscape to carve out a decent subsistence. Set against these seasoned frontiersmen, the new arrivals could look lame indeed: "Mrs. Norris had come out in 1912 and taken up adjoining land and becoming [sic] his wife. I was always under the impression that she or both of them had come west in hope of regaining their health, as she suffered from tuberculosis. Both fine, cultured people, but seemingly so ill-suited to life on a claim" (106). Given the sheer weight and variety of work—building a shack, digging a well, plowing the prairie, planting the seed, harvesting the crop, caring for the livestock, watching the children, even working at jobs off the homestead—a settler would pay a heavy price for inexperience and ineptitude.

In the end, then, we have another two-voiced telling of a Montana catastrophe. The narrative must necessarily conclude with the collapse of the boomtown created by the land rush: "Houses were moved away to other locations and little by little the town just withered away like some plant that dries and loses its leaves so slowly that the owner continues to hope for survival" (130). Yet Wollaston is as glowing about the power of hope and community as Robertson: "There were people from almost every walk of life and status of education, but they learned little of each other beyond what each planned to make of his place and plans for the future of the community. The next meal might be potatoes and water gravy but you didn't hear anything about hardship unless somebody burned out or broke a leg" (112). This dual response has left its imprint on Montana culture down to the present moment. Surely the legacy of failure, the memory of devastated crops and withering dreams, haunts the region's culture. The late historian Richard Roeder put it best: "The end of the boom erased a pervasive innocence and optimism about taking up the land and controlling one's future and that of one's community."[7] That uncertainty produced radical movements on the plains in the early twentieth century, breeding such groups as the Nonpartisan League, dedicated to revolutionizing agricultural production by instituting a state-run network of finance and produce-processing centers.[8] Such movements must be counted as important precursors to the extremist eruptions of our own time, extremism inspired in part by crises in the production and distribution of agricultural products. If such organizations seem far removed from our present predicament, we should attend to the words of the contemporary rural psychologist Glen Wallace: "You can't treat people the way rural Americans have been treated without them eventually organizing and fighting back."[9]

My wife and I know a couple who practice dryland farming on beautiful but parched land less than two hours from Billings. The farmer has often said that he would do anything to avoid moving to the city, the route taken by many homesteaders who couldn't make the farm pay. Year in and year out the two sweat the rainfalls, the crops, and the prices. At times the stress seems almost unbearable; the wife suffers recurring fears for her husband's safety and the farm's solvency. Their commitment to the place, replete with insecurity and love, often translates into what looks to my eyes like a radically conservative politics. The distrust of federal agencies, of liberal politicians, of pointy-headed academics (such as myself) goes deep. Because these are decent people, fully invested in their lives, in their farming, I cannot dismiss them as crackpot or paranoid. Yet their political and religious beliefs veer toward the apocalyptic, the cataclysmic. Perhaps their personal sufferings seem so immense, so unfair, so unmotivated, that only such an elaborate explanation can make sense.

Yet the very emphasis on community written into the homesteader memoirs suggests an alternative to despairing, tragic resistance. As one historian asserts, "a sense of 'community' or cohesiveness quickly grew where these sodbusters took up residence. They formed groups spontaneously, from the grass-roots level up, and their actions demonstrated a putting aside or combining of private desires to achieve mutual benefit."[10] It has been easy to focus on the losses, the disappointments, the failed crops and busted dreams. And it would be foolish to ignore these harsh lessons altogether. As with the displacement of indigenous peoples and elimination of wildlife such as the bison, the homesteading bust reminds westerners of limitations to desire, the boundaries put upon us by the carrying capacity of the place. We are reminded, in other words, of a necessary ecological relationship with the region. If the Poppers' proposal for a buffalo commons seems daftly romantic, it has the virtue of forcing tough questions: What have we made of the place we appropriated from other cultures? What lessons have we learned from our trials and errors? Contemporary writers return again and again to a notion of relationship, even love, the concept of a caring, reciprocal connection with the life forms and landscapes of the West. Those writers have aptly turned back toward those homesteader experiences to recover an ethos of responsibility that gets lost in the shuffle of doom-and-gloom analysis. Read of Percy Wollaston's first Thanksgiving on the Montana plains, the moment when he first met his neighbors: "I don't remember any details of the day or the dinner other than seeing these young men arrive in a group and learning some small detail of each one, yet that meeting somehow bound us together as a group or community from that day forward" (13). Or take in Pearl Price Robertson's fond memory of another holiday: "Christmas Day the neighbors gathered at my home for a community Christmas dinner. None had much, but all brought something, and assembled, it seemed an abundance" (541).

So let me conclude with my favorite of all homesteader narratives: Dale Eunson's *Up on the Rim*. Eunson matches Wollaston's humor, his sense of the absurdity and quirky delight of making a go on the plains in the 1910s. The narrative focuses on the first two years of the Eunson homestead, tracing the development of the farm and ranch through the vision of the six-, seven-, and eight-year-old Dale. Having migrated from Wisconsin with dreams of a speculative killing (Dale's father is sure they will be able to resell the land at a considerable profit), the family moves into the tarpaper shack that was standard issue for the "sodbusters." Between the salty but kind father and the idiosyncratic but loving stepmother, Dale undergoes a series of initiations on the wheat ranch. He describes the familiar ups and downs of settlement: the sheer physical beauty of the plains and distant mountains; the exultation at planting the first crop; the devastating (and terrifying) hailstorm that wipes out that very crop; the relentless winters that send howling winds and cutting snow; the emerging spring that reawakens hope; the drought that curtails the yield; and the harvest that nonetheless satisfies.

In the midst of these wonders and traumas, Dale manages to grow up in stop-and-go fashion. He befriends the drifty hired hand Jim, only to see that exotic figure wander off when a love interest evaporates. He endures the routines and boredom of the rural school, often the only pupil for the marginally trained teacher. He discovers that he can be a bully to a friend who is two inches shorter than he but who is otherwise a swell fellow. But above all, Dale develops a most peculiar relationship with his dog Shep: he becomes convinced that he can converse—in human language—with his pet. This unusual belief sets in motion a series of comic scenes with the often distracted parents. The mother turns to a Christian Scientist to pray the madness out of the boy. An uncle tells a sorry tale of a young man sent to an asylum in Wisconsin for similar behavior. And the father finally attempts to give away the dog, both because of this unhealthy bond and because Shep seems overly fond of killing chickens. But in the end Shep returns to his beloved friend, and the two of them set off on an adventure that will provide a fitting climax for the book.

The ending of *Up on the Rim* brings to mind the film *Heartland*, surely one of the most authentic "Westerns" ever made, and a local project at that. After enduring disappointments, including the death of their first child, Clyde and Elinore Stewart determine to go forward with their shaky ranching operation. The film makers conclude the action with the birth of a calf, reinforcing that sense of possibility, of starting over, of recovery. Similarly, Eunson chooses to end his narrative with the birth of a baby brother, a true surprise since the ranch kid had not even realized his stepmother was pregnant! Between the father's being away and the young boy's difficult journey to a neighbor's house for help, the situation borders on fatal. But Dale overcomes an understandable fear of a howling wolf with Shep's companionship, he completes that journey, and help arrives from Billings in time. Eunson hints that the parents' homesteading venture collapsed after five years, yet that's not the dominant tone of this affecting memoir. We're left with an image of the family, surrounded by caring neighbors and relatives, welcoming a new member on a brilliant January morning on the high plains of Montana. That could be something to build on: "We were hailed out, dried out, washed out, and blown out, yet my life was enriched and rewarded beyond measure by the experience."[11] We risk sentimentality when we focus on such moments, and rampant emotionalism is anathema to westerners. After all, this is the land of the brave and the home of the reticent. We shouldn't expose ourselves too much, either to the weather or to the ridicule of others. But perhaps it's time Montanans and their neighbors risk a bit of ridicule to reaffirm the value of people and place.

PART II

The Tragic Sensibility

1940-PRESENT

Farming out here has been a trap, a sure way to break your back and then find you were working for the bank all the time. The homesteads were too small, the returns too uncertain. The Indians were robbed, but the ones who came to rob took a beating in the pocketbook, the kind of hurt they could feel. The real loser was the country itself, the land.

—DOC EDWARDS
in *Wind from an Enemy Sky*

EARLY MONTANA WRITING PROVIDED A HERITAGE OF FRANK ENGAGE-
ment with transformations to people and places. The demise of tribal
independence, of the open range, and of the homestead movement
sent shocks of recognition through the region's inhabitants. But Montanans could also sense a change of luck as World War II approached.
While depression arrived early in Montana, and certainly exacerbated
the troubling conditions that predated that economic collapse, the
1930s also brought a huge infusion of federal aid, especially in the form
of the Fort Peck Dam project. The decade also marked the expansion
of electrical and phone service to rural communities, as well as the
improvement of roads and other infrastructure through programs such
as the WPA.[1] Ironically, then, the depression may be seen as a turning
point in the state's fortunes, as citizens built upon the dire knowledge
absorbed from the previous failures. The emergence of prosperous
cities such as Great Falls and Billings, towns relying not exclusively on
extractive industries but on retail and white-collar professions, provided another index of improvement.

Yet the region's most important writers continued to produce strikingly cataclysmic prose. It is as though Montanans suffer some fever
in the blood, some infection of dread that cannot be easily expunged.
D'Arcy McNickle, A. B. Guthrie Jr., Richard Hugo, Thomas McGuane,
Jim Harrison, Richard Ford, Joseph Kinsey Howard, and K. Ross
Toole reiterate prospects of doom in sophisticated, classic writing that
deserves its rank as a major regional literature. This state has produced engaging, memorable, poignant, transformative prose. Yet how
dire the tones, how fearful the prospects. Think of Bull, Pell, and Rafferty's deaths in McNickle's *Wind from an Enemy Sky*, or Hugo's hapless personae adrift in failed space, or Howard's impassioned jeremiad

against Big Capital. Even Norman Maclean's touching tale of two brothers, *A River Runs Through It*, carries the mood of loss, of failed love, though the novelist also places that catastrophe in context of a Christian theology that assuages the pain. How can we account for this enduring woe?

First, these writers echo the history of loss we uncovered in part I. These thoughtful recorders rightly see it as their mission to bring to light the processes of displacement, settlement, and exploitation that had been suppressed in official narratives of the state (especially those provided by the Anaconda Copper Company) and fanciful myths (especially the popular Western). In this sense the historians Howard and Toole best represent the impulse driving these more recent tragic texts, for these two historians embody a muckraking tradition that has served us well. Many of these writers are also products of the depression, and so were radicalized by the worldwide economic collapse and the extreme politics of the pre–World War II years. Similar to their western counterpart John Steinbeck, these writers responded to crises in the economy and in national faith, producing what sometimes read like Montana versions of *In Dubious Battle* or *The Grapes of Wrath*. Since Montana's economy has continued to follow a boom-bust pattern that brings out the "colonial" status of the region (for example, the oil and timber collapses of the 1980s), that critical, even radical, position retains some credibility.

We must consider as well of the legacy of the world wars and the subsequent cold war. It wasn't Ezra Pound alone who imaged civilization as "an old bitch gone in the teeth." The sheer carnage, waste, and idiocy of the two wars profoundly shaped the mood, the tone of much twentieth-century political and literary writing. Marx's eschatological political theory spoke convincingly to human beings suffering the apocalypse of total war. And what hope seems conceivable after the Holocaust? It's not by accident that existentialism and a general sensibility of post-theistic searching took root in the twentieth century's last half. It's hard to embrace a divine agency in the aftermath of such devastation, such senseless horror. That combination of angst and desire could only be exacerbated by the frenzied visions of a technological utopia that never materialized. In fact, the machines that should save us often proved our most relentless pursuers. Hugo has evoked, better than anyone, the utter despair and terror for the live human soul in the heart of mechanized World War II air combat.

No event makes the contrast between technological utopianism and reality more transparent than the forty-year-long cold war. Paranoia became the official reality of the United States. Communism seemed to rear its ugly head everywhere, in all places, simultaneously, ubiquitously. Nuclear weapons became the tool of balance, the necessary means of survival in a MAD world. Montanans daily lived with the reality of that strangely abstract, yet terrifying, nuclear deterrent. Scattered throughout the high plains, in fenced-off facilities that were readily recognizable during a Sunday drive, were missile silos that meant we lived in the eye of the hurricane. If war should come, we would be at the heart of destruction. As the narrator sarcastically notes of the MyWay Cafe in *Nobody's Angel*, "It seemed ready for a nuclear attack."[2] Or consider Grandpere's contemporary Ghost Dance vision in Dan Cushman's *Stay Away, Joe*: "No more factory for make penicillin, pretty soon white men die. No more big town like Havre to buy wheat, buy beef. No factory for build skunkwagon. No skunkwagon, no use for roads. No factory build barbwire. Boom! Big bomb blow 'em all up. Horses come back, buffalo come back, good country again."[3] So despite the resilience of this remarkable place, the grandeur of the scenery and the persistence of some life forms, nuclear winter threatened us all. It is no wonder, then, that major writers continued to generate tales of catastrophe, narratives of doom, first initiated by the earlier recorders of the Montana experience. As we saw with those earlier witnesses to vanishing dreams, however, the despair is frequently offset by a sense of possibility, of belief. We can embrace that dialectic of dread and hope in our millennial turn.

I didn't feel too friendly toward A. B.
Guthrie right then. It was The Big Sky
and the rest of the mountain man books
that had gotten me into this mess.

—PETE FROMM,
Indian Creek Chronicles

Chapter 4

A TALE OF
TWO NOVELISTS

STUDENTS OF WESTERN AMERICAN LITERATURE TYPICALLY TREAT
D'Arcy McNickle and A. B. Guthrie Jr. as separate voices, divergent
and apart. Guthrie, after all, became a famous, best-selling author in
his late forties, and in turn became a Hollywood screenwriter and
widely consulted authority on the western experience. McNickle, by
contrast, rose to prominence with the Bureau of Indian Affairs and
made his mark through historical and anthropological writings (his
study of Indian/white contact, *They Came Here First*, remains a classic).[1] Yet he too was a fictionist of great significance, though that
importance did not emerge until the 1970s, too late for him to relish
the recognition during his lifetime. Of course, the difference that
makes it easiest to segregate these writers resides in race. McNickle
was, after all, part Indian, the son of a Metis woman and himself an

enrolled member of the Confederated Salish-Kootenai Tribes. As we will see, that "mixed" status profoundly shaped his fictional themes and techniques.

Yet despite these apparent differences, Guthrie and McNickle have far more in common than one might suppose. They were virtual contemporaries (Guthrie was born in 1901, McNickle in 1904). They both attended the University of Montana during the 1920s, both fell under the powerful influence of H. G. Merriam, and both worked on his important regional magazine, *The Frontier.* Both left the region to make their marks, McNickle working in Indian affairs, Guthrie laboring as a journalist in Kentucky. Both retained the dream of the writing life planted by Merriam, and each would in time produce major fiction about this region. That writing would be the result of long years of apprenticeship, disappointment, and even failure. (McNickle's first novel was rejected at least five times; Guthrie renounced his first novel, *Murders at Moon Dance,* as a disaster.) Both saw fiction as an almost moral activity, dedicating themselves to cutting through false mythologies of the American West to recount the actuality of the place. In this sense, similar to Norman Maclean and others of their generation, Guthrie and McNickle studied at the American School of Realism and Naturalism, encompassing writers such as Frank Norris, Ernest Hemingway, and William Faulkner. They wrote with special rigor about betrayal in a land of astonishing beauty, betrayal of native peoples and the life forms that preceded white settlement. And so both were remarkably frank about the costs of white invasion of the high plains and mountain valleys.

But McNickle and Guthrie share this as well: their best-known writings, *The Surrounded, Wind from an Enemy Sky,* and *The Big Sky,* fall into the tradition of tragic narration of the western experience. The novel's protagonists, Archilde, Antoine, and Boone, bear the weight of woe that has recirculated on this terrain. Those books carry an almost melodramatic ferocity, an insistence on the devastating climax, the violent resolution. Archilde is arrested, Antoine's grandfather Bull shot down, and Boone's best friend, Jim Deakins, butchered. Readers often feel they have no exit from the catastrophe; there's no place to go, imaginatively or politically, at the end of these narratives. *Wind from an Enemy Sky*, for instance, concludes with these haunting, unassuageable words: "*No meadowlarks sang, and the world fell apart.*"[2] In this sense, both talented writers translate into sophisticated literary technique the despairing messages of Native American memoirs and tales of lost paradise among white settlers in the region. And one would be hard pressed to question that move. Surely those stories had to be retold, had to be laid before a contemporary audience in an idiom that could speak to them. Yet these three texts obscure a crucial truth about these two writers: their lives and other writings bespeak an alternative approach to western traumas, an approach we might rightly call pragmatic, thoughtful, even hopeful. McNickle's important work with Native Americans in their quest for self-determination and Guthrie's depiction of Montana "after the fall" in his later novels point to possible resolutions of the terrible crises evoked in the familiar works.

Yet all too often these vital alternatives are forgotten. It is as though contemporary readers, whether living inside or outside the region, would prefer tragedy to ameliorist, pragmatic writing. No doubt we are bumping up against an aspect of human nature: pessimism sells. Many cultural commentators have noted the rise of a "Gothic America," a culture in love with sex, terror, and mayhem. I would suggest that this is an intensified resurrection of a far more deep-seated tendency in the human psyche. We'd rather be scared to death than bored by the facts. Western landscapes and history from Cooper's *Last of the Mohicans* to Larry Watson's *Montana 1948* have provided fodder for this Gothic imagination. We can't get enough of the stuff. But if we grant that voice of disaster complete authority, if we allow that vision of the West complete control of our self-imagining, we turn ourselves into victims of history and chance. To be scared out of our wits is to become empty and immobilized.

Both *The Surrounded* and *Wind from an Enemy Sky* are shaped by promising beginnings and disastrous endings. Each recounts the irreconcilable differences between white and native cultures on reservations in northwestern Montana. The young male protagonists, Archilde in the first novel and Antoine in the second, embody the search for a coherent identity in the contorted Indian world of the early twentieth century. Both characters finally must face a form of defeat. In *The Surrounded*, Max Leon (Archilde's father) and Father Grepilloux return again and again to the belief that Archilde represents a new beginning, a new chance for the Salish people. He is, quite literally, a messiah in the eyes of these aging witnesses. His promise is set off against an earlier "great red hope." As Father Grepilloux puts it:

> I have been thinking that this Archilde is the answer we were looking for one day. You remember I told you the story of Big Paul, and we were asking ourselves how it had happened that certain bad ones had come among us and spoiled the fruit. We could not see how it would end. Our vision was short, as it always is. It was inevitable that a new age would come. It is beginning now. And your boy is standing there where the road divides. He belongs to a new time.[3]

In the priest's millennialist vision, Archilde becomes the antitype to Big Paul's type, the later incarnation that will realize the promise of the earlier model. If Big Paul was cut down by the combined hatred of his own people and whites, Archilde can transcend mere contingency to represent a new way of being for the Salish people. He will become the exemplar, the bearer of possibilities for young Indians. Yet true to the tragic form of the novel, circumstances take up this potential messiah and turn him into a mere prisoner of the white establishment. His brother, Louis, is killed in ridiculous fashion by the jumpy game warden; his mother, Catharine, strikes down that killer with an axe; Max dies and leaves a fortune to his youngest son; Elise enters the scene as a provocative love interest; she in turn convinces Archilde to hide out in the mountains when he might have turned himself in and short-circuited tragedy. It is really a string of happenstance that hems in or surrounds the male character. Archilde is in many senses the classic antihero of modernist prose. He is oddly passive, distant, acted upon. Events come at him without his recognition or anticipation. We are witnessing here the legacy of naturalism in early-twentieth-century prose, the sense that fatality sweeps us up and carries us whither

we know not.[4] In the end, the priest's millennium turns into a bitter
failure.

The same holds true for Antoine, the appealing fourteen-year-old
protagonist of *Wind*. Like Archilde, he is a product of the boarding-
school system, and so he carries within him two sets of cultural codes:
those of his white teachers, and those of his grandfather Bull. He acts
as the intermediary between the weary, enraged, but hopeful Little
Elk people and the diverse whites who circle around them. He literally translates the wishes of his people for the invaders, and in turn
tries to make plain the desires of the whites to his elders. Antoine too
is "standing there where the road divides," but he is clearly learning
to thrive at the crossroads, to live in a kind of negative capability, not
choosing but standing still, listening and absorbing. Because of his
youth, he is in many ways less judgmental than Archilde, who after all
frequently imagines leaving his Indian identity completely behind.
Portland and urban culture in general call to him. He fantasizes about
disappearing into the mainstream. Not so Antoine, though truly we do
not gain the kind of inside view of his character that we get with the
older Salish/Spanish character. Yet where does Antoine's story arrive?
As the critic Louis Owens sees it,

> McNickle offers some hope for future generations in both *Wind
> from an Enemy Sky* and *The Surrounded* in the forms of Mike and
> Narcisse . . . and Antoine. . . . But those elements of future prom-
> ise are nearly hidden by the sheer enormity of failure in both
> books. . . . For this important and seminal figure in American
> Indian literature and politics, the world he had spent his lifetime
> trying to make whole—the Indian-white world of America and the
> mixed blood world within himself—fell finally and, it seems, inex-
> orably apart.[5]

At heart, these catastrophes result from conflicting, even mutually
exclusive, world views. As Owens further notes, "language, McNickle
insists, is the darkling plain upon which Native and Euramerican cultures clash."[6] McNickle is justly renowned for his ability to inhabit
and disclose these conflicting worlds. The sequence of chapters in
Wind, moving from the BIA agent Toby Rafferty's visits with Little Elk

farmers to Veronica's reflections on her aging husband to Adam Pell's discussion of manifest destiny with a judge friend to Two Sleep's vision quest, provides a brilliant rendering of these diverse worlds. The legal and biblical justifications for the white invasion of the West—which still resonate in the twenty-first century—bring out the stakes and the consequences most starkly:

> With kindly hands, they [Pell's lawyer friends] led him through the jungle of the law: to John Marshall: *By common accord, the nations of the world recognized the right of each to chew off what it could, and to keep what it could hold;* to Vattel: *The nation with superior skill could appropriate to its own use the domain of a less accomplished people.* They even led him to the Christian Bible: *Multiply, and make the earth bear fruit.* (190)

This highly literate culture encodes and preserves its mores in sophisticated but heartless documents. By contrast, Bull's people prefer their communications in oral, person-to-person form. These confusions, these divergences of thinking and expression, are further highlighted by the convoluted processes of translation that punctuate the novel. The Boy's and Antoine's strained efforts at transcribing and transferring highlight the impossibility of bridging the divides created by antithetical maps of the mind. Only Bull is really honest about this harsh reality; the liberal Pell and Rafferty learn at their own expense about the incompatibility of the agrarian and tribal cultures.

McNickle is actually involved in a process not all that different from Mourning Dove's in her earlier novel. As we saw in chapter 1, *Cogewea* deploys the conventions of cowboy romance to clear a space for the grandmother Stemteema's stories. By this means the writer can smuggle in harsh indictments of white interference in Okanogan ways. The novel looks two ways, toward the meaningful past and toward the more ambiguous future. So also *The Surrounded* and *Wind from an Enemy Sky*. In the former, for instance, McNickle presents an almost kaleidoscopic series of impressions of the cultural life of the Salish people. This technique allows expressive space for diverse world views. Since Archilde is not the one in control, the power at the center of the action, since he is in fact more reflector than lamp, we are granted an intimacy with various approaches to the ongoing action and, especially, rapport with the values of Catharine and the tribal elder Modeste. Shifting from Modeste to Father Grepilloux to Max to Catharine, the narrative incorporates the prehistory of the tribe, the arrival of the missionaries, and the incursion by white farmers and ranchers. Hovering over this series of accounts is Max's despairing question: "He had images of Father Grepilloux working like a peasant, of the Indians perishing of hunger and disease, of the outside world pouring into this sheltered valley, a paradise in its original state—and what had been the purpose?" (148). Clearly the mother's rejection of Christianity is central to McNickle's design for his book, presumably because that turn marks a recantation of a religious and ideological system that suppressed the more sustaining ways of the Salish. Similarly, the passive protagonist is pulled toward recognizing the futility, even cruelty, of the Jesuit way, especially in their dealings with the energetic nephew Mike.

Yet William Bevis is surely right in emphasizing the "homing plot" in McNickle's narratives.[7] Set against this dire dramatic structure are remarkable insights into people and place, insights that mark an intimacy, a care, even a love. Before the devastating climax of the action, *Wind* presents a series of reborn or newly formed relationships: Antoine and his people; Henry Jim and Bull; Son Child and Bull's camp; Rafferty and Henry Jim; even, tentatively, Pell and Bull. Still more memorably, the writer recreates the landscapes of the Salish and Little Elk people. Perhaps McNickle wrote out of a deep nostalgia for the place he would never call home again (much as Guthrie would compose his own remarkable landscape pieces while living in Kentucky, Massachusetts, and Vermont). I once asked the writer Debra Earling, herself a member of the Confederated Salish-Kootenai Tribes, whether it was difficult to write about her Montana home from the vantage of Ithaca, New York, where she was attending Cornell at the time. She responded that, if anything, the distance intensified her memories, giving heft and texture to her sense of place. In *The Surrounded* McNickle also shows the ability to evoke a landscape or a season in vivid, sensory prose. He can literally take this reader's breath away with a representation of the Mission Mountains or the valley that runs north toward Flathead Lake:

> The season had changed. The sun was always seen through a mist. There were forest fires lingering in the surrounding mountains, and on some days when the wind was right the world seemed to wander all at sea in a warm fog. The nights sparkled with a promise of frost, and mist rose from the earth until the middle of the forenoon. Sounds hung in the air so that sometimes men talking in a distant field sounded near at hand. The world had become enchanted. (84)

I would put that paragraph up against Keats's "To Autumn." The narrative is especially compelling on seasonal change, the transformation of the air and light and land as time shifts from summer, to autumn, to winter, to spring, to summer, and back to autumn. In part, McNickle uses these shifts to signal the mood of the action. As the narrative moves inexorably toward its violent climax, the landscape takes on the aura of Eliot's *Waste Land*. Yet these memorable transitions also hint at a seasonal cycle that may endure beyond the specific tragedy of Archilde's story. In other words, the seasonal change may point to a counter-rhythm to the protagonist's grim march toward doom.

As critics often point out, *The Surrounded* tells of Archilde's gradual reincorporation into the "old ways" of the Salish people.[8] The chapter focusing on Archilde's attempt to help a gaunt mare brings to a focus McNickle's sense of his character and that character's evolution. In many ways the male protagonist acts like a liberal white: paternalistic, caring, and dangerous all at the same time. Archilde so desperately wants to save that animal, clearly an embodiment of his people (and especially his own mother). The mare becomes a symbol for the Salish people's traumas and for Archilde's own Catholic-induced guilt. He can't help himself—he must rescue the animal from the waste land she inhabits with her young colt. The result is a poignant, painful comedy of errors. The horse evades the helper, wanting only to be left alone to endure in her own way. She simply wants the freedom to exist on her own terms, even if that means relative pain and poverty.

Archilde cannot fathom this possibility; he cannot accept that he has no help to offer her. In heavy-handed irony, the scene concludes in a predictable fashion: the male character must shoot the creature he most wanted to save. He had literally run the weary animal into the ground, driven her toward death. This weird, dreamlike sequence signals that for all of mainstream, urban, white America's best intentions, the answer to the crisis on reservations may be withdrawal rather than intensified engagement. For all that the Americanized Archilde would like to rehabilitate the mother horse, his actions only result in more pain, more disappointment, more heartache. If ever we sought an allegory of self-determination for native peoples, this is it.

Which leads to my lingering doubts about the conclusion of *The Surrounded*. Why, in the end, must Archilde, the "child" of the people, go down to defeat? Why can't the narrative grant him the limited freedom of Modeste and his nephews? Why his almost catatonic behavior after his mother's death? Why surrender his will so completely to Elise? For the sake of argument, let's agree that Archilde is suffering a trauma, a deep wound to his understanding of the world. In more academic terms, we can agree that he has suffered an epistemological crisis—the universe no longer makes complete sense to him. That gap in apprehension opens when his mother rejects the priest's aid (though the domineering priest goes forward with Extreme Unction in any case). Apparently this protagonist must learn over and over again the lessons that reservation life forces upon him: the old way must return to power; the Black Robes brought not salvation but guilt and disappointment; Modeste's stories carry far more meaning than any lesson taught in the still-frightening church. But granting this difficult process of reeducation for the mixed-blood character, why must he become the victim of two acts of violence? Why is he the fall guy?

Years ago, I had a fine teacher talk about the dangers of the thesis-driven novel. He was discussing *A Farewell to Arms* and the trap Hemingway had set for himself: in a novel about the meaninglessness of the world, Catherine must die in childbirth. The author was powerless to evade this outcome, since the novel had so thoroughly taught the lesson of nihilism. If Catherine and Frederic were granted a child, wouldn't that signal hope, a possible future for these war-torn characters? The result is a famously grotesque (and forced) climax to an otherwise elegant, moving novel. I sense the same dilemma here for McNickle. An editor at Farrar and Rinehart, Constance Lindsay Skinner, made a salient point when she observed that "he seemed torn between telling a good story and delivering a sermon."[9] McNickle rightly calls attention to the indecency of the reservation system; he rightly requires his main character to recognize that immorality; he force-marches Archilde through a series of encounters, including the deaths of both parents, to put him precisely at the place where he can understand, fully, his relationship with his Indian past. Surely no one would expect a "happy ending" here; there's no way that Archilde can simply resolve the tragedies of his people's defeat and incarceration. Yet is it really necessary to conclude with Archilde's pathetic arrest? Isn't he then, in the language of the novel, just another failed Indian?

Dorothy R. Parker points out that *The Surrounded* allowed McNickle to explore his options as a mixed-blood through the character of Archilde. Like his troubled protagonist, the writer faced three options: taking up the ranching life near and dear to his father; turning to "the blanket"—that is, adopting a native way of living; or, "one McNickle only alluded to in fiction, . . . the one he himself chose."[10] The biographer refers to the author's decision to leave the reservation, to journey far afield, to Europe, New York City, and Washington, to "find himself" and to become fully the advocate for Indian rights. McNickle's is certainly a far more promising story than Archilde's. Which returns me to that lingering question: Why couldn't the novelist write that story, his own story, into either *The Surrounded* or *Wind from an Enemy Sky*? Perhaps McNickle opted for the pyrotechnics of plot precisely in order to highlight the tragic possibilities for the mixed blood and native alike. He wanted to drive home his sermonic message through memorable incident. Once again, we cannot forget that McNickle wrote in the shadow of great modernist writers such as Hemingway, Fitzgerald, and Faulkner, all of whom veered toward existentialist tragedy. In fact, it's not too much of a stretch to compare *The Surrounded* with Faulkner's masterful *Absalom, Absalom!*, also published in 1936. As the southern writer narrates in fractured, postmodern fashion the failure of Thomas Sutpen's dream of plantation greatness, McNickle shows how the Leon family has been torn apart by the clashing desires of its members. Much as Sutpen is ultimately undone by his inability to deal with the racist legacy of the South, so Max is harmed by his inability to understand or openly love his Salish wife. If both white men are dreamers of that old American dream of possessing an agrarian paradise, both are linked by their failure to sustain the legacy.

If this comparison between two American tragedies holds up, we can speculate that McNickle turned to fiction as a mode for communicating the tragic possibilities of Native American life. History and anthropology, on the other hand, would serve to inculcate more sober, practical lessons about making the culture work. Perhaps these novels also allowed the writer to vent pent-up rage that he could not express in his capacity as politician, advocate, and anthropologist. I suspect McNickle was also up against wider audience assumptions about Montana, the West, and Native Americans that cut against the grain of a comic resolution. In his first version of the novel, the writer granted Archilde a happy ending as a successful rancher. The publisher rejected this version, no doubt in part because of its amateurishness. But one wonders if the publishing and reviewing establishment desired a more dramatic—that is, more despairing—conclusion to an Indian saga. (It's interesting that Mourning Dove struggled so mightily to get her less polished novel into print. Perhaps, again, the relatively upbeat tone of the ending played a part.) We might agree with Parker that Archilde's story organically led toward defeat: "The essential truth about Archilde's situation was not a 'happily-ever-after' fairy tale but a deeply moving tragedy."[11] Or we might suggest that McNickle, like many Western writers since, was "surrounded" by reader expectations that demanded violence, chaos, a good murder, a good chase, and a bit of Indian lore thrown in. This argument, of course, reads like a cynical view of the cultural establishment of the United States.

Yet consider the persistent fascination with the Western, a form dedicated to melodrama. After all, the endings of both *The Surrounded* and *Wind* involve gunplay in the Western mode. Sheriff Quigley is twice described as being cut in the mold of the "Old West." When Elise shoots him down, it's like a parodic inversion of all those episodes when the powerful white male gets his Indian. Think, especially, of Wayne's character in John Ford's *The Searchers*. Elliott West has captured the ideological force of this popular genre:

> The two basic narratives that compose the Western—that of imposing an outside order and that of escape into prehistory—have been carried into the country and acted out upon it. The result has been a kind of narrative colonialism, but in this case outlanders have not extracted valuable resources. Instead they have exploited the West by using it as a blank screen where they can project and pursue their fantasies.[12]

Perhaps because of the seemingly barren landscape, readers project fantasies of moral struggle onto what seems a tabula rasa. Or perhaps these desires for violent action reflect a lingering memory of the interracial conflicts and messy process of settlement throughout three centuries of American nation-building. In any case, Archilde's and Antoine's stories diverge remarkably from that of their maker.

But let's allow the writer the final word on his approach to storytelling. He wrote to a colleague that "Indian storytelling presents a contrasting view of man's role in historical process; the coyote tales are especially good for this. Coyote is rarely a hero, or if he starts out to be a hero invariably he ends up a scoundrel or he finds himself outsmarted. There are no mounting crises, no gratifying denouements. Life is an arrangement of reciprocal expectations and obligations, and no one is allowed to set himself up as a power unto himself."[13] Though this illuminating comment emerged many years after the composition of *The Surrounded*, it provides a revealing gloss on the problems plaguing reader responses. McNickle suggests that the "hero" must, of necessity, be brought to earth. The central figure, like Coyote, must be humiliated, must be shamed, to signal his place in a larger scheme of "reciprocal expectations and obligations." Reading Archilde's story through this lens, we might see that his arrest is a necessary punishment for his crimes against humanity. His capture might in fact be, as John Lloyd Purdy suggests, a kind of triumph over his own shame. Difficult as such a theme may be for this Euramerican reader, that meaning may be the heart of the matter for McNickle, singing his Indian song. If that is the case, *The Surrounded* carries a message of humility and belonging that can endure beyond the apparent catastrophe.

McNickle's contemporary A. B. Guthrie Jr. certainly valued humility and a sense of place. His hero Dick Summers is a classic American stoic, blessed with wide perspective and a large dose of self-mockery. Summers is surely the writer's middle-aged surrogate, his voice in the text. His presence lightens the otherwise grim plot of *The Big Sky*, adds local color to *The Way West*, and generates whatever narrative virtues one can find in *Fair Land, Fair Land*. But Summers's grim death in this last novel points toward the cataclysmic heart of Guthrie's writing, for as Thomas W. Ford has put it, "what [*Fair Land*] does is to make even more pronounced the elegiac tones of the series."[14] While I will argue that Guthrie's later novels carry another possible meaning, Ford has it essentially right: Guthrie returns again and again to the tragic resonances of the westering experience. The writer himself reveals this preoccupation in his fine autobiography *The Blue Hen's Chick* (for my money, the best of all his books). Writing of *The Big Sky*, Guthrie observes: "I had a theme, not original, that each man kills the thing he loves. If it had any originality at all, it was only that a band of men, the fur-hunters, killed the life they loved and killed it with a thoughtless prodigality perhaps unmatched."[15]

Here we can look to Guthrie's own education to garner a clue about his pessimism: "Hardy awakened me to universal tragedy, and for years I walked in his dark shadow and to some extent still do."[16] True to his generation's commitments, Guthrie sides with the naturalists, viewing life as tragic. I can't overstate the importance of World War I (and later, the Second World War) for Guthrie's generation. Imagine cutting your teeth on *A Farewell to Arms* and *All Quiet on the Western Front*. And Guthrie after all, as a native Montanan (though born elsewhere), witnessed much of the destruction and waste attending various settlement attempts in the state. It's not coincidental that he was a good friend of Joseph Kinsey Howard, that great proselytizer for a catastrophic reading of Montana history. Tragedy cast a spell upon people enduring world wars, the flu epidemic, world-wide depression, dire political changes in Russia, Germany, and Italy, and Montana's own legacy of conquest:

> Guthrie lets no one off the hook, from mountain man to pioneer schoolmaster. The history of the westward movement has been a series of aggression [*sic*] in the name of freedom and opportunity: aggression against the land, against the Blackfeet, against women like Teal Eye and Callie and May Collingsworth, and finally against the future, as Guthrie, drawn himself to the dream of idyllic splendor in the mountains, hammers down his lesson. *Every man kills what he loves.*[17]

Any other reaction may seem, on the surface, unseemly, even immoral. But as we will discover in part III, for other witnesses to the events of the state's history catastrophic tragedy is not the only choice.

For better and for worse, Guthrie's legacy centers on the canonical *Big Sky*. In some ways this is a cruel twist of fate for the writer, who composed a complex series of novels to move beyond Boone Caudill's downfall. Yet for most Montanans (and one would guess, most westerners) none of the other novels, including the Pulitzer Prize–winning *The Way West*, comes close to moving and infuriating in the way the first novel does. There's a dreamlike quality to this mountain-man saga that Guthrie could never quite summon again. The writer is caught up in a Romantic sublime that elevates the prose to landscape poetry. The circumspect Guthrie gets it right when he observes in his autobiography, "My manuscript was two-fifths finished when I set out for Bread Loaf. Looking back at my loneliness, renewing in my recollection my almost physical hunger for the West, sometimes I think that whatever *The Big Sky* is, it owes much to nostalgia."[18] We noticed the same process of transmutation in McNickle's remarkable novels, especially in *The Surrounded*. Yet the novel's heart lies in Zeb Calloway's words to his nefarious nephew: "She's gone, goddam it! Gone! . . . The whole shitaree. Gone, by God, and naught to care savin' some of us who seen 'er new."[19] Zeb's dire words, his unassuageable sense of loss, form the emotional and ideological center of the novel. Indeed, Zeb's vernacular description of paradise lost drives the entire plot of Boone's failure.

This tragedy in five acts renarrates the American fall from innocence. But the novel leaves us no exit, no sense of what to do about the collapse of another great dream. The novel's apocalyptic structure, destroying Boone's (and our) dreamworld, reveals no alternative, no means of redress, no goal for amelioration. In this way the seminal Montana book generates a curious resignation, even fatalism, that has an enduring currency in the region.

To restate my interpretation in medical terms, the novel infects the reader with the disease of self-pity originating in an irreparable break from past greatness. Zeb carries the germ of loss in his bitter self and transmits it to Boone, who in turn transmits it to the reader. By the novel's end, Jim is dead, Teal Eye abandoned and disgraced, Dick Summers puzzled and passive, and Boone a misanthropic drunk. The Big Sky country has been abandoned by the key white players, left to lick its wounds perhaps, but never to be the same. This germ of self-pity is carried more precisely in a mythology of the lost Eden analyzed by Bevis.[20] As the literary critic observes, Guthrie's novel has a curiously romantic quality, one founded on the myth of the American Adam celebrated in a male tradition of writing. The success of the narrative, then, depends upon Guthrie's giving that Adamic dream heft and credibility, and so he does. For this reader, returning to *The Big Sky* many times out of personal and pedagogical necessity, what endures are the haunting landscape descriptions, the sense of absolute space, of nature untouched by Euramerican greed. In these descriptive moments, the gap between the narrator and the main character collapses, revealing the writer's full commitment to the awestruck quality of Boone. There can be no mistaking the novelist's investment in the vision of Montana as pre-fall Eden. And given the dominant Judeo-Christian theology of American culture, what other outcome can we imagine than the destruction of the Garden and the casting out of the protagonists?

As contemporary readers invariably detect, this is an intensely male fantasy. Annette Kolodny has critiqued the male archetype by showing how literary Adamism translates into visions of deflowering the natural world.[21] *The Big Sky* is a case study in such wish fulfillment, though I must be sure to acknowledge Guthrie's partial consciousness of what he's about here. In the erotic subtext of the novel, Teal Eye becomes the embodiment of nature (or more specifically, Montana), and so Boone's quest to "have" the Indian female becomes his quest to "have" the Big Sky. The antisocial male character penetrates feminized nature on the Missouri River, merging imperial and sexual possession. Narrative logic dictates, then, that once Boone has deflowered Montana/Teal Eye, the game's up. The plot has reached its necessary but self-defeating climax, for the conquest of paradise means you can never have it over again. By definition, to penetrate the place is to lose what you value most. As Zeb puts it, "She's gone."

My readers might at this point object that Guthrie was far more circumspect about this mythology than I have allowed. Boone's decision to help Peabody find a path through the mountains, for example, appears pigheaded and morally suspect. As though to reiterate and criticize Caudill's male violence, Guthrie also has him sexually abuse a young white woman on his return to Kentucky. These actions suggest a character deeply flawed, made violent and destructive by his horrific upbringing. For these reasons Boone may be interpreted as the counterexample, the instance of the failed westerner, the warning to us all about our possible depredations. But if the writer has skillfully undermined his main character, he has left intact the mythology of possession that powers his plot. As with the landscape descriptions, the narrator's presentation of Teal Eye seems fully in sync with the character's. I do not detect irony in those longing gazes toward the female. Guthrie in fact reinforces the image of Teal Eye as nature embodied through the sympathetic character of Jim Deakins. There can be no doubting the sexual and ideological appeal of this Indian maiden.

Furthermore, if Guthrie desired to censure Boone and Boone alone, why must he destroy Jim and drive Summers out of paradise? In a literal instance of overkill, Guthrie has his character murder everything. The only outcome must be a total catastrophe. As Boone tells us, echoing his uncle, "It's like it's all sp'iled for me now, Dick— Teal Eye and the Teton and all. Don't know as I ever can go back, Dick. Goddam it! Goddam it!" (366). Invoking a near-biblical judgment in those final two exclamations, Boone emphasizes his utter alienation from the place he loved. In the end, we, like Dick Summers (again, surely meant to be the male reader's surrogate), scratch our heads, wondering how it all went so wrong, and sink into our easy chairs, resigned to the attenuated bitterness of living after the fall.

My readers might still object that Guthrie relies upon a theory of history that takes us beyond Boone's disaster. The novelist went on to compose five more novels in his narrative cycle. Surely this rich texture of stories fills out Guthrie's vision of settlement, his sense of Montana's destiny. These six novels, that is, collectively narrate the historical process of settling the northern plains, a process that moves beyond Boone's juvenile misconduct to the mature actions of Ben Tate in *The Last Valley*. As Fred Erisman astutely comments, "The Arfive novels are 'local' stories in the very best sense, and the smaller scope serves Guthrie well. The older author focuses here upon characters concerned with community as much as with self.... Now the characters must take up the task of turning wilderness into community."[22] Much as the homestead writers Percy Wollaston and Pearl Price Robertson located a source of possibility in community, so Guthrie, in his later narratives, senses hope in collective action. And in the final novel especially, the writer goes out of his way to critique precisely the frightening extremist views now touted by the Militia of Montana. Guthrie incisively and bravely attacked the KKK's presence in an emerging Montana community, asserting that there's no room for that value system in the West of his memory and desire.

Yet, granting that Guthrie aspired to this revision of the apocalyptic story, his tactic does not work for two obvious reasons. First, his lead novel in the hexalogy so completely dominates our sense of Guthrie's achievement (and our teaching of western literature) that the other texts have receded into obscurity. For most readers, Guthrie's accomplishment is summed up in his first and most famous novel. If we consider his cultural presence, then, his influence on the wider society, *The Big Sky* carries his charge. Guthrie's novels also subtly reinforce cataclysm by reproducing the argument of James Fenimore Cooper's Leatherstocking Tales. Cooper's historical vision was profoundly cyclical, that is to say, apocalyptic. Writing as a conservative suspicious of American claims to a special destiny, the New York novelist demonstrated repeatedly the venality of humans and the failure of human institutions. His hero Natty Bumppo ironically advances the cause of settlement through acts that only assure Eden's demise. Summers echoes Bumppo's complicity, explaining to Boone that "There was beaver for us and free country and a big way of livin', and everything we done it looks like we done against ourselves and couldn't do different if we'd knowed" (366). Guthrie has thus carried over into our historical epoch a grimly pessimistic vision of historical change.

Yet something endures beyond these disasters. Thomas W. Ford is persuasive when he asserts that a sense of place is central to Guthrie's art.[23] As I have already suggested, those marvelous landscape descriptions continue to pull us in long after we know the sad outcome of Boone's story. And Guthrie's most beloved landscape, the region around the Teton River, continues to loom up like a judgment and hope in all six novels. (It's tempting to think that Guthrie modeled his technique on Thomas Cole's *Course of Empire*, which features a single identifiable mountain peak as the recurring base or subtext of the ongoing tragic narrative.) Ear Mountain bears witness to the entire narrative cycle. And that sense of place, that wonder in the natural environment, that belief in an enduring wilderness presence, raises a possibility only glancingly considered by Guthrie himself: Can we imagine an ethos that counters the notion that we kill the thing we love, an ethos grounded in that very place he loved so much? To answer that question fully will be the burden of part III. Yet let me pause a moment to consider this option. This past week, my family and I lived in a cabin on the edge of Flathead Lake in northwestern Montana. This largest freshwater lake west of the Mississippi is surrounded by those same Mission Mountains that influence McNickle's characters. (In truth, we were staying on the Salish-Kootenai Reservation, on land appropriated from the tribes.) The landscape is comparatively lush, covered in pine and ash. Storms move on and off the lake, creating a dramatic effect. As Thoreau wrote of his pond, a body of water can become the eye of the world.

Now, in a strong sense, that stay on Flathead was a homing experience for me. I was born in Polson in the mid-1950s. My parents later moved to Bozeman, then to the Midwest, but the lake continues to exert a powerful pull on me. Since my mother-in-law and two siblings are buried in the cemetery that overlooks Flathead, we had many occasions to journey to high ground, to witness the place, to think about matters spiritual and communal. There's no question that Flathead country has been overrun by development. There are far too many resort homes, far too many loud sport utility vehicles (including my own), far too many speculative land deals. But despite the noise, the booming logging trucks, and the trendy restaurants girding the lake, something endures that we can't manage to kill. That's obvious from my own tears as I stand in the cemetery, thinking of my late mother-in-law, thinking of my own deceased parents, thinking of my own life's circle. It's obvious when I stare at the face of the Mission Mountains, reflected in that remarkable body of water, much like Guthrie's beloved Ear Mountain. The busyness of humans can recede to nothing in such moments. I'm not foolish or blind—we've overdeveloped one of the most beautiful places on earth. We've polluted the lake. We've squeezed each other out so that only a few can enjoy private views of the water. But it isn't all gone. We haven't killed the thing entire. If we can gather our senses, recommit to the place, and stop dreaming of owning it all, we might just stop the madness and retain the dignity available to us.

It is remarkable how many people will do anything to live in the Flathead region. I met people working two and three jobs just to make ends meet, just so they could stay on the shores of Flathead Lake. These are not people who dream of glamorous powerboats on the water or trophy houses on the islands. These are people who feel at home, who wait for the tourists to go away. These people have a sense of place. It's not dead.

Chapter 5

MOONS FOR
THE MISBEGOTTEN

RICHARD HUGO'S BEST-KNOWN POEMS TELL TIME AND AGAIN OF absolute, pure loss. His confessional voice carries the woe of the lonely, the estranged, the misplaced, the misbegotten. His personae enunciate with uncommon clarity and frankness the loneliness of the long-distance poet. Montana's wind-scarred landscape carries the metaphorical weight of this woe, the pain writ large. Similar to Guthrie, Hugo endured beyond these poignant cries of the heart, composing more balanced and kinder "letter" poems, for instance. But as with Guthrie, the posthumous Hugo remains a victim of his own genius, his harshest, most daring, most existentially terrifying poems calling to us, enthralling us. In this sense, Hugo is typical of a collection of talented "outlanders" who have found in Montana a fit habitation for their lugubrious stories. Jim Harrison, Thomas

McGuane, and Richard Ford have composed similarly heartbreaking tales, using the region's landforms as a tabula rasa for the enactment of farce and tragedy.

By no means would I want to live without Hugo's poetry. He is among the most talented, most compelling, most *interesting* writers to emerge in this region. We need him, we need his bluntness, offbeat humor, and acuity. As an undergraduate at the University of Montana, I shied away from his courses, mainly because I've never thought of myself as a poet, but also because friends told me of the man's rigor, his painfully direct criticisms (though they were often delivered through a cigarette-induced, smoky, laughing cough). Yet one of the best poetry readings I've ever attended occurred in Madison, Wisconsin, when Hugo came through on a tour promoting *The Right Madness on Skye*. The audience seemed more polite than involved in the poems anchored in Scotland, but once the poet turned to his Montana materials the air became electric. Hugo brought his presentation to a climax by shouting (not reading, not saying, but shouting) "Degrees of Gray in Philipsburg." I wasn't the only one who felt the top of the head come off when he finished that heart-wrenching performance. I knew then what Yeats was getting at when he wrote about the gaiety of tragic art, the painful joy of artful sadness. When we think about Hugo's Montana lyrics, then, we can't slump into simple despair or grim malaise. Hugo wouldn't allow it—he was too funny, too quirky, too ambivalent for that. While I read his poems, I'm often on the verge of bursting into laughter (though I hope it isn't sheer hysteria). Hugo dispenses tragedy and humility in a single dose. There is something delightfully irreverent about his brand of dread. In that way Hugo sets himself apart from a cluster of regional writers who can only strain for comic effects; in that way, he has more in common with our cowboy poets than with A. B. Guthrie Jr. or D'Arcy McNickle.

Still, I can't evade his outlander status, the sense in which Montana was more metaphor, more figurative landscape, than a literal, real, historically bounded, determinate place for Hugo. The title of his autobiographical essays, *The Real West Marginal Way*, hints at this status. After all, Hugo suggests, I do get at the real thing, the West itself, but I do so by attending to the marginal experience and by myself remaining marginal to the enterprise. And he says as much in his collection of essays about the art of poetry: "Contrary to what reviewers and critics say about my work, I know almost nothing of substance about the places that trigger my poems. Knowing can be a limiting thing. . . . I would never try to locate a serious poem in a place where physical evidence suggests that the people there find it relatively easy to accept themselves—say the new Hilton."[1] (Contrast this approach with Ivan Doig's compulsive need to research his subject matter inside and out.) Even mentioning this issue of "insiders" and "outsiders" makes me uneasy, mainly because Montanans (and westerners in general) can be embarrassingly chauvinistic. How many times have visitors to the state, friends or colleagues, been told (basically) to leave the place to "us locals"? How many arguments have I witnessed over how the "outlander" can't write authentically about the region? (I recall here a gripping, half-playful, half-earnest disagreement between Tom McGuane and William Kittredge at an informal gathering of writers and artists during Montana's centennial year.) I do not invoke the term *outlander* to discredit Hugo or others. Instead, I'm raising what seems an important technical matter: the writer who grows up elsewhere and has absorbed other repertoires of language, landscape, and history may well have a different relationship to the language, landscape, and history of this place than the native child. Think about the almost desperate nostalgia of McNickle's and Guthrie's prose; you're unlikely to encounter that vivid sense of irrecoverable innocence and wonder in texts made by writers who grew up in Michigan, or Mississippi, or Washington. The writer who adopts the place is likely to edge toward an almost allegorical relationship with character and landscape. To phrase that point in less fancy terms, the writer from elsewhere will often see Montana in much the same terms as Hugo articulates above: the precise specifics of a place matter less than the internal responses triggered and then released through art.

Notice, also, that it's not just any place that stimulates this particular poet: it must be a site where people find it hard to accept themselves. The artistic deck is stacked from the start. In his posthumous autobiography, Hugo explains that he grew up essentially an orphan, raised in a tough town outside Seattle by his worn-down grandparents. As Hugo would explain in a "Self-Interview," discussing how his generation's subject matter differs from his students': "The Depression, threats of poverty and dispossession, loyalty to defeated people we still love and desire not to be like, and then a feeling of having violated our lives by wanting to be different—oh, very complicated matters."[2] We also learn of his traumatizing experiences in World War II, the thirty-five missions that haunted him. (The photograph, reproduced on page 132 of the autobiography, of the exhausted bombardier after a raid is one of the most revealing war photos I've ever come across.) Hugo knew in his bones what total devastation, what heartless harm looks like. "His own sense of abandonment," as William Bevis has written, "dovetailed with the region's history of disaster: the crushing of the Indians, the fur trade boom and bust (1825–45), the mining boom and bust (1860–1900), the homestead boom and bust (1909–19; 66 percent failed), the oil and lumber booms and busts (to the present), the water boom and bust (in full swing now)."[3] Bevis goes on to assert that Hugo's poetry is finally about endurance, about getting through, about surviving the hard falls and disillusionment. Maybe. But I have a hunch that the critic reads Hugo's verse as a friend here. Yes, it's true that certain poems, even collections, point toward the more hopeful reading. Look, for instance, at *31 Letters and 13 Dreams*. Hugo consciously constructed a bridge to possibility, working through a series of harrowing dreams to arrive at the "Good Dream": "Storms are spotted far off enough / to plan going home and home has fire."[4] And individual poems, written in a relaxed and personable, if sometimes anxious, voice, make real the possibility of love, of belonging. In one of my favorite of all Hugo poems, "Letter to Levertov from Butte," the persona first discloses the children "Degraded by drab homes" but then finds his way to this notion of endurance:

And I want my life
inside to go on long as I do, though I only populate bare
landscape with surrogate suffering, with lame men

crippled by more than disease, and create finally
a simple grief I can deal with, a pain the indigent can find
acceptable. I do go on. (307–8)

In a sense all he offers is the staying power of the witness, the one who knows, the Tiresias of Butte, of Montana, the one who empathizes. It's a lot—it's more than most of us can aspire to.[5] But can we really think of Hugo as a poet of hope?

Quick now, when I mention Richard Hugo, which poems come to mind? The answer will no doubt vary depending upon the reader's age, location, and amount of time spent with the poet's collected works. For me, the list would read: "Degrees of Gray," "The Lady in Kicking Horse Reservoir," "Montana Ranch Abandoned," "Missoula Softball Tournament," "The Milltown Union Bar," "Driving Montana," "Bear Paw," "Silver Star," "Ghosts at Garnet," and then I would have to pick up the collection and begin to think. Granted, this is what a sociologist would call a small sample, a pitifully small sample: one literature professor. So one could assert that my reading of Hugo depends upon my quirky reader response, my idiosyncratic selectivity, my thesis-driven quest for catastrophe. But I don't think so. Test this out with other avid readers of western American literature and see which poems rise to the top (like those trout that swim so seductively through Hugo's lyrics). What's at stake here is the legacy, what endures. Hugo could well be smiling at this moment, since he sagely asserted that "[w]hat endures is what we have neglected." So the poems I've isolated may provide hints of other voices, other possibilities that will last beyond the harsher poems full of degradation and even self-loathing. And my list is by no means unabated woe: consider the hair lighting the wall at the end of "Degrees," or the beautiful wives at the softball tournament, or the simple fact that many of these poems are dedicated to friends. As Hugo reminds us in *The Triggering Town*, poems are often best addressed to someone intimate, someone who matters, and the very act of composing can be felt as a reaching out, a connecting beyond the shameful self.

But think again about the dominant imagery of all those triggering

MOONS FOR THE MISBEGOTTEN ᏕᎠ 81

places in Montana: grayness, cracking, disheartening wind, weathered buildings and lives, sagging prospects, empty roads, clownish failures. It's not a pretty picture, nor is it meant to be. And add this: Hugo's poems have achieved what art must, changing our way of seeing the world, of experiencing the self, of knowing others. On a road trip to northern Montana in the late '90s, I could not escape either Raban's *Bad Land* or Hugo's "Montana Ranch Abandoned." Abandoned shacks called to me. The restless wind coursed through my memories and dreams. I will never see Montana without the lenses provided by this compelling poet. And as Bevis's list of Montana catastrophes reminds us, there's plenty of grist for the elegiac mill here. That's why, I suspect, my students often cringe when they first encounter this verse. It cuts close to the bone.

But let's remember that Hugo spoke true when he asserted that his poems have no obligation to reality, only to the "truth about your feelings." As a confessional poet who takes readers to the edge of psychological and existential abysses, Hugo dances in the subjective rather than the objective. He is, by his own admission, a biased, slanted respondent to Montana, which suggests that he not be granted the final word on the meaning of this place. His gifted former student James Welch, for example, might take us to a different end of the road as he represents Montana traumas.

Consider also other important Montana poets. Think, first, of Wallace McRae, the rancher/poet who writes with a political fervor that often spills over into sentimentality and open pleading. With McRae's cowboy verse, you know someone's at home in this place and willing to risk ridicule to protect that sacred space:

I'm s'posed to ramrod all them beasts
on land, in air and sea.
But the earth and all her critters
has got dominion over me.[6]

Paul Zarzyski writes with an eye and ear for the specifics of place, often combining keen wit with an almost hypnotic attention to the actual. To take a striking example, this onetime outlander has cleverly, even shockingly, brought to our consciousness the presence of those ballistic missiles on the Montana landscape:

> Silos against Augusta:
> honeybee with Hutterite with family ranch—
> the Minuteman launching pads
> against everything from Dearborn River
> to jackfence to cowhorse and combine.[7]

The poem makes us confront the absurdity of locating weapons of mass destruction in the midst of natural wonder. Zarzyski veers toward an almost tendentious style here, but one that stimulates, that moves. And finally, take the case of Sandra Alcosser, surely one of the best writers presently working in the state. Her poems are sensual, wildly imaginative, funny, and almost painfully disclosive. Her art suggests vital differences between male and female ways of imagining. If Hugo concentrates on the absurd loneliness of the displaced self, Alcosser bears down on the explosive connectivity of the placed body. Compared with Hugo's tough-guy spareness and understatement, her style appears almost baroque in its lavishness and metaphorical play:

> All that I will ever know is right here
> in the wash and till of my own ten acres.
> Frost tonight and behind it the whole summer
> so brief I can still see the bronco-faced calf
> born to the bloody pasture and the brown trout
> suspended in its first glittering insect hatch.[8]

Harrison, McGuane, and Ford, while strikingly different in voice and approach, also treat Montana as a perverse field of dreams. The place and its layered history provide a scrim upon which to project their fables of failure. A brilliant but slightly crazed writer once told me that *Legends of the Fall* is her favorite Montana book. I pushed her: better than *The Big Sky* or *A River Runs Through It* or *This House of Sky* or *Fools Crow?* The writer was persistent, inflexible. Harrison's stuff is the best. To be honest, this conversation took place before I'd actually read the now-famous novella. Having since spent time with the narrative, both as a book on tape and a book on the page, I can see her point:

the voice is incredibly seductive. The narrator is sure, graceful, and at times stunningly poetic. The tone is dramatic, expansive, even apocalyptic. And Harrison covers some serious ground, locating the reader in northern Montana, World War I France, the Caribbean, China, San Francisco, Helena, etc. Yet, when all is said and done, I don't believe a word of it. It all seems over the top, worked up, fabricated. Harrison has himself been seduced by melodramas of the West every bit as suspicious as *The Virginian* or *Riders of the Purple Sage*. I struggle to find an actual human being in the story.

Like all romances, *Legends* has an intense, dreamlike quality. It's as though we're watching our archetypes strut around in front of us, enacting our fantasies and fears. The characters in Harrison's novel are larger than life, vivid, melodramatic, incredible. Tristan, the Brad Pitt character, is the most outrageous of all, beginning as a wild savage and coming full circle to something like maturity at the end. He manages to slaughter and scalp Germans, engage in gun and opium smuggling, work as a bootlegger, and kill some nasty Irish gangsters in gruesome fashion. More than enough action for one life, for several lives. As his father speculates at one point, "So perhaps Tristan in a genetic lapse had become his own father and would like Cain never take an order from anyone but would build his own fate with gestures so personal that no one in the family ever knew what was on his seemingly thankless mind."[9] At the risk of seeming a big bore, I can't help contrasting this action with Guthrie's Arfive stories, set in exactly the same location—Choteau, Montana, within view of the Rocky Mountain front—in roughly the same years. Though Guthrie was not at his storytelling best in *Arfive*, something like the actual works its way into the novel: the by-turns Victorian and sexually needy principal Benton Collingsworth (based on Guthrie's own complicated father); the tough, likeable cowboy Mort Ewing; the troubled young woman Julie. Guthrie is tracing out how a community takes up habitation on the frontier, how citizens gradually build a home on land more suited to buffalo ranges and hunting-and-gathering cultures. He is also trying to understand how sexuality figures into the processes that meld a town, a bold move for a Montana writer. Harrison's West is, by contrast, child's play; it's still the Wild West, still the world of the 1860s and '70s, still the place of insanely outsized and manic lives. It's Yellowstone Kelly with a great lyrical style. And sex is sex, raw, good for destroying lives but not much good for anything else.

William Ludlow, Tristan's eccentric but brilliant father, may be more grounded than his outrageous son, but he also bears witness to some significant history. We learn early in the novella that Ludlow served as a scientist on Custer's infamous Black Hills expedition, the predetermined outcome of which led to Custer's final defeat. Ludlow recalls his pleasure at learning of the Last Stand (which Harrison inaccurately locates in 1877). So we have an enlightened immigrant who has raised three remarkably different sons, the future politician, the wild man of the mountains, and the fragile victim of mechanized violence. Harrison's tactic reveals itself here: he has written a virtual fable of western settlement, an allegory of expansion, mistakes, mistreatment, and final disaster. The three sons provide templates of western personality: the aspiring civic leader, the renegade, and the mama's boy who can't make it. It's as if Wallace Stegner had determined to compress his 600-page epic of the West, *Angle of Repose*, into 100 pages. Telling would for sure dominate showing, and you'd have to cut a few corners (or angles) along the way.

In addition to Custer's defeat, Harrison incorporates many of the catastrophic events that have circulated through Montana history: the savage defeat of the Nez Perce (231); the dispiriting homesteader land rush (197); union/capital strife in a brief mention of Frank Little's lynching in Butte in 1917 (241); and the arrival of the Great Depression (251). Harrison is plainly drawn to the catastrophic extremes of the region, the incidents of crisis. As the narrator explains, "there is little to tell of happiness—happiness is only itself, placid, emotionally dormant, a state adopted with a light heart but nagging brain" (253). These events provide the base or subtext for the covert competition between Alfred and Tristan for the love of Susannah, casting a spell of unease over the rapid-fire narrative. The brothers' rivalry can be read as a conventional clash of ideologies: the hierarchical, shrewd, cynical, pro-Company stance versus the democratic, untamed, callously naive, pro–little guy values. The narrator clearly sides with the latter set of principles, showing up the hapless Alfred as a shallow coward. While

Tristan can be casually cruel, he is alive and giving. But grant Harrison credit for outlining an important struggle for the soul of the West. He highlights a political, even spiritual, battle that has preoccupied writers and historians such as Guthrie and Howard. Tristan is an avatar for contemporary varieties of rebellion.

The crazed energy of the narrative finally finds vent in the madness and death of Susannah. Harrison's descriptions of her manic-depressive cycle are among the most impressive stylistic effects in the novella. She seems a medium for the wildness, desire, and anger of the entire cast of characters. She is, in a sense, the Cassandra of the story. It's not by accident that late in the novella Isabel and Ludlow are reading Melville's *Pierre; or, The Ambiguities,* a story of the failed, tragic life of the naive child of an aristocratic upstate New York family. As Lucy, Isabel, and Pierre must all die pathetically in Melville's tale of sorrow, so also must Samuel, Two, and Susannah. And like the faith-starved Melville, the narrator of *Legends of the Fall* dwells upon the missing presence of God, the absent meaning-giving center of the universe. Tristan and his family have indeed fallen, into an abyss of hurt, a memory of woe, without the balm of belief. We are left with the legends, the retailed memories, and little else.

Whereas Jim Harrison's prose is outlandish and archetypal, Thomas McGuane's is cool, ironic, and patently absurdist. Reading a McGuane novel is like plunging your hand into the Boulder River during late autumn—the prose is chill and elusive. We catch the mood of his taletelling when we recognize that the writer has renamed Livingston "Deadrock." McGuane has staked out his own Montana terrain: the experience of the prodigal son, the loner in search of love, the drifter at odds with himself and the world. Like *Rancho Deluxe,* the film sendup of the western experience that McGuane scripted, *Nobody's Angel* focuses on the "new West" of affluent immigrants, disillusioned cowboys, and campy sex. Beneath it all you can almost hear Elizabeth Ashley's plea for "some Gothic ranch action." If Harrison reiterates the West's woes with a kind of feverish, hallucinatory intensity, McGuane treats that history with a cynical sneer. Here Patrick Fitzpatrick, the ne'er-do-well native son come back from cold-war soldiering, reads a casting call for a movie that's supposed to be shot around Deadrock:

"In order to reflect the hardships endured in the West in the 1880's, we would especially welcome the physically eccentric, those with permanent physical injuries, such as scars, missing teeth, broken limbs, broken noses, missing limbs, etc." (14). McGuane's technique is heavily inflected with cinematic effects. The opening chapters of *Nobody's Angel* read like a long montage, a series of briefly realized scenes that are artfully spliced together. But such an approach also points toward disconnection, the lack of narrative through-line, the loss of a telling action. That sense of incoherence applies to characterization as well. Personalities seem an assemblage of parts, an accretion of partial identities. When Fitzpatrick remembers his youth in Montana, it's as a private montage of superficial experiences.

Still, cool and ironic as the novel's technique may be, Fitzpatrick is clearly haunted by ghosts of prior demise. He has a sickness of the soul, a radical homelessness, of a piece with the nihilist terror that afflicts Tristan and his clan. He is a fallen angel, of course, bonded to the shattered pilot he finds in the mountains above his family's Heart Bar Ranch, the pilot who could be his dead father. Contemplating his grandfather's tales of a cowboy past, complete with paranoid theories about the changes wrought by modern technology, Fitzpatrick realizes his necessary commerce with the legends of the place: "As then, when he felt the old man's past, or when he went among the ancient cottonwoods that once held the shrouded burials of the Crow, Patrick felt that in fact there had been a past, and though he was not a man with connections or immediate family, he was part of something in the course of what was to come" (63). For all that, "the cowboy captain felt stranded on the beautiful ranch he would someday own, land, homestead, water rights, cattle and burden. He had no idea what he would do with it" (65). In sum, he is one of the "[l]ost souls on the big sky" (75).

Similar to Harrison's Susannah, Patrick's sister Mary carries the burden of family disease, manifesting the emptiness at the heart of the ranching clan: "Patrick had wandered away and Mary had flown into the face of it, the face of it being the connection they never had, an absence that was perilously ignored" (86). If the male can come at

his sadness-for-no-reason obliquely, and temporarily evade the imme-
diacy of those blues through ranching, sex, and domestic duties, Mary
confronts profound despair straight on, almost in a loving embrace.
She is more than half in love with death. As such, she serves as the
reflector of the deep griefs that Patrick can only mumble.

If the reader pauses to wonder why these events are set in Montana, the best answer seems to be: the contemporary West occupies an
interstitial space between lost, even discredited, stories and anything
like a meaningful alternative. The grandfather mourns his lost cowboy
youth and dreams of "the Australia" he'll never know; Patrick sardon-
ically observes the "boomer town" and various émigrés to the region,
restless souls who look for something like solace in a stunningly beautiful environment that concedes nothing: "the West, the white West,
a perfectly vacant human backdrop with its celebrated vistas, its
remorseless mountains-and-rivers and its mortifying attempts at town
building" (134). Montana seems to be in a funk, a permanent blues,
and Patrick is just the man to wallow in that condition. For McGuane,
he's truly a native son. And since the narrator looks upon religion,
especially Catholicism, as a defunct belief system, it's hard to imagine
an alternative to this depressing Montana on the mind. Patrick's angry
dismissal of the priest during his sister's funeral takes us right back to
that essential nihilist Ernest Hemingway and the bitter conclusion to *A
Farewell to Arms*. (The mention of Hemingway is not gratuitous, since
McGuane cleverly echoes *The Sun Also Rises*, especially in his characterization of Claire as a kind of latter-day Brett Ashley.)

McGuane's narrator does allow "that friendship was somewhere
possible" (167), and so David Catches and the fantastical Marion
Easterly are the closest thing to a salve offered in this grimly funny
book. Yet even love, a solution available to some of our most down-
and-out existentialists, especially one Richard Hugo, seems a mistake. Patrick's relationship with Claire drives toward madness and
death. After all, Claire and Patrick's last stand in the cabin is imaged
"like an English couple eating marmalade in an air raid" (193). Yet
their final session of lovemaking cannot rise to the level of Custer's
pallid glory: "He was not so far gone as not to note that the West's last

stands were less and less appropriate to epic poetry and murals" (223). It's a satirico-tragic vision of homelessness on the range. Appropriately, the novel's final words read: "he never came home again" (227).

There's something distinctly autumnal about the Montana books discussed in this chapter, and no writer better demonstrates that allegiance to the season of change and death than Richard Ford. He composes in the spare, minimalist, underhandedly comic style that characterized much of the best writing of the 1980s, including the work of Raymond Carver and Bobbie Ann Mason. But that observation leads to the realization that in many ways Ford's Montana is primarily a backdrop for tales of loneliness, economic marginality, and pain that could take up habitation in any number of places. The western landscape becomes a useful metaphor for the desiccation and emptiness of the characters' lives, as we will see especially with the title story of the collection. The soon-to-be convict Bobby summarizes this sense of the place in his memorable lines, "I don't know why people came out here. . . . The West is fucked up. It's ruined. I wish somebody would take me away from here."[10] In such moments Ford's characters sound strikingly similar to Uncle Zeb and his nephew Boone.

Because of that tone of loss and disappointment, Ford comes closest to Hugo among the three fictionists treated in this chapter. As he describes an impromptu reading with Carver and Tess Gallagher, Ford testifies to the poet's influence:

> I distinctly remember Tess reading Hugo's great poem "Degrees of Gray in Philipsburg," and as the last phrase sounded . . . feeling a moody silence come over us all, a slightly embarrassed wordlessness about the fact that we were so frankly letting this poem *in*, with all its blunt intimations of death and lust and boom-towns gone bust and beautiful girls you'd never get to visit again. It's a sentimental poem and a wonderful one from a wonderful and rather sentimental poet who never got his due. And it carries strong feeling the way a hod carrier totes bricks. But we all subscribed to it.[11]

Ford approaches the elegiac, dreadful poignancy of the master poet in several of his stories, taking us to the abyss and beyond. He composes in the blue-collar blues. He also has that uncanny ability to involve the reader in these characters' traumas, establishing a rapport reminiscent of poems such as "The Lady in Kicking Horse Reservoir." Ford will not allow the reader to settle into a comfortable, complacent distance from the sadness let loose in the narratives. His stories imitate that peremptory "you" that leaps off the page in Hugo's poems. We feel as though attention must be paid.

Ford's characters are quintessential drifters, crossing through Montana on their restless searches for something like meaning, something like drama. Typically petty criminals, out-of-work loners, and hopeful if depressed survivors, they are "marginal" to what passes for ordinary, middle-class life. Suffering some ineradicable ennui, an indifference similar to Patrick Fitzpatrick's, they long to jumpstart their lives by action, however silly or deviant. As one character puts it succinctly, "Les wants more" ("Winterkill," 152). Though paradoxically vain and insecure at the same time, the male character in "Going to the Dogs" jumps in the sack with a tough but willing huntress, only to discover later that he's been robbed by her partner during the act. In "Empire," Vic Sims sleeps with an ex-biker chick out of boredom and lust, only to find himself threatened with blackmail. The tawny plains, incipient chill, and apparently pointless small-town life of Montana provide effective symbols for these sorry lives. The narrator of "Children" suggests this correspondence between the allegorized place and his own offbeat, sad story: "Claude Phillips was a half-Blackfeet Indian, and his father, Sherman, was a full-blood, and in 1961 our families rented out farm houses from the bank in Great Falls—the homes of wheat farmers gone bust on the prairie east of Sunburst, Montana. People were going broke even then, and leaving. . . . and . . . I would be long gone from there myself, and so would Claude" (69).

"Rock Springs" summarizes the strengths and appeal of Ford's collection. Written from the point of view of a failed criminal, the action follows his comically inept efforts to take himself, his daughter, and his lover to Florida, a cross-country journey that would signal his break from the Montana that sends people to prison for writing bad checks. Perhaps better than any other story (though "Empire," "Optimists," and "Communist" carry a similar force), "Rock Springs" builds the reader's identification with the speaker/protagonist. His overwhelming desire for normalcy, for an intact family, for a modest affluence, courses through the story. He steals an ophthalmologist's cranberry Mercedes-Benz, then presents himself as that very ophthalmologist when he checks into the Ramada Inn in the Wyoming town. He borrows the phone of a black woman and her mentally retarded grandson, claiming a marginal superiority because his daughter is healthy and normal, yet he struggles to leave behind that homelike trailer. And in the haunting closing sequence, the narrator looks the reader right in the eye and asks a series of dead-on questions:

> And I wondered, because it seemed funny, what would you think a man was doing if you saw him in the middle of the night looking in the windows of cars in the parking lot of the Ramada Inn? Would you think he was trying to get his head cleared? Would you think he was trying to get ready for a day when trouble would come down on him? Would you think his girlfriend was leaving him? Would you think he had a daughter? Would you think he was anybody like you? (27)

Here Ford creates the "There but for the grace of God" effect that recurs throughout the collection. The writer cannily shows that the border between our so-called normalcy (our complacency) and the troubled, even desperate, lives of his characters is permeable, friable, dissolvable. He suggests that the walls we place around our lives constitute psychic Maginot Lines. Is the speaker of the story all that different from most of us? Why have we, perhaps, found an approximation of comfort and sureness while he wanders in the dark?

Ford exploits to perfection the western setting for the action, once again establishing a meaningful correlation between the inner life of his characters and the outer world that ensnares them. Rock Springs and its surrounding environment present both an El Dorado and a Waste Land, both the miragelike dream of absolute wealth and the valley of dry bones. This blended, paradoxical vision of the West as the Big Rock Candy Mountain and the Great American Desert often dominates our national consciousness. And so this conjunction of fear and possibility opens out the action to an almost mythological dimension: "And sure enough [Cheryl] had seen something I hadn't, which was Rock Springs, Wyoming, at the bottom of a long hill, a little glowing jewel in the desert with I-80 running on the north side and the black desert spread out behind" (8). When the narrator's eye rests squarely on the heavily industrialized gold mine itself, this taunting sense of possible wealth becomes even more intense: "I stared out at the big, lighted assemblage of white buildings and white lights beyond the trailer community, plumes of white smoke escaping up into the heartless Wyoming sky, the whole company of buildings looking like some unbelievable castle, humming away in a distorted dream" (18). Prosperity is just so near and so far for the everyman narrator, so completely real and illusional in the same moment. In this way, Ford employs the linked myths of western dream and nightmare to create a subtle but telling subtext to the overt story of a man's failed life. Without overplaying his hand or beating us over the head, this writer exploits the allegorical possibilities of setting to show what defeat looks like at the most personal level. Ford takes us out of the abstractions of politics and makes us feel what despair is like in the blood and bones of the lonely self: "I was beginning to think of Rock Springs in a way I knew I would always think of it, a lowdown city full of crimes and whores and disappointments, a place where a woman left me, instead of a place where I got things on the straight track once and for all, a place I saw a gold mine" (25).

Harrison, McGuane, and Ford tap into a dilemma that recurs in writing by western males: How to make a meaningful self out of the flotsam and jetsam of personae thrown up by myth and media? Hugo writes feelingly of his troubled search—lasting well into his adulthood—for a credible masculine identity: "You'll notice that the men I wanted to be are strong men, men in control. Humphrey Bogart. Herbert Marshall. Each in his own way, tough. My urge to be someone adequate didn't change after the war. When I gave up fiction as a bad job and settled back into poems for good, I seemed to use the poems to create some adequate self. A sissy in life, I would be tough in the poem."[12] Given McGuane's fascination with media such as film and country-western music, this passage is especially relevant to Fitzpatrick's case. Men pick up and try on selves that appear strong, glamorous, self-reliant, sexually potent, etc. Living in the shadow of the myth of the western male, embodied by John Wayne above all others, and living in an often tough terrain that strips away the social structures and leaves the self one-on-one with weather, land, work, and economic failure, and living within a culture that prizes silence as much as communication (depriving the male of confidence, of a sure sense of accomplishment), western males have embarked on the manic search for a way of being believably adult.

As is so often the case, it's the women who see this most clearly, and none better than Mary Clearman Blew, daughter of a true cowboy who ultimately comes to a sorry end: "Pressures on young men in the West? Living up to the myth may be harder on men, in the long run, than on women. And the strictures of the Western code of silence apply specifically to men."[13] As we will see in Chapter 9, no writer is better able to capture the malaise of unstable identity than William Kittredge. *Hole in the Sky* evokes the divergent and empty selves "Kittredge" tries on and discards during his troubled journey toward mature self-possession. To take a final example of this dilemma, James Welch's nameless narrator in *Winter in the Blood* tells us at the beginning of his haunted search for himself, "I was as distant from myself as a hawk from the moon."[14] This novel, along with *Fools Crow*, will provide a vital counterpoint to McGuane's and Ford's farcical, sad-for-no-reason chronicles. Welch's male characters, though caught by a deracination far more devastating than any white American male can know, approximate composure and selfhood. They are among Montana's most important avatars of masculine maturing.

Chapter 6

JEREMIADS

TO TURN FROM THE IRONIC, SAD, OFTEN DISJOINTED WORK OF Hugo, Harrison, McGuane, and Ford to the work of Montana historians is to suffer a shock. The tone of our classic historians is bracing, even defiant. Joseph Kinsey Howard and K. Ross Toole embody the role of historian as preacher, as conscience of the people. Coming of age between the Progressive era and the Great Depression, these writers absorbed the traditions of muckraking journalism and analytic or critical historical writing. They also emulated fervid public intellectuals such as Walter Lippmann. Scholarship should reach beyond the academy to shape public policy, even our sense of ourselves. There's more at stake than the historical record here. Many readers of the anthology *The Last Best Place*, which has defined the canon of Montana writing, have wondered about the absence of the historians, and they have a point.[1] These critics suggest that history often fuses with art in the region, and that we ignore an important self-analysis if we slight historians. It is fascinating how genres tend to blur on "the frontier," history merging with poetry merging with fiction merging with personal narrative. As we revisit the work of Howard and Toole, then, we are not simply taking up another academic overview of our shared past. Instead, we are interpreting highly colored recastings of that past, versions that have had a profound influence on our sense of ourselves and our collective destiny.

These two writers remind us that the cataclysmic style of western discourse is not limited to right-wing radicals. In fact, extremism has a quality of "reversibility": opposing militant positions often begin with common assumptions about the root causes of the crisis but assert competing, even mutually exclusive, solutions. As the examples of the Populists, Wobblies, and the Montana Society of Equity suggest, left-wing militancy has a long tradition in this region as well. To take one of our more dramatic contemporary examples, Earth First! is a militant environmentalist group that advocates biocentrism, placing the needs of nature above those of humanity. To defend "Mother Earth" against the depredations of humanity, Earth First!ers have deployed tactics such as tree spiking—placing heavy nails or other pieces of metal in old-growth timber so that loggers risk injury when they harvest those trees. It's a terrifying act, truly a form of eco-terrorism. Yet this group has attracted notoriety, grudging respect, and even the kind of romantic allure we associate with Robin Hood and his Merry Men. Earth First! argues that such tactics are not just useful but necessary, since they are waging a final war for the survival of the natural world.

This analysis is not meant to suggest that we turn away from the historians' texts. They can still inspire citizens to reflection and action. That is, after all, the power of the jeremiad: the capacity to involve, to motivate, to activate the reader. And while these two political preachers at times take liberties with historical fact, they make a convincing case for the unseemly influence of eastern and international capital in the lives of citizens on the ground in Montana. Both writers argue with verve that decision making must rest at the local level, in the place itself. Howard and Toole both acted on this assumption, the former in his work with the Montana Study, the latter in his political activism on issues of taxation and land use.[2] As we will see in part III, recent philosophers and writers have attempted to expand upon that very approach to dwelling in the region.

The jacket for the Bison edition of *Montana: High, Wide, and Handsome* proudly declares that this historical text "was chosen in 1981 by the readers of *Montana: The Magazine of Western History* as the most significant book on the state."[3] Think about it—a political diatribe that assaults big business, false dreams, and foolish settlement prospects, chosen as the most telling, most important book about the region. While we might wonder about the method of polling, and while that poll was conducted at a specific moment in time with its own historical and political imperatives, the very fact that this book would rise to the top suggests its currency, its persuasive force, its representative status. Since I assume that popularity signals something about our collective judgments and values, the appeal of *Montana: High, Wide, and Handsome* confirms the region's tragic sensibility.

Howard wrote in the classic voice of the American jeremiad, the political sermon that argues we suffer terrible afflictions for our sins of commission and omission. This long-standing tradition, reaching back to the Puritans, provides a call to action, often proffering horrible consequences if we do not rise up to take arms against our own and others' venality.[4] Howard, a talented journalist from Great Falls, wrote with precisely this fervor and purpose when he composed his enduring account of Montana settlement. Written in the immediate aftermath of the depression, this 1943 narrative traces the recurring processes of settlement and failure in the state. In one sense, Howard's book is a recapitulation of the trends examined throughout this study: waves of dreams that come to naught on the high plains and in the mountains; betrayal by word and deed of native peoples and later immigrants; a surliness toward each other that takes root in this deprived soil.

The book's title is at least partly ironic. As Howard asserts early in his discussion of James Brisbin's *The Beef Bonanza, or How to Get Rich on the Plains*, a popular "how-to" manual for immigrants to the region, "It was an invitation to high, wide, and handsome looting of a virgin empire."[5] This sentence captures not only the predominant tone of the book but its major claim as well. Again and again we witness the foolish or greedy despoliation of a naturally sound, ecologically balanced place. Early in his capacious book, as he derisively catalogs the actions of the buffalo hunters, Howard invokes what seems a prescient sense of the complex interaction of life forms on the plains: "with this orgy of destruction the natural economy of the northern Great Plains perished, and none of the white man's devices has yet sufficed to restore the perfect balance of Nature, man, and food in this grim and unforgiving land" (22). It is not too much of a stretch to describe such a passage as biblical. The book's voice is by turns bemused, querulous, impatient, and even a bit patronizing. Howard generally follows the sequence of settlement attempts discussed throughout this book, but he feels no obligation to pursue chronology or analytic logic slavishly. His digressions into peculiar characters or events provide many of the highlights of the study. When Howard pauses to describe the sorry plight of a half-breed youth who fiddles the night away before being hanged as a rustler, the reality of vigilante violence comes home to the reader.

Given the general tenor of the book, it makes sense that Howard reserves some of his best writing for two commonly cited catastrophes in Montana's abbreviated history: Butte mining and the homestead boom. Both events bring out his colorful prose and rising ire. Discussing the mining boom in general, Howard sourly observes, "Here in Montana was a no-man's-land, to be looted by the strongest and, as soon as possible, abandoned. One owed it no allegiance" (48). In his five full and memorable chapters on the evolution of the mining industry in Butte, Howard outshines himself in exposing the mendacity and rapacity of the city's dominant figures, especially, in the end, the Anaconda Copper Company:

> Butte is the black heart of Montana, feared and distrusted. From the sixth floor of one of its office buildings go forth the corporate commands to politicians, preachers, and press, all the pensioners

and servile penny-a-liners of corporate capitalism. Butte is a sooty memorial to personal heroism, to courage and vigor even in rascality; and it is a monument to a wasted land. (85)

Having traced the mining and financial maneuverings of one of the three dominant figures in Butte history, Howard concisely concludes, "F. Augustus Heinze, Robin Hood of copper, did Montana incalculable harm" (83).

Howard writes with edge, conviction, and commitment when he characterizes the forces of ill that shaped Montana's copper industry. At times he allows the colorful, "boisterous" life of the city to percolate to the surface, capturing some of the allure that emerges with full force in Myron Brinig's *Wide Open Town*. But more often than not, the miner, the embodiment of that touted "personal courage," represents that most famous of lines about the state: "Montana, subject colony, has been the end of the cracked whip" (3). Translating the metaphor, the miners of Butte (and the homesteaders on the plains) were the victims of vast economic processes about which they had little or no say. Most tellingly, Howard presents a lucid and gripping account of how Standard Oil backed down Heinze and the governor of Montana by virtually shutting down the state's economy in 1905. If you are looking for a textbook instance of domination by external forces, that one nicely fills the bill.

If Howard can at least acknowledge the appeal of the mining culture of Butte, he can barely squeeze out anything other than scorn for the saps who participated in the farming boom in the first two decades of this century: "Honyocker, scissorbill, nester. . . . He was the Joad of a quarter century ago, swarming into a hostile land: duped when he started, robbed when he arrived; hopeful, courageous, ambitious" (178). Howard's analysis of Jim Hill and the homesteading debacle is surely the stylistic and political high-water mark of the text. What he saw as the fantastic idiocy of it all went beyond reason, beyond comprehension. In a telling aside, Howard concludes the ranchers' skeptical view of this land rush by suggesting, "Had not a horde of avid newcomers who had heard of the cattle bonanza descended upon these families, they probably could have established a permanently prosperous economy for the state: theirs was the ideal agricultural system for the plains" (170–71). Here Howard reiterates his faith in John Wesley Powell's grounded vision for settlement of the plains, lapsing into something like his own utopian nostalgia (to indulge an oxymoron). By contrast, the land rush produced a virtual nightmare, a hellish vision on the landscape: "The dreams of great men often live a long time, as dreams. That of Jim Hill, which he sought to bring to life in fact, became a witless nightmare. His trains rattled empty through dying towns. His neat little green fields were transformed as if an evil spirit had sped overhead, laying a curse upon them" (196). But we have to remember that Howard wrote in the shadow of economic collapse, a vast outmigration of failed farmers, and the haunting dust storms that carried much of the plains' topsoil eastward. He wrote under a literal pall, and that specific catastrophe colored his disillusioned prose. As Pearl Price Robertson, Percy Wollaston, Dale Eunson, and my own grandmother make clear in their writings, the homesteading experience went beyond folly, delusion, and failure. Some did, after all, survive the hard times, and others garnered a remarkable training in community building and resilience. On the environmental issue, however, it is difficult to challenge Howard's wrath.

When *Montana: High, Wide, and Handsome* shifts to a scathing analysis of the Federal Reserve System, a reader may be tempted to roll his eyes out of tedium. Here we sense the gap between the contemporary and the near past, for the muckraking journalist typifies the obsessions of those who were still weighing the costs and causes of the Great Depression. Howard relentlessly pounds the deflationary policies of that system, showing with stark clarity the dire effects of banking policies on agricultural communities. And therein lies the fascination and importance of this material. Howard outlines with unusual directness a plague, an obsession that continues to haunt Americans living in the "rural outback." Here, for instance, he excerpts an extensive journalistic piece on the causes of depression in the northwestern states:

> The cause, did you say? It is that the government, having moved the farmer dangerously to increase his production for reasons of patriotism, left him afterward to the mercy of bankers, who outra-

geously deflated him, the Federal Reserve System assisting; it is that big business is organized against the farmer to exploit him; it is that industry receives the benefits of tariff protection while agriculture does not. (227)

Compare this passage, published in 1924, with a more recent analysis of Roosevelt's banking reforms, appearing in 1996 on a website headed "Billings or Beijing?": "The farmers were being hoodwinked out of their land with fictional foreclosures. A few anointed plutocrats could manipulate the stock and commodity markets, create boom and recession—even war—at their own whims, and generally whipshaw [*sic*] the economy in any direction at any time they chose."[6] Or compare that earlier analysis with this more careful, fairly moderate survey of rural conditions published in 1995:

> Many consumers do not realize that this emerging corporately controlled food system raises serious questions about: 1) the quality and safety of their food; 2) the long-term sustainability of a system heavily dependent on fossil fuels and exploitation of soil and water resources; 3) the moral and ethical issues of low wages and dangerous conditions for workers; 4) the flight of profits from rural communities and the increase in rural poverty; 5) the depopulation of farming areas and the sense of powerlessness, alienation, and frustration that leads to community conflict, individual depression, and the rise of radical social movements.[7]

Howard's jeremiad leads us once again toward the startling realization that the despair of earlier Montanans circulates and recirculates, reemerging when the optimum conditions arrive. His diatribe also points up what I have referred to as the "reversibility" of radical politics. The journalist/historian is very much a left-of-center thinker, advocating government intervention to alleviate the rural crisis. The writer of "Billings or Beijing?" goes on to advocate the antigovernment position of the Freemen. This is one reason that extremist arguments pose dangers, even if, in the short run, they seem to favor our position. Once we collectively grant certain premises—for example, the powerlessness of farmers and ranchers in the face of impersonal industrial and governmental forces—we are left with few options other than radical, often violent responses.

In the final fourth of his big book, Howard subtly changes tone, shifting from the gloom-and-doom prophetic voice to that of the more moderate, progressive thinker. Perhaps Howard sensed that his tough, sometimes cynical language could depress rather than elevate the spirits of his local readers. Or perhaps he saw the first three-fourths as the necessary prelude to the activist chapters that complete *Montana: High, Wide, and Handsome*: "There is not much use determining the nature of a malady unless the process suggests some course of treatment" (321). Of course, many of Howard's contemporaries distrusted his political motives, especially when he publicly supported the Missouri Valley Authority.[8] The fact that the Montana Study was underwritten by the Rockefeller Foundation undoubtedly added a layer of suspicion to the project. Howard clearly asserted the value of collective planning, a notion likely to rile many westerners raised on the notion of individual rights.

It's a relief, in any case, to arrive at something like hopeful prose, something like a program of action. The concluding chapters are of a piece with *Montana Margins*, an attempt to energize community building by illuminating a rich cultural context for Montanans. As Howard asserts in the introduction to his anthology of writers from the state:

> The participative attitude toward art or literature, or toward any other human activity, can be most easily encouraged through emphasis upon native and regional values of the culture. The fully functioning community will provide even the experience of beauty for its citizens: in Montana, it will help them to interpret in music and painting, in drama and literature, the elemental values of life in this State which have been too often overlooked—space and freedom, sun and clean air, the cold majesty of the mountains and the loneliness of the plains, the gayety of a country dance, the easy friendliness of the people. These are the margins around the sometimes fretful business of earning a living. These are what Thoreau meant when he said, "I love a broad margin to my life."[9]

As with Guthrie's Arfive novels and Hugo's kinder, gentler letter poems, Howard's anthology marks his recognition of a need to overcome the obstacles he exposed so ruthlessly in his more famous work. He shows in these words that for him, as for Stegner, the West could be the native home of hope.

K. Ross Toole looms for me as a white-haired presence standing before an assembled throng in a cavernous, crepuscular theater on the campus of the University of Montana. It was the final quarter of my senior year in college. I'd already been accepted to graduate school and had enrolled in all the courses I'd been meaning to take for four years. To say that my commitment was at low ebb would be to understate the situation drastically. I took Toole's course because my brother-in-law, a soil scientist then as now, told me that the history professor was simply the best speaker he'd ever heard. And my brother-in-law was right. Toole had refined his content and delivery to the point where he seemed the voice of revelation. The man had been to the mountain top and received a vision. His tone was that of the prophet, the seer, the radical. His style combined urgency with a dab of bitterness and a large portion of pain. At the time (1978), Montana was again in the midst of economic turmoil, mainly surrounding decisions about what to do with the huge coal reserves underlying the plains of eastern Montana. As a diehard populist who preached the colonial status of Montana, Toole urged his awestruck listeners to take up arms against the vast companies that would once again lay waste to the state, both by strip mining and by running massive power lines from the site of coal-fired power-generating plants to the West Coast. I've never really recovered from these more contemporary jeremiads, and I am not alone. Toole's rhetoric shaped the political assumptions of several generations of Montanans.

The relationship between Howard's and Toole's work has been apparent to many, most notably the eminent Montana historian Merrill G. Burlingame: "Howard influenced Toole profoundly, and they had much in common. Both were historical activists, both were especially gifted writers and speakers, both were perceptive, incisive, intrepid. Both were motivated by a genuine affection for Montana."[10] Tellingly, the same poll that ranked Howard's book as first in significance listed Toole's *Montana: An Uncommon Land* as third (right after

Guthrie's *Big Sky*). And so once again I am compelled to consider the appeal of our catastrophic writers. Toole famously intones early in his strongly interpretive history, originally published in 1959, "The Montana pattern has been brief, explosive, frenetic, and often tragic. The economic picture has often been one of exploitation, overexpansion, boom, and bust. The political scene has been equally extreme—from fiery, wide-open violence to apathetic resignation."[11] No wonder "[o]ptimism has alternated almost monotonously with despair" (9). If Howard's prose can at times seem patched together or incohesive, Toole's style is smooth, assured, and consistently witty. It may have helped to be writing in the shadow of Howard, for the older author carried the burden of arguing for a highly critical interpretation of the Montana past. Toole advances much the same argument, but without the sense of having to begin from ground zero, of having to build from scratch. He cleverly echoes the title of that important precursor when he writes of the state's geographic placement, "High, wide, handsome, and remote, this area resisted penetration longer, perhaps, than any other" (12). If *Montana: An Uncommon Land* lacks some of the more memorable anecdotes in Howard's essays, the book often compensates with snappy quotes and one-liners: "[The managers of Standard Oil] were used to high financial maneuvers, massive squeeze plays, mergers, combinations, and impersonal dealings. But how did you deal with a corrupt district judge in the tough city of Butte with eggs in his beard and larceny in his heart?" (202).

Another noticeable difference between the younger writer and his mentor is Toole's feel for the land and the climate. Howard excels in his analysis of "the natural economy of the northern Great Plains," yet the emphasis falls on "economy" in the narrow sense of the exchange of goods and services. Writing in the lingering shadow of the Great Depression, the older chronicler searches restlessly for causes and solutions to the most fundamental problems of political economy. Toole, by contrast, often waxes poetic in his rendering of the mountains and plains, demonstrating a rapport, a familiarity, a fondness for the physical place. This discovery points toward a central theme in *Montana: An Uncommon Land*: the organic nature of many of the state's strengths and weaknesses. Toole clearly believes that the violent, cataclysmic events that have transpired on the plains and in the mountains largely erupted from the place itself. Hence the title: Montana history is unique because it has emerged from an uncommon land. And so the historian will on occasion lend an almost human sentience to the place: "The great quiet land and its original inhabitants had all the advantages" (51), or, "There was a pause of twenty years, during which the wealth of the land lay hidden by the land's own formidable ramparts" (63).

Proceeding from this premise, Toole composes a classic narrative history, leading from the prehistory of the state to the depression. It may be that the tragic theme appealed to Toole in part because of its utility for good storytelling. If you are determined to chronicle Montana history in sequence, and you desire to make that tale alluring, you might well feel a pull toward the cataclysmic. Of course, that writerly concern went hand-in-hand with Toole's genuine political commitments. Still, it is striking how often the jeremiad uncovers countertrends, tendencies that defy the nasty, brutish, and short theory of Montana history. In his analysis of the gold-mining camps of the 1860s, for instance, Toole makes an excellent case for the stabilizing forces that countered the rough-and-tumble mining culture: "Gunmen and violence were there, but beneath the primitive and raw surface churches were emerging, and social and economic institutions of substance were taking form" (76). Or as he later asserts, the gold camps "were the wedge of settlement, and thus their contribution was lasting" (80–81). And after detailing the bizarre political processes of the Montana Territory, he concludes: "The political scene in Montana between 1864 and 1889 has the superficial appearance of disorder, chaos, and even comedy. The fact is that there was deep consensus concerning the maintenance of the Union, there was a basic agreement about what the Territory needed, and Republican and Democrat alike shared a conviction that Montana was destined for great things" (114).

Toole reserves some of his most engaged, vivid prose for the political machinations of the early Territory. Thomas Francis Meagher has proven one of Montana writers' most durable characters, and Toole does him particular justice. The blustering, restless, self-promoting

Irishman seemed to hold a special power over the historian. Toole also sketches with verve the political chaos of the early Territory, resulting largely from the conflict between the defiantly Democratic Territory and the stubbornly Republican national government. In this way, *Montana: An Uncommon Land* highlights two tendencies that have found renewed vigor at the turn into the twenty-first century: a "copperhead" commitment to southern values, and a submerged desire for a break from "the States." While other historians tend to downplay this southern streak, it's surprising how prevalent that influence remains at this moment in Montana's history.[12] Perhaps because both the South and West were "last frontiers," immigrants to the northern tier felt a rapport with the marginalized condition, the isolation from the centers of political and economic power, and the blatantly white supremacist arguments that surrounded Indian affairs. Montana might well seem the last enclave, the home of white manhood, the sanctuary of a "true" American way. Fortunately, Montana's politics and culture have evolved to a point where that poisonous nonsense struggles to find a comfortable home, except in isolation, a true separatism.

Beginning with his analysis of the sordid Indian policy of the 1870s, Toole returns to his central theme: repeated political and economic miscalculations, resulting in disaster after disaster. Of Indian-white relations he concludes, "All that can be done now is to deal both understandingly and practicably with a people whose final heritage consists of a built-in and ineradicable tragedy" (138). Of the open-range era of the cattle industry, he memorably opines that "in the shockingly short span of six years the whole empire came crashing down. It took only a brief malevolence of nature and a few years of man's abuse" (144). Of the climactic struggle in the war of the copper kings, he asserts: "This was no mere strike or shutout; it was the bludgeoning of an entire state" (207). These shocks to Montana's system seem, on the whole, to buttress Toole's tendentious conclusion:

> The land was far away from the main stream of American life. Its wealth, almost without exception, was of such a nature that it could only be converted into coin of the realm by devices and methods created and paid for outside of the region. The raw mate-

rial could rarely be fabricated on the spot because of the simple economics of distance. And so the land—what was on it and in it—was given over to others. Distance meant cost, cost meant capital, capital meant absentee ownership, absentee ownership meant absentee control, and absentee control meant operation in the essential interest of outsiders with local interests a very secondary consideration. And so it was with beaver, beef, sheep, silver, copper, oil, and, to a lesser extent, even with lumber and wheat. (249)

I can still remember the fervor with which K. Ross Toole spoke nearly these very words to that assembled throng in 1978. I literally felt a chill run down my back as he intoned this dire insight. And even though he goes on to present a paean to the beauty of Montana and the friendliness of its citizens, you know that this interpretation forms the heart of his belief, his vision of the place.

Yet this reader is left with the impression that the lucid narrative that precedes it does not fully support so stark a summary. As noted earlier, Toole uncovers cores of stability and culture even in gold mining and territorial formation. In his analysis of the Progressive period between 1910 and 1924, the historian brings out ethical politicians and an initiative that increased the taxes on the mining interests. During his terse, almost sympathetic account of the homesteader boom, he discusses at least two phases of adaptation, marking a learning curve on the plains. And most interestingly, during his analysis of the disaster wrought by the Dawes Act of 1887, an act that effectively stripped reservation Indians of much of their land, Toole makes a critical point:

In 1910 [the Confederated Salish-Kootenai Tribes] had owned 1,250,000 acres. By 1930, 750,000 acres of their best land had been lost, their stock industry had been to all intents and purposes ruined, and 1,400,000,000 feet of their timber had been dissipated. Under the Reorganization Act, 192,425 acres have been redeemed, tribal income from its enterprises has been good, and tribal management has been competent. Not all tribes have shown equal acumen, but in the main the Indians' situation showed marked improvement after 1934. (137)

While on first acquaintance that passage might seem dry, overburdened with statistics, consider its implications: after a calamity in the form of a shortsighted piece of legislation designed to make farmers of the aborigines, the "Flathead" recovered an impressive amount of land and so recouped some of their dignity and economic prospects. By no means does that recovery make up for the losses, but it signals a resiliency and endurance. This upbeat message speaks not only to Toole's claims but to the meaning of D'Arcy McNickle's remarkable novels. On the one hand, we can further appreciate the context for the despair written into *The Surrounded*. After all, Max Leon represents the non-native landholders who had claimed huge chunks of reservation ground. The conflict between the agrarian and indigenous value systems that is so well rendered in both *The Surrounded* and *Wind from an Enemy Sky* has a clear basis in historical fact. Yet on the other hand, one wonders why McNickle did not have more to write about the recovery and its attendant pride and self-determination.[13] The Confederated Salish-Kootenai Tribes did not prove mere victims of fatality.

For all that I admire *Montana, High, Wide, and Handsome* and *Montana: An Uncommon Land*, at times I find their rhetoric strained, extreme, hyperbolic. These texts are very much products of their historical moments; the tough, almost slashing style bespeaks their genesis in an era dominated by the intense conflict between large, identifiable corporations and the "little guy." It may be time to absorb many of the lessons offered by these dynamic thinkers, while moving toward a more balanced, more modest, more forgiving rhetoric. At our epochal moment, it may be time to adopt the voice of respect and compromise rather than the voice of gloom and doom so familiar in major writing emerging from the state over the past sixty years. It may be time to create a true dialectic between our harrowing tragedies and more hopeful texts.

PART III

Provisional Hopes
1940-PRESENT

You can have your Utopian orgies:
I should prefer an orgy with the
Montanans.

——JACK KEROUAC,
"On the Road Again"

Comedy on the frontier . . . can be a kind
of bravery for meeting the dangers of the
frontier and what lies ahead. Comedy is
the western way of playing down big
things.

——NORMAN MACLEAN,
quoted in Sue Hart,
"'Eyes to See'"

Using stories as the common coin of social
discourse, people share their experiences of
place and thereby construct a collective
understanding of their lives there. From
that understanding, expressed in stories,
past and present, oral and written . . .
people weave their own history of place.

——BARBARA ALLEN BOGART,
"Knowing Our Place"

THE VOICES OF CATASTROPHIC TRAGEDY ARE LOUD, BOLD, AND compelling. They have drama and some history on their side. It's bracing to pick up *The Surrounded*, *The Lady in Kicking Horse Reservoir*, or *Montana: High, Wide, and Handsome*. Each oracular text gives our nervous systems a jolt, a jumpstart. Our faculties become fully focused, involved. We know we are in the presence of engaged, thoughtful, ethical writers. We know that these books carry at least a partial truth and, in the best of circumstances, we are motivated to absorb the knowledge embedded in these readable texts.

Yet the catastrophic voice carries dangers as well. Visions of cataclysm can contribute to a culture of despair and thereby disempower as much as empower the reader. When Montana citizens read over and over again of failed dreams, dashed prospects, and helpless settlers, they may be tempted by self-pity, even resignation. As we have discovered throughout this study, however, countervoices articulate other interpretations, other possible responses to political, economic, and cultural struggles. Even that most apparently tragic of chronicles, Howard's 1943 critical history, carries the germ of hope. The journalist dedicates the final fourth of his book to practical solutions to the crises he has outlined so vividly: taxing mining interests; employing strip farming in wheat country; developing countywide plans for land use. An activist to the end, Howard proposes thoughtful, collective action to countermand the decrees of history. In that pragmatism he reinforces the cautiously hopeful forward glances of writers such as Pearl Price Robertson and A. B. Guthrie Jr.

We have available to us, then, an alternative representation of our dilemmas and prospects, a voice that espouses engaged, careful, concrete, caring responses to the pressures that continue to exert themselves on the rural West. The most notable of these voices is that of Wallace Stegner, near-contemporary of Guthrie's, Howard's, and Toole's, a dyed-in-the-wool westerner who'd seen it all and lived to write that "the West at large is hope's native home, the youngest and freshest of America's regions, magnificently endowed and with the chance to become something unprecedented and unmatched in the world."[1] If anyone else had written that, I'd immediately check my wallet to make sure I hadn't been taken in by another huckster or wild-eyed promoter. But this is Wallace Stegner, after all, and he's earned his hopefulness. This is the same fellow who, in *Beyond the Hundredth Meridian*, wrote a scathing, brilliant satire on William Gilpin's manic boosterism; the fellow who told his own tough, gritty, antiromantic story in *The Big Rock Candy Mountain* and *Wolf Willow;* the fellow who wrote the best non-Indian novel about the West, one full of sorry dreaming and unintended sorrow, *Angle of Repose*. For Stegner to write so fulsomely (it seems) suggests that he's on to something many of us haven't quite figured out, and indeed, I think he was (and is). He suggests that the land itself, in its glory and toughness, can shape a politics of pragmatic hope; he suggests that we can learn from our foolish miscalculations and tragic mistakes; he suggests that we can listen to each other better, and absorb wisdom from our apparent enemies. In short, for Stegner, we are better than a stand-alone catastrophic theory would allow.

If Stegner is the attending genius of our provisional hopes, Montana philosophers can lend their voices as well. In a charming essay entitled "A Philosophy of the Open Air," Bill Borneman asserts that something like a home-grown approach to living well has emerged in Montana over the past forty years. He takes Henry Bugbee's *Inward Morning* (1958) as the originary moment of this down-home philosophy, commenting with real affection that Bugbee's book "remains, in essence, an invitation to awakening. . . . the kind of awakening that occurs when we simply open our eyes; not the world as 'revealed' mystically, nor as 'explained' scientifically. Just the everyday world as humbly real."[2] Turn away from the abstract theories, the vast explanations, the overarching models, and look at what actually confronts you, here and now. Stop with the arguing, the declaiming, the self-promotion, the narcissism, and listen, listen to the world, listen to what others might have to tell you. That, simply stated, is what Bugbee seems to be about. He's not alone, since he has inspired many others along with Borneman. Consider the writings of Albert Borgmann, Daniel Kemmis, and David Strong, all composing their deeply committed books under the influence of Bugbee's distinctly American style of pragmatism.[3] All three urge a turn toward the place itself, toward meaningful practices, toward dwelling through careful living and respectful communion with others. And so Borneman seems to be on to something here—there has emerged a philosophy of the good life that can counterbalance fear and despair.

Some might immediately object that I've been seduced by "Missoula," regional shorthand for a left-of-center, off-balance, starry-eyed approach to Montana's problems. But before we shout down these voices of humble decency, let's spend time with at least one of their books. Let's focus on Kemmis's *Community and the Politics of Place*, since it is the most accessible of these writings and since its author grew up in eastern Montana. If we want to dismiss this antitheoretical philosophy as some Missoula conspiracy, we should at least acknowledge that Kemmis writes intimately, with an insider's knowledge, not only about the mountain valleys but about the plains as well. To narrow our focus even more carefully, consider Kemmis's widely reprinted chapter, "Barn Raising." Here the citizen-philosopher brings his argument home to a western reader.

He tells a simple story of the relationship between his mother, prim and proper, and Albert, a neighbor who enjoyed off-color stories and general rowdiness. Kemmis explains that these two, while dramatically different and in many contexts incompatible, had no choice but to cooperate on the Montana plains of the 1940s and '50s. They needed each other. And so, when it came time to replace the Kemmises' crumbling barn, Albert was there, contributing with gusto, if offending Dan's mother all the way. The citizen-philosopher rightly asserts that such relationships seem almost unthinkable in our intensely privatized contemporary culture. Yet because we close ourselves off from others who seem "different" or "offensive," we lose something far more significant:

The kinds of values which might form the basis for a genuinely public life . . . arise out of a context which is concrete in at least two ways. It is concrete in the actual things or events—the barns, the barn dances—which the practices of cooperation produce. But it is also concrete in the actual, specific places within which those practices and that cooperation take place. Clearly, the practices which shaped the behavior and the character of frontier families did not appear out of thin air; they grew out of the one thing those people had most fundamentally in common: the effort to survive in a hard country. And when the effort to survive comes to rely upon shared and repeated practices like barn raising, survival itself is transformed; it becomes inhabitation. To in*habit* a place is to dwell there in a practiced way, in a way which relies upon certain regular, trusted habits of behavior.[4]

Kemmis invokes that semimystical term *place,* an idea that has taken on added significance in the region's conversation with itself. Stegner tellingly quotes Wendell Berry's memorable assertion, "If you don't know where you are, you don't know *who* you are."[5] In some sense, in many senses, we must settle down, take stock of where we are, what has happened here already, who our neighbors are, what their needs consist of, what we imagine to be a good life. In part, of course, we are discussing an ecological sensibility, a thoughtful assessment of the distinctive features and carrying capacity of the land we inhabit. And that ecological sensibility must open out to consider not just our parochial "homes" but the wider place, the streams, mountains, and plains affected by our actions. But dwelling in a place must, of necessity, involve economics as well. Many have pointed out the etymological connection between "ecology" and "economy"—both are rooted in the Greek word for "home." One reason so many in this region distrust environmentalists is that they have a strong hunch that those wilderness advocates are affluent outlanders who do not know what it means to survive in this part of the world. It's difficult to feel a deep empathy for old-growth timber if you can't feed your family. A commitment to place must embrace diverse economic possibilities, but possibilities that operate within the limitations imposed by the land and climate itself. We should also acknowledge historical practices, activities that have stood the test of trial and error and survived on the northern plains and in the mountain valleys. It seems harsh, for instance, to berate the ranching and farming communities as exploitive, when on average those folks are deeply attuned to their landholdings and often eke out a living.

Montana and the West in general have shown impressive economic resilience over the past decade, in part because of woes in other places, California in particular. Our economy is now more diversified, "softer," less extractive. We have turned toward tourism, high-tech industries, reclamation projects, and alternative crops, including flax and canola. This "New West" paradigm exists in uneasy alliance with "Old West" industries such as mining, timber, and ranching, but there's no need to make some absolutist choice about which West, Old or New, we must advance at the expense of the other. These are subtle, negotiable issues deserving attention and commitment. To take a famous example, an out-of-state company proposed developing a gold mine on the boundary of Yellowstone Park. The clash between an extractive industry and its contemporary alternative—tourism—could not have been more stark. Add to that the feared environmental degradation resulting from the highly obtrusive gold-mining process. The federal authorities intervened to provide a classic capitalist solution: the U.S. government would exchange other federal land in the state for the company's holdings outside the park, thereby preserving a nearly sacred place while protecting private property rights.

There are necessarily dangers inherent in this diversified economy, dangers that may seem starkly familiar:

> In the new economy . . . with its very different slant on the commercialization of the outdoors, new forms of capital are transforming the western landscape on an unprecedented scale. Sage deserts are being remade into elegant golf courses, ridge lines are increasingly dotted with huge luxury homes, and fashionable and upscale shopping centers are blossoming everywhere near those growing population centers. Despite the over-weaning [*sic*] self-confidence and arrogance of the developers, there is little to give

assurance that the emerging new economy is any more permanent than the old extractive one.[6]

Ask low-wage "service workers" in Bozeman, Polson, and Whitefish about the pitfalls of this innovative economy. And look around any prospering western community. In Billings, citizens have allowed far too much private development of some of our most precious land-forms, especially the distinctive "Rims" that bound the city to the north. We must make a conscious effort to think through our develop-ments, to consider planning for the long term, planning with an entire region in mind. Yellowstone County might consider protecting agricul-tural land that circles the existing and still-expanding city to ensure a "green belt." And more fundamentally, as Kemmis asserts:

> Ideals like building strong, stable local economies by encouraging import substitution, or nurturing indigenous businesses, cannot go far in this part of the country unless colonial patterns are inter-rupted. Specifically, the building of strong, indigenous communi-ties requires that states and localities have the capacity and the will to keep some locally generated capital from leaving the region and to invest that capital creatively and effectively in the regional economy.[7]

There are signs of hope, of "investment" in all forms, in Billings, for example. Local businesspeople have worked together to landscape some of the oldest, most neglected streets downtown, encouraging many to venture back into an area that seemed demoralizing, even threatening. The city has set aside an island in the Yellowstone River as a nature preserve, saving one of its most precious ecosystems from thoughtless destruction. You can walk along the shore of that august river and imagine William Clark and Nathaniel Pryor floating by 190 years ago. The Institute for Peace Studies at Rocky Mountain College has created an economic development program with Russians that funds exchanges between farmers. Montanans can share their expert-ise in wheat growing and cattle raising and learn a thing or two in return. The Montana Association of Churches advocates for the dig-nity and rights of those who have been marginalized by this economy, calling citizens' attention to inequities in income and, especially, struggles in the agricultural community. These are modest but meaningful signs. People are looking ahead, thinking locally and globally, not settling for simple resignation. They are working toward living up to the place they inhabit.

Writing can also play its part in helping us achieve authentic "inhabitation." We can look to narratives that offset the tragic with the realistic and the comic, that place beside the sublime drama the tempered and thoughtful, that skirt despair and journey toward possibility. We should attend to those texts that may be termed "pragmatic comedies," narratives blending the search for solutions with a comic tone and plotting. Because these are Montana stories, they do not necessarily point toward an overtly optimistic outcome. Comedy in this climate is typically tentative and cautious. As James Welch has so memorably phrased it, the result may be "a happiness that sleeps with sadness."[8] Writings by Welch, McFadden, Walker, Blew, McNamer, Kittredge, and Doig show, in detail, just how westerners have achieved that paradoxical state of being. History is not solely a nightmare from which we are trying to awaken; it is also the source of learning, inspiration, and possibility.

Chapter 7

THE RETURN OF
THE NATIVE

A GOOD PLACE TO BEGIN IS WITH AN ENDING: "BEFORE HE DIED,
Black Elk called up a rain shower out of a blue sky in an effort to nour-
ish the roots of the withered sacred tree. The Indian spirit was, and
remains, hard to break."[1] Those concluding words to an account of the
Indian Holocaust on the high plains signal the difference between
James Welch and earlier Indian writers, including memoirists and the
novelist D'Arcy McNickle. Welch's characters are indeed hard to
break, whether we consider the nameless narrator of *Winter in the Blood*,
or *Fools Crow*, or Sylvester Yellow Calf in *The Indian Lawyer*.[2] *The Death
of Jim Loney* is as close as Welch comes to composing wholly in the
tragic mode of western writing, and so, perhaps not surprisingly, I will
have little to say about that stark, haunting book. In fact, I want to
focus on what I consider his two major achievements, two novels fram-
ing the Indian experience in past and present, *Fools Crow* and *Winter in*

the Blood. A colleague in sociology has carried on a running debate with me about which novel is Welch's best. He asserts the superiority of *Winter,* stressing its concision, surrealism, and humor. I have always leaned toward the later novel, drawn to its epic scope, poetic language, breadth of vision, and magical, dreamlike passages. Since they cover a range of history as well as style, and since they can be read in revisionary relationship with earlier narratives we have discussed, these two novels make an ideal representation of Welch's contribution to regional discourse. If "comedy" risks overstating their appeal and their meaning, at least we can agree with Louis Owens when he writes, "*Fools Crow*—like the story of Feather Woman—is about returning, about going home to an identity, about looking back through the hole in time. . . . If the reader can pass through that conceptual horizon, if the reader acknowledges and accepts this reality, he or she experiences an Indian world. . . . In *Fools Crow,* Welch has accomplished the most profound act of recovery in American literature."[3]

Before considering this act of recovery with more precision, we should pause to reflect on Welch's role as a writer and citizen in Montana culture. At first glance, this may seem an unnecessary digression, a distraction from the matter at hand: writing that confronts our worst crises and takes us toward dread or hope. But this brief journey into Welch's wider life tells us a great deal about his commitments as a writer, as a re-creator of native experience in the West. I had the privilege of reading the citation when Welch received an honorary doctorate from Rocky Mountain College. To say that it was a thrill is to underestimate what that moment meant to me. Yet after the ceremony, Cliff Murphy, a retired professor of philosophy who had worked with Welch on prison issues, made an essential point: he commended the citation, focused as it was on the writer's literary achievements, but he wondered why we didn't pay more homage to Welch's work with the wider community. This remark took me aback but has stuck with me since. Murphy was exactly right: why did we stress so insistently the individual literary achievement and neglect the social contributions? The answer has since occurred to me: because Jim Welch is himself so quiet about this extensive work. Welch has served on the Parole Board, participated on the editorial board for *The Last Best Place,* written an introduction for a new edition of *Winter Wheat*, helped edit Hugo's autobiography, written the screenplay for *Last Stand at Little Bighorn*, and served both his Blackfeet and his Gros Ventre people in countless ways I cannot begin to know. This is, I'm sure, a small portion of the work he's done beyond his familiar literary achievements.

Consider the implications of these achievements, consider the implications for the writer's role that such a life proposes. Clearly for Welch it is not enough to write well. It is also critical to give back in a variety of forums. The writer, then, has larger obligations or affiliations than to the word or to a specific audience. The writer must advance social well-being through action and generosity. Now it's surely true that these other obligations have lent a balance to Welch's life and given him grist for his artistic mill. Certainly *The Indian Lawyer* is unimaginable without his experience on the Parole Board, and *Killing Custer* emerged from his film-making experience with Paul Stekler. But as the writer confides in his prologue to that historical narrative, every such commitment curtails the amount of time spent on an arduous writing process. I can only conclude that Welch operates within an ethical and communal world view that contrasts sharply with the prototypical American artist's pursuit of insight and expression by means of a separation from the wider community. We like our writers dark and alienated, caught up in their private visions, Dionysian and explosive. Welch's life and writings implicitly argue for a different kind of subjectivity, what I might call an intersubjective subjectivity. The artist should not stand alone, isolated from the currents of the wider culture, somehow immune to the immediate and the political. Instead, the writer should participate in and transmute those materials into the very stuff of our fiction and history. And that's what Welch, better than anyone except Ivan Doig, has done.

To put Welch's literary achievement in context, it is important to see his writings in relationship to Indian memoirs and McNickle's novels, as well as the generally pessimistic works of Richard Hugo and Thomas McGuane. But it is also useful to see how Welch's two major novels interrelate with other modern writing about Montana Indians, specifically the texts of Dorothy M. Johnson and Dan Cushman. These two white writers have presented their own versions of the Native American experience on the high plains, treatments that veer away from tragedy toward sympathy and comedy. There seems to be a tacit agreement within the scholarly community not to say much about either Johnson's Indian narratives or Cushman's *Stay Away, Joe*. In part, I suspect, we are embarrassed by the datedness of these two authors' stories, the sense that their writings belong to an earlier, less sensitive generation. Certainly Cushman's hilarious novel at times comes across to a contemporary ear and eye as unselfconsciously racist. And Johnson's tales can seem slick, polished to a point of overdone sophistication or cleverness. They are well-made stories at a time when we may prefer the messiness of the postmodern collage or the confessional purge. Yet for many western readers, Johnson and Cushman provide compelling, entertaining reading, and their accounts of native life are not as demeaning as one would initially suppose.

What I propose to do, then, is read *Fools Crow* and *Winter in the Blood* in revisionary relationships with *Buffalo Woman* (1977) and *Stay Away, Joe* (1953). I cannot "prove" that Welch consciously set out to remake the representations of Johnson and Cushman. I can, however, point to significant similarities in plot and character. And given the popularity of these writers' works, it seems logical to wonder if the gifted Indian novelist wasn't reacting to the existing tradition of representing Indians in the region, especially in the widely read work of white writers. We do not have to assume an overtly hostile rejection of these earlier texts. At a conference on Guthrie's *Big Sky* commemorating the fiftieth anniversary of its publication, Welch spoke with obvious affection about Guthrie's mountain-man novel and expressed real respect for the author's skill and vision. At the same time, Welch's Pikunis seem a far remove from Guthrie's oversimplified Blackfeet. Influence is not purely a matter of resistance and antagonism; influence can combine rapport and reimagining.

Fools Crow, though published twelve years after *Winter*, can be read as a vital pretext for Welch's account of contemporary Indian life. As we will discover later, the nameless narrator of *Winter* comes to know his connection to his Blackfeet ancestors through his visits with Yellow Calf. In those moments, and in memories of the dead grandmother, the narrator briefly evokes an entire world, a way of being, that is elusive and fragile in the present time. In the historical epic, as Owens suggests, Welch manages to embody that world fully, to help us see and know what has been lost, and what must be remembered. Perhaps we should think of *Fools Crow* as the novel *Winter*'s narrator was enabled to write by his spiritual and emotional odyssey.

Welch has discussed his use of sources such as George Bird Grinnell's *Blackfoot Lodge Tales* and James Willard Schultz's *My Life As an Indian* to help him reenter that lost world.[4] And in *Killing Custer,* Welch emphasizes the role of his great-grandmother as a witness to the atrocities on the northern plains (39). These, along with Welch's own memories, experiences, imagination, and art, provide the vital influences on his remarkable novel. Yet surely he must have been sensitive to the portrayals of Native Americans in other writings about Montana. Admittedly, during a radio interview, Welch adamantly rejected my suggestion that *Fools Crow* is in part a response to Frank B. Linderman's *Plenty-coups.* Yet writers are often reluctant to acknowledge such intertextual relationships.

Johnson's *Buffalo Woman,* focusing as it does on the coming-of-age story of an Oglala Sioux woman, makes an excellent companion piece for *Fools Crow.* Much as Welch uses the growth of White Man's Dog to figure the changes in Pikuni life at large, so Johnson cleverly performs the same magic with her protagonist Whirlwind. Yet reading Johnson's novel shows just how daunting a task a writer faces in re-creating the pre-reservation life of the Plains Indians. White writers in particular confront a nearly insurmountable challenge in entering into the daily habits, rituals, and values of native peoples. That is so, in part, because the plains cultures remain forever elusive. No matter how much we study the photographs of Edward S. Curtis, or read the accounts of Yellowstone Kelly and Andrew Garcia, or spend time with Pretty-shield and Two Leggings, we feel as though we are in the presence of ways of seeing, feeling, and believing that are not just unfamiliar, but radically incompatible with our Westernized way of

being. We also must confront the layered history of white representations of native peoples, stretching from Shakespeare to *Dances with
Wolves*. Indigenous cultures have been translated into archetypes of
precivilized savagery, demonic heathenism, and noble barbarity.
These archetypes have proven both convenient and irresistible to
writers as different as James Fenimore Cooper, Henry Wadsworth
Longfellow, and Thomas Berger. Often we translate the Indian into a
child of nature, a figure who worships Mother Earth, it's true, but one
who also speaks in the simple tones of the preadult, even the preado-
lescent, self.

I hope I am not unduly harsh when suggesting that Johnson falls
into some of these traps in *Buffalo Woman*. Through research and good
faith, Johnson attempts to take us inside the adapting but threatened
Sioux culture of the nineteenth century. Yet the writer employs a series
of strategies to make her predominantly white readership comfortable
in the presence of these alien peoples, and those strategies create a
tone of special pleading, even condescension. The controlling voice of
the novel, for instance, can at times seem simplistic and singsong. In
such moments we are right back in the now-embarrassing voice of *The
Song of Hiawatha*: "And so they moved on, that band of The People,
noisy and happy, with much shouting and dogs barking and babies crying, through a country rich in game, a land to which their nomadic lives
were completely tuned. Now and then someone broke into a short
prayer song of gratitude to the Great Mystery and the other spirits,
because they were The People, fortunate above all others, and they
were happy."[5] Johnson also insists on leading off each part of the novel
with a cast list, as though readers would become lost or confused if she
did not remind them of the names and ages of the major players. Yet
American readers will spend hours with foreign novels without similar
distancing aids. Finally, there's a kind of desperate moral earnestness
to it all, an earnestness that depletes the characters of human ambiguity. Welch will substitute humor, misjudgments, sensuality, and confusion for this nearly one-dimensional native type.

But to give Johnson her due, she writes with an anthropological
rigor that takes us beyond the Cooper/Longfellow mode. Part of the
writer's seriousness arises from a palpable desire to recreate the

densely ritualistic lives of the Plains Indians in the years before and during the Indian Wars. That's one reason the text reads more like a telling than a showing: there's a documentary precision to the proceedings that seems at odds with novelistic narration. To phrase this response in different terms, much of the careful detailing of the sungazing ceremonies, vision quests, Buffalo Girl ritual, etc. seems external to the interior lives of the characters. We have an uneasy sensation of inhabiting two universes at once, the universe of the individual characters (especially Whirlwind), and the universe of the tribe. Johnson might reasonably respond that the two worlds drive toward a merger: as the female protagonist grows up, she becomes more and more fully a part of the tribal culture, and so we observe the very process by which a young person is absorbed into the latent values of her people. If the rituals seem distant and strangely artificial at the beginning of the novel, by the end Whirlwind is a revered participant in those same processes and so has become identical with the values of the Lakota. As she remarks to her father upon attending a dance, "then I was a little girl, watching from the outside. . . . Now I am grown up and everything is different!" (96).

Johnson also skillfully shows how that ritual-based, whole, grounded culture comes under terrible pressure with the increasing presence of the Wasichu. She covers much of the same ground as *Killing Custer,* though Welch devotes far more space to Sitting Bull and his convoluted, painful maneuvers to avoid capture. Johnson saves some of her best prose for the period after Little Bighorn, the time of indecision, confusion, and dissension. Like Welch, she demonstrates just how a culture comes apart when put under the thumb of a technologically superior, ruthless society. In the words of Mad Plume, a failing leader in *Fools Crow,* "Look around you, White Man's Dog, do you see many of our young men? No, they are off hunting for themselves, or drunk with the white man's water, or stealing their horses. . . . There is no center here. That is why we have become such a pitiful sight to you" (97). *Buffalo Woman* presents with clear-eyed and unsentimental precision how young warriors must forgo vision quests to fend off the Blue Coats; how the sacred rituals surrounding the building of tepees must be suspended in favor of expedition, of haste; how families disintegrate as members die from sickness and war wounds. We also witness the increasing hunger and disease resulting from forced removal to unfamiliar hunting grounds as the various bands seek safe haven from the Americans. In the midst of these crises, Whirlwind, aging and revered, suffers her own ominous wound: a grizzly bear sow attacks her, ripping away part of a leg, leaving her lame for life. Yet the grandmother is able to save her grandson, earning the notice of so august a figure as Crazy Horse, who renames her "Saved Her Cub."

That sequence is typical of Grandmother Whirlwind's late life. Even as she must bear witness to and suffer the horrors of white invasion, she demonstrates uncommon courage and a devotion to her people. It's fascinating to observe how Johnson steers away from the obvious grim conclusion to this blended fictional biography and ethnography. The reader hears of the massacre at Sand Creek, confronts the attack on Whirlwind's own band, and watches the slow dying of the grandson she had saved from the grizzly. Yet the novel concludes with a paean to the old woman, wounded in spirit and body, who surrenders herself for the stricken Lakota. She understands that the "good of all the people was more important than the survival of one person" (242). And so she does not fear death, realizing as she does, "*I was never the least among my people, and I need not be humble among my people in that other country either*" (244). Whirlwind not only bestows her new name upon her dying grandchild, but she acts as though she must save all the cubs, the "children" who force march themselves toward Canada. Her death, then, is a sweet one, full of the courage of self-sacrifice and a glimmer of contentment. And even in death she performs a crucial role: she seems to act as a spirit helper, bringing a revitalizing chinook to the winter-weary people. She has lived up to her two great names.

Welch incorporates the anthropological astuteness of a Dorothy Johnson into an effective storytelling voice, and in the process plunges us directly into the probable universe of the Pikunis. He does so in large part by means of his lyrical gifts. By trusting to humor and metaphorical vividness, Welch goes beyond a kind of intellectual respect for native peoples to a rapport, a fully invested empathy with them. If a poetic image can evoke "an intellectual and emotional complex in an instant of time,"[6] Welch's multiple, rich, interwoven images take us inside a complex of feeling and thought for one Plains tribe in 1868:

> Now that the weather had changed, the moon of the falling leaves turned white in the blackening sky and White Man's Dog was restless. He chewed the stick of dry meat and watched Cold Maker gather his forces. The black clouds moved in the north in circles, their dance a slow deliberate fury. It was almost night, and he looked back down into the flats along the Two Medicine River. The lodges of the Lone Eaters were illuminated by cooking fires within. It was that time of evening when even the dogs rest and the horses graze undisturbed along the grassy banks. (3)

The action begins in medias res. We are immediately introduced to the troubled protagonist, an eighteen-year-old youth of little luck and less belief in himself. He is betwixt and between the dramatic natural world and the peaceful village life of the Pikunis. He seems both very much somewhere and absolutely nowhere. He is emplaced, yet without a fix, a mark, a settled sense of himself.

And so Welch launches us on a journey with the young man soon to be renamed Fools Crow. The novel follows a two-part movement: the coming-of-age of White Man's Dog, and the displacement of the Pikunis by American invaders. On the surface that is a classically tragic structure, showing how the individual man of greatness is laid low by fate. But Welch carefully modulates the plot lines to point toward survival rather than pure loss. Fools Crow is anything but the hubristic overreacher of the European tragic tradition. (For this reason, Welch's book is dramatically different from Chinua Achebe's *Things Fall Apart*, another important novel tracing the devastating impact of European colonization on tribal cultures.) He is more like Two Leggings, the Crow warrior who overcomes youthful exuberance, vanity, and folly to recognize his place in a larger scheme of creation and destiny. Fools Crow's growth leads toward sustaining wisdom, a full understanding of his modest role in the spiritual and material life of his people. In that sense, he is also much like Johnson's Buffalo Woman. And while it is true that his rising stature will be checked, even arrested, by the massacre on the Marias River near the end of the novel, Fools Crow sees a purpose, a vital mission for himself beyond that horror. He practices what Johnson's narrator calls "a different kind of courage from that of yelling warriors, painted and armed, riding into battle, facing death" (245). Like Buffalo Woman, Fools Crow must lovingly provide his people what he can: stability, faith, and a vision of the difficult future. He must also be sure that the stories of the Pikunis are handed down. Catastrophe might be the necessary means to another beginning, though a difficult, even terrible, beginning. And that is why Fools Crow comes to know "a happiness that sleeps with sadness" (390).

Welch compresses these two patterns into a little over a year of action, achieving something like the classical unity of time. That compression allows him a density, a specificity, a roundness to the narration that is missing from *Buffalo Woman*. He practices showing rather than telling. White Man's Dog rises up from the ashes like a phoenix, gaining horses, coup, a family, and an incipient medicine power under the tutelage of Mik-api. The novel provides a startlingly vivid sense of the interior life of this aboriginal people, showing that native tribes often operated with a concept of meritocracy every bit as elitist as Euramerican culture. After all, White Man's Dog must earn his respect and his power through brave deeds and bold action. There's an evident give-and-take between private initiative and sacred support. No wonder my students sometimes compare the Pikuni male to Ben Franklin! The narrative also stresses that old truism, "Try, try again." White Man's Dog's first vision quest resulted in disillusionment. Yet as Fast Horse advises early in the novel, it can take many attempts before the quester finds his true power animal, his spirit helper. Once the protagonist meets the Skunk Bear in the mountains, he seems destined for high status within the culture.

Welch cleverly deploys a series of foils to highlight Fools Crow's virtues. Fast Horse is the ultimate petulant, self-assured, cocky, ill-fated young man. He is painfully reminiscent of other doomed male characters: Boone Caudill in *The Big Sky,* Tristan in *Legends of the Fall,* Paul in *A River Runs Through It,* and Alec McCaskill in *English Creek.* Ultimately Fast Horse brings out the homelessness, the nihilism of the warrior who has turned against the sacred foundations of the Piku-nis. Operating outside the ethical norms of his people, he drifts into an abyss of pointless violence. Fools Crow's brother, Running Fisher, demonstrates the fate of one who breaks the taboo surrounding a son's relations with his near-mother. His banishment highlights the protagonist's morality, his attention to the sacred and profane laws structuring a man's life. Owl Child, meanwhile, shows the route of armed but depraved resistance. For all that Mountain Chief seems willing to defend this young renegade, he seems mean and rootless. There's little redeeming value to his murder of Malcolm Clark; it's scorn for scorn, humiliation for humiliation. The reader may feel a grudging understanding for Owl Child's sense of shame and desire for vengeance. In fact, there are moments in the novel when I wonder whether the hero shouldn't be more assertive, more violent, more willing to take the path of a Crazy Horse or Sitting Bull. Yet Owl Child's behavior only incites the fury of the blue-coated seizers and the immediate harm to Heavy Runner's band. And his resistance is literally pointless—it leads nowhere.

Contrasted with these narrow, petty characters, Fools Crow is immersed in a universe both magical and dreadful. Welch has written in another context, "Stories 'eased the way' through life by instructing, entertaining, shaping one's view of the world and its creation, by *placing* one within the great scheme of things."[7] Fools Crow's second name emerged from his attraction to the old storyteller Victory Robe White Man. From an early age he was drawn to the circle of language, of myth, of sustaining legend. As he matures toward full manhood, White Man's Dog absorbs a series of transformative stories. For instance, when he asks Mik-api how the elder became a many-faces man, the singer-for-the-sick reveals that his change occurred at the very same time of year as the protagonist's own, during the moon of the falling leaves. When he narrates the particulars of his calling, Mik-api enters into a lyrical voice that discloses the interconnectedness of body, soul, and world:

And so, still weeping, I left [Head Carrier] there and wandered back into the brush. I could hear his death song getting fainter behind me. I found a slough and sat with my head in my hands. Oh, I was sad. All around me the green-singers were tuning up. I had never liked frogs, but as I cried I became aware of the beauty of their song. It filled me with so much sadness I thought my heart would fall down, never to rise, and I cried louder. Soon the biggest of the frog persons came up to me and said, "Why do you weep when all we mean to do is cheer you up?" (67–68)

The Frog Chief will prove a powerful helper to "Spotted Weasel" (Mik-api's earlier name), journeying far under water to acquire the salve to heal his dying friend. The story indirectly confirms White Man's Dog's own encounter with his power animal, and it more broadly articulates the vital relationship between the Pikunis and the animal persons. Mik-api implicitly argues that the Blackfeet cosmos works, and that gifted, dedicated, disciplined human beings can cooperate with the higher powers to comfort and heal. This pattern repeats itself in Boss Ribs's recounting of the Beaver Medicine story later in the narrative. The lesson is clear: White Man's Dog will become a healer for his people in the profoundest sense possible.

But White Man's Dog's confusing dream of the white-scabs victims in the Crow camp and his later terrifying encounter with the mountain man remind the reader that the ways of vision are not always transparent or easy. In contrast to a stereotypical image of the native healer as a kind of otherworldly shaman, prescient and superhuman, Welch shows the intense, almost heartbreaking humanness of the many-faces men. Similar to Johnson's account of Grey Bull, the proud warrior who is transformed into a contrary by a powerful vision, *Fools Crow* reveals the sacrifice, doubt, and sometimes failure that accompany the healer's role. That's why humility is so essential a quality for the apprentice—the role would break the spirit of a prouder man.

These visionary qualities are doubly significant as Fools Crow journeys toward his ultimate insight, the pictographic telling of his people's future. Welch consciously slows down the action in parts 3, 4, and 5, breaking the narrative flow that seemed to sweep the protagonist toward his rightful status as leader of the Lone Eaters. In place of the dramatic urgency of the first two sections, we experience a hesitation, a perplexity, a confusion of action, a sense of imminent disaster. In part the novelist captures the seasonal rhythms of the Pikuni existence, showing how the people huddle in their lodges during the bitterly cold winters, sojourning for necessities such as game, but generally hunkering down. But the increasing threats from the Napikwan, along with the threat of white-scabs disease, cast a deeper pall upon the winter camp. Increasingly divided attitudes toward the invaders cause dissension bordering on anarchy. Owl Child is only the most outlandish, most outspoken renegade. Chiefs dispute with chiefs; younger warriors argue passionately for armed resistance. When smallpox hits with full force, these divisions only widen, for individual bands must now turn away relatives who might carry the disease.

It is in the midst of this mounting sense of dread that Fools Crow follows Nitsokan toward his meeting with Feather Woman. The arduous, disorienting journey mirrors the pain and confusion of the Pikunis at large. Fools Crow truly carries the woes of his people on his back and in his soul. The unfolding vision discloses a series of catastrophes: smallpox, massacre, the eradication of the buffalo, and the boarding-school nightmare. Through the scenes in the yellow world, Welch has foreshadowed and reinforced the tragedy of Pikuni history. Yet when the protagonist turns toward Feather Woman, a being who knows much about loss and grief, she urges restraint, even resilience, in the face of horror. Above all, she emphasizes care for the children, the ones who must endure the changed world: "Much will be lost to them. . . . But they will know the way it was. The stories will be handed down, and they will see that their people were proud and lived in accordance with the Below Ones, the Underwater People—and the Above Ones" (359–60). Fools Crow has clearly absorbed this lesson in survival, for when he discovers the stunned victims of the Heavy Runner massacre, he urges the people to remember that "[i]t is good that you are alive. You will have much to teach the young ones about the Napikwans" (385). He reminds them as well of their duty to the ancestors: "But this is the land of the Pikunis. This is where the long-ago people were born and lived and died. They would be angry with us if we just gave it up" (385). In these hortatory words to the violence-shocked survivors, Fools Crow performs that most vital storytelling function of all, locating the listeners in a continuum of time that offers memory and purpose, a sense of belonging to an order of life, a reason for continuing. It is Welch's role as well.

The conclusion of *Fools Crow* is famously ambiguous. Welch summons a vision of the return of spring and the buffalo, hinting at a healing, a recovery for the Blackfeet peoples. Yet we know that the grim reservation life, complete with the horrifying Starvation Winter of 1883, looms for Fools Crow's tribe. When I discuss this passage with students, they often speculate that the novelist is describing life in the Sand Hills, the life after life, the life after a passing away from this troubling existence. Spring and the buffalo come only to those who have died and entered another plane of being. But when I asked Welch about this conclusion during a radio interview, he gave a fascinating, even startling, answer: the ending suggests that the people do not know what awaits them, the future is not clear to them, and they take pleasure in the familiar cycles of rebirth. Only the title character understands the full extent of the catastrophe. Fools Crow knows that he must serve to perpetuate the soul of the Blackfeet through story-telling and political leadership, "even though he was, like Feather Woman, burdened with the knowledge of his people, their lives and the lives of their children, he knew they would survive, for they were the chosen ones" (390). That's why a colleague of mine may well be correct in his assessment of this puzzling conclusion: the novel itself constitutes the escape from "a den with only one entrance" (216). By instilling the lyrical intensity of the Pikuni past in the contemporary reader, Welch has in fact performed the function Owens credited to him: he has achieved the most significant act of recovery in American letters. That act in and of itself signals a resourcefulness, an endurance that may surprise the non-native reader. In this sense, then, the novelist bears out the belief that "if we learn his language, we can beat him with his own words" (122) . Yet it will take another Welch novel, written earlier than, yet logically a sequel to, *Fools Crow* to demonstrate how a contemporary native man can find sustenance, even pleasure, in living after things fall apart.

Stay Away, Joe is a wild, carnivalesque story about the "breed" Big Joe (his father is Metis, his mother Assiniboine), a larger-than-life, Falstaffian character who makes his way through the world with a combination of physical strength, guile, and charm. The novel conforms to the homing plot that Bevis finds in native writings: Joe returns to his father's ranch (actually, his own allotted land) as a veteran of World War II and the Korean War. Joe is a Zorba the Greek of the high plains, minus the brooding, semimystical meditations of Kazantzakis's novel. There is no dark, Dionysian edge to the Indian character's antics. It's all in good fun. At the start of the action, Joe finds his father in possession of a cattle herd granted him by the government as an experimental project. A local congressman, facing reelection, wants to appeal to liberal voters by demonstrating his commitment to improving life for the down-and-out indigenous peoples. In this way, Cushman skillfully satirizes the paternalistic white attitude toward Indians, much as McNickle calls into question those same attitudes in his two major novels.

It's apparent where this plot is headed: the boisterous Joe will use his father's cattle to capitalize his drinking, whoring, and generally enjoying life. Cushman's descriptions of parties on the reservation are the most extravagant this side of Sherman Alexie's *The Lone Ranger and Tonto Fistfight in Heaven* (though again, without the sadness, even self-loathing, we find in Alexie's natives). The novel makes for a curiously divided experience for the contemporary reader, or at least this contemporary reader: I often laughed out loud, but I also often groaned at patently condescending stereotypes of breeds and Indians. But lest we are left with the impression that Cushman is an obtuse, insensitive observer of modern reservation life, we should attend to one of the best lines in the novel. When Mama gets it into her head to remake her home to placate a white woman (a soon-to-be in-law), Louis observes to the distressed Grandpere, "That's just the point.... We are not living in the old days. These times a man has to keep up with the Joneses."[8] It's a pleasure to pick up a Montana book that makes us laugh a deep belly laugh. Cushman has more in common with our funniest cowboy poets than with the highbrow stylists such as Harrison and Maclean. And I suspect that Welch found a great deal to work with in this sometimes embarrassing book, at least based on *Winter in the Blood.*

Begin with the similarities between the two novels: both are set on or near Indian reservations in north-central Montana (Rocky Boy in Cushman's case, Fort Belknap in Welch's); both focus on the home-coming of a protagonist who has journeyed far; both attend to the physical wounds those travelers carry home; both generate effective humor out of the conflict between the heavily drinking male character and his surrounding relatives, especially a female figure; both take us to the edge of an almost surreal sexuality; and both concentrate on the relationship between the protagonist and a traditionalist grandfather. Given these correspondences, I am tempted to suggest that the name of Welch's anonymous narrator is Joe Champlain. But there, of course, I overstate my case. If Welch begins with some of Cushman's prem-ises, he takes us inside an entirely different sense of native reality and, in the end, guides us toward an *earned* sense of belonging that can sustain the character and the reader long after the book is set aside. It's like the difference between farce and tragicomedy. Both texts drive toward what we can loosely term a "comic" effect, but the second kind of text gives us substantial food for feeling and thought.

Winter often generates the same manic, even hysterical, humor as Cushman's novel. The entire bizarre episode with the airplane man in Havre has the zaniness of Joe's wild dealings with Callahan. The hap-less protagonist, passive in the manner of Archilde in *The Surrounded,* literally goes along for the ride with a manifestly insane white man. We are in true absurdist country here, experiencing dialogue straight out of *Waiting for Godot*:

> "Pigs," I said. "Once I caught a ride up here with a man who was delivering pigs."
>
> "Is there anything up there?" He pointed to the top of the hill.
>
> "Not that I know of."
>
> "Did you see any back there that interested you?"
>
> "What?"

"Cars, for Chrissake."

"Oh!" I turned around. "Well, that's a different story."

"Pigs, you say." He sounded disgusted.

"What?"[9]

But this farcical interlude culminates in a bitter illumination: "Again I felt that helplessness of being in a world of stalking white men. But those Indians down at Gable's were no bargain either. I was a stranger to both and both had beaten me" (120). In such passages the narrator reminds us of doomed Big Paul in *The Surrounded*.

For its first two-thirds, Welch's novel is largely an elegy for the lost father, lost brother, and lost world of the native peoples. The narrative technique circles around the deep griefs that depress, even suppress, the thirty-two-year-old narrator. First Raise, Mose, and Yellow Calf circulate like ghosts through the story, sporadically emerging as memories, dreams, or wraithlike reality. Welch deploys a surrealistic technique as the narrator moves in and out of drunken states, blackouts, and hallucinatory nightmares. The narrator's dream visions are the ironic and terrible inversions of Fools Crow's meaning-drenched magical moments. In these uncanny passages Welch matches Hugo's technique stroke for stroke. Compare, for example, "The Lady in Kicking Horse Reservoir" with the narrator's drink-induced horror show in Chapter 16:

> I awoke the next morning with a hangover. I had slept fitfully, pursued by the ghosts of the night before and nights past. There were the wanted men with ape faces, cuffed sleeves and blue hands. They did not look directly into my eyes but at my mouth, which was dry and hollow of words. They seemed on the verge of performing an operation. Suddenly a girl loomed before my face, slit and gutted like a fat rainbow, and begged me to turn her loose, and I found my own guts spilling from my monstrous mouth. (52)

The dream manifests the protagonist's oppressive guilt and rage. He is haunted not just by death, but by the inescapable sense that he has aided and abetted the forces of destruction. (In case we had any doubts about these fatal powers, an old man collapses and dies in his bowl of oatmeal while the narrator looks on.) He carries within the belief that he has killed his brother and, indirectly, his father. If the novel were to wallow in this despair, leaving the reader no exit, no sense of possibility or resolution, we would be justified in leaving Welch in the company of Hugo's wandering poets and McGuane's Patrick Fitzpatrick. Surely we reach the emotional nadir when the narrator enters a Camus-like indifference to one of his casual lovers: "And I was staring at the sobbing woman with the same lack of emotion, the same curiosity, as though I were watching a bug floating motionless down an irrigation ditch, not yet dead but having decided upon death" (123).

But what we witness, instead, is a gradual coming to terms with this radical homelessness, this sense of distance from the self and the world, this Cain-like sensation of abandonment and guilt. Mose is the central figure in the narrator's troubled fantasy life, and over time that figure takes on a clearer and clearer impression for the taleteller and the reader alike. Rather than settling for the grim elegy, then, the narrative has the effect of gradually revealing or disclosing the lost brother, bringing him ever more vividly before us, giving him a posthumous life, a reality, a substance. It is as though the narrator's unconscious is slowly, painfully summoning the ghost, in order to express his sorrow and to put the horror behind him. To indulge a classical allusion, it's not all that different from the homeless and wracked Odysseus confronting the ghosts of Erebos in order to journey home. None is more haunting than his mother, and none more wrenching than his dead comrade Achilles.

The emotional climax of the novel arrives with the full-blown recollection of Mose's death. We understand, completely, the significance of the title, for that cold, snowy dying infects the narrator with winter in the blood:

> "What use," I whispered, cried for no one in the world to hear, not even Bird, for no one but my soul, as though the words would rid it of the final burden of guilt, and I found myself a child again, the years shed as a snake sheds its skin, and I was standing over the awkward tangle of clothes and limbs. "What use, what use, what

use . . ." and no one answered, not the body in the road, not the hawk in the sky or the beetle in the earth; no one answered. (146)

In this terrible return to his brother's calamity, the narrator becomes a child again; he is reborn through this grim epiphany. He faces squarely the guilt of the catastrophe, his sense that his own awkwardness distracted Mose and delayed him on the highway. He also acknowledges his complete and utter loss of faith, his sensation that no one answered his terrible question, "What use?" No voice spoke to him, no words comforted him, no meaning was forthcoming. The narrator lost not only his beloved brother but anything like faith that cold, cold day. The world had been drained of significance, of purpose.

Yet the narrator must also come to terms with the lost father, especially in light of Lame Bull's absurd and painfully funny attempts to play the father to the "boy." He takes comfort from his father's evident competence, his sense of humor, his ability to get along. Yet that death in the borrow pit (the very pit in which the narrator pisses at the start of the novel) hovers as the prophecy of the protagonist's own destiny. If he carries the winter in his blood, it is merely a matter of time before he succumbs to the external forces of destruction. Given his binge drinking and manic behavior, can he be long for this world? Unlike Joe Champlain, who seems indestructible, and who after all has the apparent affection of his father, Louis, and of his Grandpere, this confused character seems fragile, vulnerable, doomed. It's difficult to imagine what will save him, even after he encounters fully and finally the tragedy of Mose's death.

Remarkably, he is rescued by finding a genealogy, a lifeline leading from the heroic past to the diminished present. It is as though the narrator had discovered that Fools Crow was his ancestor. (Not entirely farfetched, since Yellow Calf turns out to be a displaced Blackfeet warrior.) Welch demonstrates real command of narrative pacing and tone by saving the Yellow Calf revelation for late in the narrative, thereby doubling and tripling its emotional impact. Here the analogy with *Stay Away, Joe* seems most credible and telling. Surely, outside of the title character himself, Grandpere is the most memorable figure in Cushman's novel. And after all, Grandpere is granted many of the best scenes, as in his fantastic vision of nuclear destruction I quoted at the beginning of part II. If Joe seems one-dimensional and unthinking, the good-time kid with amazing stamina and resourcefulness, Grandpere takes on a more substantial role, colorfully summoning memories of a great tribal past among the Cree. (The narrator makes a point of stressing that Grandpere is pure Cree, in contrast to his son Louis, who is Metis.) The 105-year-old elder lends a surprising significance to Joe, casting the roustabout veteran as a latter-day warrior.

Yellow Calf unexpectedly extends a similar kind of legitimacy to the narrator of *Winter in the Blood*. On the heels of his full-blown recollection of Mose's death and his own fearful wounding, the narrator rides the 100-year-old Bird to see the aging man. It's not clear what motivates this journey, although he recalls a visit as a young boy with his own father. As the narrator poignantly realizes later, "Although he told me nothing of it up to the day he died, he had taken me that snowy day to see my grandfather" (162). So some suppressed memory, some homing instinct seems to guide the speaker toward his ancestor. The scene of revelation is handled with Welch's distinctive understated humor. Yellow Calf refuses to gloat or pontificate; because the old man has few teeth left, it's not even clear if he smiles during their illuminating conversation. Yet when the realization strikes home, it's as though the winter in the soul has finally broken: "I began to laugh, at first quietly, with neither bitterness nor humor. It was the laughter of one who understands a moment in his life, of one who has been let in on the secret through luck and circumstance. 'You . . . you're the one.' I laughed, as the secret unfolded itself. 'The only one . . . you, her hunter . . .' And the wave behind my eyes broke" (158). Suddenly, the narrator is not so alone, so desperately disconnected, as he had imagined. He now has a male ancestor, one to replace, in part, the only people he has ever loved, his brother and his father. He can claim the legacy of heroism, the strength in a dark time, the time of his people's destruction. He can turn toward a man who cared for a woman, even to the extent of defying his people's distrust of her disturbing beauty. It is crucial as well that Yellow Calf is fully of this place, this landscape and weather, is attuned to the rhythms and sensations of the High Line environment. He fully belongs, and now the speaker may have a chance at the same way of being.

The following strange episode with Bird and the cow is surely meant to defuse the sentimentality of this recognition scene. There is something programmatic about the narrator's discovery of his vital genealogy, something a bit too willed about this resolution. Bird's collapse and the cow's death seem the young writer's ironic counterpoints to that forced solace. Readers often puzzle over this interlude, asking whether it should be read in a positive or negative light. Does Bird die? (Yes, he does.) Does the cow live? (No, she apparently doesn't.) Depending on the individual's answers to these questions, one can build an interpretation of despair or hope. But that controversy misses the point: the narrator has reached a stage where he can actually care enough about anyone or anything to take so much of a gamble, to put himself at physical and emotional risk. After all, the attempted rescue is painful and dangerous. The narrator is himself nearly swallowed by the mud. And his leg, injured so grievously twenty years earlier, buckles and nearly fails him. And Bird, whom the narrator has blamed for the catastrophe in the snow, proves himself a hero in his death throes. Welch suggests an analogical relationship between the horse and the old warrior Yellow Calf, conferring a linked dignity to each. He also hints at a symbolic connection between the warrior and the cow, perhaps a perverse way of representing the old man, but touching nonetheless: "Something about those eyes had prevented me from looking at him. It had seemed a violation of something personal and deep, as one feels when he comes upon a cow licking her newborn calf" (151). (It is difficult to do justice to the symbolic density and intricacy of this short novel. Welch often plays upon such metaphorical relationships, adding a rich subtext to the story.) After the terrible scene in which the narrator strikes his lover, and his general indifference to women, including his mother and grandmother, the attempt to rescue the mother cow suggests he has passed beyond this coldness, this neglect.

The funeral scene that ends the novel confirms that the narrator has arrived at something like adulthood. Though thirty-two years old, he has often been treated as a boy. He clearly has not arrived at his majority, a confident sense of himself, through most of the novel. Only when he confronts Mose's death head-on and discovers his true family can he begin to act like a capable, caring human being. The funeral scene, with its unusual combination of sadness and humor, marks this tentative (I stress tentative) arrival. Not only does the narrator bear witness to his mother's meaningful grief, not only does he acknowledge his grandmother's significance for the first time, but his final gesture signals his connection to an Indian past: "I threw the pouch into the grave" (176). In contrast to Lame Bull's typically idiotic speech, this simple gesture of love and respect speaks volumes. The narrator had earlier reflected on the traditional custom of burying the native person's effects with her. He is haunted by the lingering presence of Mose's stamp collection and other remembrances. In an act of devotion, the narrator follows the old way and places the grandmother's most intimate articles in her grave, including an arrowhead that may have been a memento of Yellow Calf. He has come a long way from the man as distant from himself as the hawk from the moon.

James Welch's fiction takes up and remakes the Indian stories handed down from native remembrancers and white writers. He transforms those materials into an authentic account of despair and survival. He shows how an indigenous westerner can grow into a confident sense of himself, come to know a place, a lineage, a purpose. That growth suggests a necessary maturation in western culture at large. As Fools Crow must embrace his role within Pikuni culture, as the narrator of *Winter* must recognize his connection to others, so westerners, native and non-native, must acknowledge their relationship with community and landforms. We are like adolescents learning to replace black/white dichotomies and physical violence with nuance and negotiation. Citizens of the high plains and northern Rockies can learn to take stock, show respect, and gain a mature identity. We must glean the stories from the past, then begin to compose our own.

Chapter 8

EVEN COWGIRLS
GET OVER THE BLUES

ONE OF THE FIRST MONTANA BOOKS I CAME ACROSS AFTER MY return to the state in 1985 was Cyra McFadden's *Rain or Shine*. I'd spent the previous few years familiarizing myself with the classics: *The Big Sky, A River Runs Through It, This House of Sky,* and Hugo's poetry. I was immediately taken by the informality, frankness, and tenderness of McFadden's memoir. It also struck me as something I hadn't come across before, a woman's telling of life in the West. It is in fact a classic account of a daughter's struggle to parse her father, to come to terms with his behavior, his silence, his disapproval, his love. I realize now that the book had an added kick in the mid-1980s because my own sisters were going through this very process with my father. We met often as siblings to talk through our traumatic, strained childhoods. It was the relevant thing to do at that moment, in part, no doubt, because

Ronald Reagan—the cowboy father—served as president. We were all working our way into our thirties, our mother had passed away many years before, and we sensed our father was drifting into a more and more distant relationship with all of us. So we would cook our breakfasts of coffee, pancakes, and bacon and share memories of neglect, benign or malign.

It dawned on me early in this process that much more was at stake for my sisters than for me or my brothers. Why? As my two older sisters recounted most honestly, they never felt embraced, or even acknowledged, by my father. He seemed a distant patriarch, one who struggled to say a kind or affirming word. My father was the true westerner in our family, born, raised, and buried in the West, moving from North Dakota to Lewistown early in his life and coming of age as a child of hoteliers in that lovely central Montana town. He absorbed his father's reticence and his mother's rectitude. It was apparent that if we at times felt unloved, my father must have suffered a double dose of that treatment from his mother, a tough woman not prone to displays of affection. But Dad also absorbed that part-western, part-late-Victorian creed of toughing it out in silence and not tipping one's emotional hand too often or too early. He frequently complained about the sentimentality of contemporary television, and I knew he spoke from the core of his personality.

So McFadden's blunt recounting of her life with father registered as a familiar western tale, a story of disconnection, followed by a final reconciliation. After I'd read through it with a kind of breathless eagerness, I urged my father to pick it up (he was an avid reader as well), thinking mainly about its Montana setting and the fact that Cy Taillon, Cyra's charismatic father, was a familiar figure from his childhood. But when my father started reading the book, he became uncomfortable, even a little surly, about it. I now realize that he may have seen there a reproduction of his own difficult relationship with his daughters. He may have assumed I'd sandbagged him, set him up, lured him into an emotional trap. I'd confronted him with his own familial "sins" through the backdoor of our shared love of literature. In hindsight, my father may well have been right, though I acted out that motive unconsciously.

Rain or Shine is a middle-aged woman's reassessment of her own and her father's linked lives. Hovering over the story from the beginning is the by-now familiar (and inescapable) western myth of masculinity: "When my father died, in April of 1980, newspapers in the West compared him with John Wayne."[1] Her father had come to embody those seemingly evanescent American virtues: gallantry, toughness, and moral righteousness. Yet McFadden knew her father as the very antithesis of this idealized westerner, for she grew up as his waiflike child on the rodeo circuit, traveling from arena to arena throughout the West with her glamorous mother and the rakehell Cy. But that family came unglued, blown apart by drinking, jealousy, and mental illness, and Cy moved on to a new family and a different identity, the selfhood encoded in countless films and popular novels. No wonder his renegade daughter, liberal and sophisticated, felt abandoned, cut off, left without a legacy or genealogy.

But McFadden's memoir does not, finally, devolve into a family tragedy, complete with broken hearts and minds. Coming to terms not only with her father's but with her husband's death, the writer takes a deep breath and recapitulates her experiences in an effort to piece them together, to find order in chaos, sense in apparent meaninglessness. In part she discovers that her father was, after all, a rounded, complex, sometimes difficult, sometimes wonderful human being. He was no John Wayne—he was both more and less than that. She also discovers bloodlines linking her irrevocably not only to Cy but to her two half brothers, Terry and Tom. In many ways this is a narrative of going home, of finding family, of discovering a legitimate self in the convoluted but serviceable genealogy of divided families: "I accept the lot of us, at last, as who and what we were: just one more group of people joined together as that mysterious and complicated thing, a family" (249). In an important sense, then, McFadden's tale has much in common with the anonymous narrator's in *Winter in the Blood*, who feels a thawing of the soul when he discovers that Yellow Calf is his Blackfeet grandfather. And so McFadden shows that a western story, especially a western woman's story, can be as much about finding a place as about being driven out or destroyed.

McFadden's is but one of many narratives by western women that represent this alternative perspective in memorable terms. Hughie Call's *Golden Fleece* (1942) is one of my favorite Montana books, though one I treat as a guilty secret since it's an "adolescent" story. A charming, well-written, down-to-earth book, it attends to the particulars of Call's daily life on a sheep ranch in the Gallatin Valley. In many ways this is a classic pastoral. Call organizes the narrative around the phases of the sheeprancher's life: breeding, lambing, shearing, and shipping. She covers in detail her daily routines such as "jacketing" and dealing with cooks. She's witty and tolerant, but amusingly perceptive. Call uses an age-old writer's trick to get the reader inside the experience: she presents herself as the greenhorn, the tenderfoot. Her husband Tom then becomes her foil, her knowing counterpoint. And so she invites the reader in by showing herself to be an outsider who moves inside. As she observes with effective understatement, "The years I've spent in Montana have taught me to look facts in the face."[2]

McFadden and Call return us to the provocative insights of Julia Watson:

> Regarding that myth of masculinity as *the* voice of Montana autobiography makes it difficult to hear the differing voices and values that many women bring to writing their lives: an emphasis on family and domestic life, on the importance of small communities, on survival rather than conquest, on generational networks, and on pleasure in place. And it obscures the myth's underside, violent male enforcement enacted on women and indigenous peoples in the name of maintaining rugged individualism.[3]

Female writers in Montana, especially those writing over the past fifty years, seem to bear out Watson's claims. As McFadden challenges the mythic stereotypes of the cowboy father, and as Call acquaints us with a settled way of living that is both comical and sustaining, so Mildred Walker's *Winter Wheat,* Mary Clearman Blew's *All But the Waltz,* and Deirdre McNamer's *Rima in the Weeds* subvert masculinist stories and assert women's narratives.[4] These three generations of writers counter the cataclysmic "heroic" tales of a predominantly male tradition with quieter, more intimate, and more enduring accounts of toughing it out, of "sticking." While each text incorporates starkly tragic elements, each offers the protagonist an opening out, a sense of possibility, a prospect. By taking us through complex passages of pain and sorrow to arrive at a sustainable hope, these women's stories provide paradigms of pragmatic comedy.

Walker's novel demonstrates the connection between the female body and place as well as any fiction this side of Willa Cather:

> September is like a quiet day after a whole week of wind. I mean real wind that blows dirt into your eyes and hair and between your teeth and roars in your ears after you've gone inside. The harvesting is done and the wheat stored away and you're through worrying about hail or drought or grasshoppers. The fields have a tired peaceful look, the way I imagine a mother feels when she's had her baby and is just lying there thinking about it and feeling pleased.[5]

The passage's combination of gritty realism and natural mythology marks a distinctive sense of place. Ellen Webb, the eighteen-year-old narrator, living on a wheat farm in north-central Montana, describes with uncommon honesty the bitter conditions that often temper life on the farm. But she concludes with a Demeter-like evocation of the satisfaction of producing good food out of that tough land. In these opening words to her personal narrative she establishes an unbreakable bond between herself and her world—the soil, the color and texture of wheat, the relentless winds, and the slick, unforgiving gumbo. She's a wheat-colored, lank, tough young woman. And she has it within her to flourish despite disaster, to come up in the spring, whole and better, despite a series of terrible winter shocks. Ellen Webb, connected as her name would imply, is indeed the winter wheat of the title. The land giveth and the land taketh away, but ultimately it sustains.

As Ellen journeys east to her new life as a student, she repeatedly compares her novel sensations to her beloved homeplace. When she visits Gil's parents for the first time, she notices that the "colors in the room were as soft as the summer colors of the prairie" (52). And when she imagines disclosing herself fully to Gil, she thinks, "I wanted him to know the terrible feeling of sadness that creeps into my mind sometimes, like rust on the wheat" (53). Because of this inescapable connection between herself and her home terrain, Ellen's relationship with Gil is doomed from the start. The son of a history professor and a genteel mother, the urbane artist/architect can only be appalled by life on the Webb ranch. He seems to have imagined a romantic Western scene, something straight out of *The Virginian*, but what he finds instead is the result of a difficult struggle to make ends meet from year to year. The house is a brownish-gray product of the wind, rain, and snow; the prairie is covered with wildflowers that seem inconsequential, even vaguely offensive; when Ellen tries to show Gil the beauty of a cactus in bloom, he is only slightly amused and a bit annoyed. The lush midwestern landscape has so thoroughly shaped this aesthete's sense of beauty that he turns in disgust from the dryland farm country. No wonder he asks Ellen if she could ever be happy living in a city such as Chicago. He assumes that Montana and the city occupy mutually exclusive social and cultural universes.

It is apparent to Ellen as well that this sophisticated young man has been put off by her mother, and this recognition leads the narrator to analyze her parents with a pitiless intensity. Since she has lost Gil, she must account for the debacle, and they provide a readily available target for blame. Ellen had already wondered at length about their relationship; what could possibly bond the Protestant, genteel young man from Vermont and the Orthodox "peasant" from Russia? As the only child of their marriage, Ellen had plenty of opportunity to observe their sometimes testy, often distant relationship. In the effective flashback section during her one year at college, Ellen recounts a series of curious episodes involving them, most memorably the strange journey to Clark City over an Easter weekend that exposed their divergent religious views. After Gil's abandonment, Ellen begins to think that her parents are not only mismatched but positively harmful for each other. She also recognizes that her mother's relationship with her father is similar to her own with Gil, and so she concludes that her parents' bond must be a sham, a convenient ruse to protect her. When she overhears her mother and father arguing over their reason for marrying—Anna had falsely told Ben she was pregnant—Ellen has all the confirmation she needs that her parents live out a lie, that they in fact hate each other.

We might pause to wonder why these important female writers are drawn to parsing parents. We have already seen McFadden's unavoidable reflection on her father's double life; we will see shortly how Mary Clearman Blew struggles with her father's death (and so, by implication, his life); and the female characters in *Rima in the Weeds* try to come to grips with their parents' treatment of them. Watson suggests generally that women are more interested in questions of relationship, of affiliation, of connection than are male writers. To be more precise, these female writers face the problem of adjusting to life as the oldest child of a family that may well have longed for a son. Blew emphasizes Jack Hogeland's desire for a male heir, and short of that, he turns to young Mary as the surrogate son. Cyra felt displaced by her two half brothers precisely because of their maleness, their ability to fill the role Cy Taillon had imagined for his scion. Ellen has become a tomboy of sorts, as comfortable in jeans as a dress, and Gil, to his credit, recognizes this ineradicable trait in her. In the terrible scene in which Gil gets the truck stuck in the clayey gumbo, the scene that marks the end of their engagement, Ellen must bail out the hapless outlander. So Ellen may well be scrutinizing this issue of gender expectations as well, the degree to which she has been made into a tough, hardworking, but unfeminine woman by conditions on the wheat farm. Certainly her mother provides a role model for that crossing-over.

These writers also puzzle through seemingly fatal patterns within families. Cyra notices that she is drawn to men with deep, booming voices similar to her father's; Mary ends up marrying a rakehell cowboy who takes her to the edge of despair, much as her father had done in his life and death. Ellen must come to terms with her attraction to an elegant man of the city, a character remarkably similar to her father. It is no wonder that Ben Webb and Gil hit it off during the young man's brief, abortive visit to Gotham. Ellen is sorting through patterns of behavior to discern her own motivations and missteps. She seems to believe that if she can only explain this family curse to herself she can somehow recover her lost relationship with Gil. With genuine misapprehension, Ellen reveals: "I felt with a sick sense of disappointment that he was going before he had seen anything, before he had any feeling for the country. But why did that matter? Wasn't I separate from the country?" (80).

Ellen enters into a deep funk, a depression, after Gil's rejection. She is more and more convinced that her life is meaningless, that her existence on the farm is ugly and deforming, that she is old before her time. She is saved, in part, by that old-fashioned elixir, hard work. Ellen works and works and works to bring in the hay and the wheat, largely to finance her second year of college, of course, but also because she senses the healing power of outdoor labor. In this sense, Ellen Webb's story is typical of a distinctive western mode of representation. As Maile Meloy writes, "By making the georgic the substance of successful self-fashioning, recent Montana literature has been characterized by an urge to escape the idealized in order to lodge in something closer to the actual. Self-fashioning is work, and it has to be done in connection with some other kind of work."[6] This insight returns us to the importance of concrete activities as described by citizen-philosophers such as Bugbee, Kemmis, and Strong. We find ourselves, the argument holds, not through some abstract analysis or institutional affiliation, but through hard work that grounds us (literally), that puts us in our place, that forces us to attend to the immediate and the local. Toward the end of her memoir Ellen puts it simply and well: "I knew now that there were times when you couldn't look ahead. It hurt too much if you tried to think what came after spring and what after summer. It was easier to go along and work so hard in the day that you were tired at night" (301). Her almost painfully detailed accounts of harvesting represent precisely this vital work ethic, this ethos of labor that binds us to a place that matters. Through her labors she recovers her equilibrium and realizes that she is more than the young woman Gil might have loved, she is the Montana woman who can drive a truck through gumbo, work a combine, and get the wheat to the elevator at ten at night after a brutal day of work. It turns out that Ellen is more and better than Gil would have allowed her to be.

Her experiences as a teacher connect her to the place in a different but complementary way: she is bonded to the people of the region, even though that relationship ultimately runs afoul of petty moralisms. Like many young women who need to make ends meet (including my grandmother and the women of Blew's family), Ellen turns to teaching in a rural schoolhouse. The move grants her a needed hiatus from her parents (despite the benefits of hard work, she's still persuaded that her father and mother live a false life, poorly concealing their hatred for each other). It also calls up skills she did not know she possessed, and it allows her the freedom to date another attractive male, though ultimately that relationship will founder. This period of gestation for the protagonist—and the winter wheat—also includes a terrible tragedy: the death of a mentally retarded boy in a dreadful snowstorm. That loss puts life in perspective, once again reminding Ellen that whatever the pain of Gil's flight, there are more serious and deadly concerns. Like all of us attempting to grow up, Ellen must realize that her suffering is not the most significant event in the world. Her response to that death also teaches her a lesson about owning up to our mistakes, acknowledging rather than fleeing our errors of omission and commission. Imitating her resilient mother, Ellen accepts her responsibility and moves on. Slowly but surely, the protagonist advances toward mature selfhood.

Her return home after her dismissal signals the last stage of her growth. But first she must learn of Gil's death, made all the more poignant by Ellen's sense that he had at last realized the depth of his love for her. She is shadowed by the knowledge that they might have been able to patch together their relationship after the war. But as Anna, the no-nonsense member of the family, observes, many young women will lose their "sweethearts" in the war and Ellen's loss is of a piece with a more general calamity. Though that insight provides cold comfort to the narrator, she is forced to confront once more her place in a larger scheme of experience—she can't dwell naively or egotistically in her private pain. News of Gil's death also triggers the final confrontation with her parents' seemingly troubled relationship. In two heartfelt conversations with mother and father, Ellen knows, completely, for the first time, that her parents love and understand each other. What the daughter perceived as spiteful, even hateful, exchanges were, according to Anna, "[l]ike ice an' snow an' thunder an' lightning storm, but they don't hurt the wheat down in the ground any" (284). And Ben lovingly explains that his Russian wife is necessarily "alien" because of her bitter upbringing in a foreign country. The conclusion seems unavoidable: the supposed hate between her parents is but a mark of intimacy, affection, and sure comprehension that can provide a template for Ellen's future marriage. No wonder Ben calls his daughter "Karmont," referring to a hybrid of Russian and Montana strains of wheat. She is a vital fusion of both parents' traits: Ben's love of learning and gift for language and Anna's astonishing energy and bluntness. It seems a pleasant combination of cultivation and true grit.

The novel follows a three-part structure that highlights Ellen's maturation: part I focuses on her journey to Minneapolis, her courtship with Gil, his flight, and Ellen's bitter attempt to work her way through the pain, events that consume one full year; part II provides further mixed blessings, combining Ellen's joy in teaching with the retarded boy's death and her dismissal from her job by petty parents, events that consume fall and winter; part III brings Gil's death, Leslie's "adoption," and Ellen's recognition of her parents' love, all leading toward the spring that signals rebirth, for both the protagonist and the wheat. The epigraph for the third section sums up this vital pattern: "*Sow the seed in the wide black earth and already the seed is victorious, though time must contribute to the triumph of the wheat*" (257). Ellen has entered and passed through her most difficult transitional state, the stage between late adolescence and full-blown adulthood. She has needed much time and many shocks to arrive at her mature self-possession. Her individual crises mirror larger crises in the ranching and farming communities of Montana. As Warren sadly observes, thinking of his own disappointments in marriage and career, "Maybe a country settled by homesteads is bound to be made of expectation and disappointment. . . . So much hope to begin with settling down into so much resignation" (220). But Ellen discovers that her parents are not "resigned" in some grim sense. Instead, they demonstrate warmth, humor, and cleverness in negotiating their wheat-farming life. Similarly, Ellen can look forward to a life full of promise, albeit promise that must grow in the shadow of death. Perhaps for this reason, *Winter Wheat* generates an unusually complex and ambivalent reader response. A friend who grew up on a Montana ranch listened patiently to my upbeat assessment of the novel, and then responded, "But it's such a sad book." Yes, so much that is sad, even tragic, occurs in the novel, yet at the end the narrator declares, "[My parents] had love that was deep-rooted and stronger than love that grows easily. It gave me faith for my own life. . . . Now I wanted to live my life with the strength of the winter wheat, through drought and rain and snow and sun" (306). That is why this novel is the quintessential pragmatic comedy. It comes to grips with the realities of making a go of Montana yet arrives at a satisfying sense that an intelligent, strong, willful, sometimes misguided young woman can embrace such a life. The world doesn't end for Ellen—it's beginning all over again. For Mildred Walker, life is more dialectical and evolving than catastrophic.

Similar to *Winter Wheat*, Mary Clearman Blew's *All But the Waltz: A Memoir of Five Generations in the Life of a Montana Family* grants space to catastrophe but finally affirms provisional hope. The book is a hard-hitting account of betrayal, failure, and occasional survival among Montana homesteaders. Repeatedly, men fail women and themselves in the attempt to translate Montana into a paying proposition. Yet something endures beyond the loss. As Blew put it succinctly in an interview, "In my family, the men were glamorous and the women persevered."[7] Though Blew does occasionally acknowledge the enduring male, especially her resourceful uncle Ervin Noel, the more typical male figure is A. P. Welch, a hapless homesteader from Canada by way of Iowa. Blew's grandfather on her mother's side, A. P. is far more gifted at social graces than at working an unforgiving terrain. He ultimately slides into madness, not an unusual outcome for men in this extended family. The narrative leads us to believe that the wind, drought, crop failures, professional inadequacy, and his wife's success as a school-teacher drive "Apple Pie" over the edge. Two photographs accompanying the text give a haunting sense of that decline: in the first image, a youngish, reasonably confident-looking A. P. is surrounded by his four daughters on the porch of a homestead house; in the latter image, an aging A. P., not long for this earth, dressed in a tidy three-piece suit, stares vacantly into the camera. If ever a graphic image defined the price of settlement in the boom-and-bust years, that second photograph does.

A. P.'s story is a kind of shadowy retelling of the more dire failure narrated earlier in this collection of personal essays: Blew's own father, Jack Hogeland, dies of exposure in 1983, for reasons not thoroughly understood. In one sense, this complex, troubled, darkly humorous book is a coming to terms with Jack's death. Described repeatedly as a cowboy living in the fading years of that dream, a man shaped as much by Zane Grey and A. B. Guthrie Jr. as by the realities of ranching on hardscrabble land, Jack comes across as both tormentor and hero to the middle-aged memoirist. The reader would struggle to reduce any of Blew's characters to mere stereotype, since the writer has the unnerving habit of approaching and reapproaching her subjects to dissolve comfortable assumptions and introduce new possibilities. The book is dominated by questioning, by wondering, by searching, and the father is surely the best example of that interrogative stance. Jack was glamorous, competent, blunt, and verbal for the young Mary. He also raised her as the son he did not have. This meant that when the oldest daughter fell off a horse, she was expected to get right back on, come hell or high water. Jack taught her to work hard, care for herself, and be strong. Yet when Mary chooses a path that diverges from her father's dream, when she chooses, that is, academia over rural teaching or ranch life, Jack cannot forgive her. In a haunting refrain for the book, he tells his daughter, "*Somewhere you got the idea in your head that you know something, but you don't know a goddamned thing.*"[8] As in all family chronicles, guilt plays an important role here, for Mary realizes that her father had given up his cherished Spring Creek ranch to move closer to Lewistown so that his daughters, especially his bookworm oldest daughter, could attend a proper high school. Her leaving first for the University of Montana, then for the University of Missouri at Columbia, felt like an especially cruel betrayal to the man who had surrendered his patrimony, the land his own grandfather had secured in 1882.

Just as haunting, just as elusive as this sense of mutual betrayal is the nature of the father's death. Leaving home ground for an unfamiliar stretch of rural outback south of Miles City, Jack lies down on the ground beside his truck and goes to permanent sleep. No doubt the daughter wonders about her own complicity in this senseless ending, her own role in killing the talented horseman's dreams. But she also wonders about a genealogy of male woe in the Hogeland/Welch families, the breakdown not just of A. P. and Jack but of her "step grandfather," Bill Hafer, who abandons Mary's grandmother when he finds he has cancer. Set adrift in the search for a cure and a second chance, "Hafer Bill" turns to miracle remedies and other women. He does not, of course, elude the ultimate sorry joke, his own lonely death. And these breakdowns only provide the prelude to a final collapse, that of Mary's second husband, Bob. The concluding essay, "All But the Waltz," takes us to the emotional center of this dauntingly frank family narrative. It is in this final movement that the reader discovers the most pressing pretext for this deep search into family history. By turns a rakehell and charmer, Bob introduces the uptight academic dean to the thrills of flying, in every sense. Yet he too goes smash, descending into a dementia brought on by illness and his own refusal to deal with that sickness. Is there a kind of grim fatality that hovers over Montana? Is the myth of the cowboy West, complete with male independence and derring-do, a repeated invitation to a personal beheading? Even her great-grandfather Abraham, the original patriarch and a success by most standards, appears a bullheaded, domineering, at times sneering overlord, at least as Mary glimpses him through his surviving papers. Though he managed to survey the land and establish a comfortable homestead in the years just after the extermination of the buffalo, he also managed to reduce Montana range to pure property and to demean native peoples with lame stories and mock dialect. Mary of course identifies with the Other here, as elsewhere she connects with the Hutterites who practice an alternative style of landholding on the desiccated high plains.

So who are the women who survive and even flourish despite these foolish men? There is, first and foremost, Mary Welch, the grandmother, wife of A. P., and the writer's namesake. She takes on more and more stature as the chronicle unfolds, circled back to again and again as the example of the one who made it despite a mad husband

and a bum deal. Mary becomes a teacher in those one-room school-houses of the northern plains, returning to the classroom after twenty years, in the aftermath of homestead and insurance-selling failures. There is nothing romantic or idealistic about her decision; Mary Welch is the ultimate pragmatist. It would be difficult to call her life as an itin-erant teacher "comic" in any sense, whether we think of actual humor or merely a story with a happy ending. Still, she endures, and she passes on to her daughters and granddaughter the life of the teacher and the possibility of living after the fall:

> Her gestures, the quick movements of her hands, are imprinted on mine. She is there when I knead bread or comfort a child or pick up a pen. Sometimes I imagine her square figure turning from the teacherage stove where she has been poking up the coal fire, and I see her face with the arched brows and the compressed mouth and the permanent lines of sadness, and for a moment it is I who turn from the stove, my face seared with the indelible lines of hers. (198)

If the older Mary is the matriarchal alternative to the overwhelm-ing Abraham, Imogene, the maiden aunt, is the second mother to the memoirist, the most beloved and engaging of all characters in the book. It is clear that Imogene combines the qualities that Blew admires most: intelligence, humor, warmth, sureness of self, and a fair amount of perspective on herself and her family. In a moment both horrific and comic, Imogene nearly loses her foot in a haying accident, only to forestall ultimate disaster with quick thinking and immediate action. It is Imogene as well who teaches the dryland girl to swim, an important symbol for Mary's emerging sense of independence and purposiveness. The fact that this aunt on the mother's side must also leave Montana, to take up a life in Port Angeles, Washington, only contributes to her importance: she models the break from the Mon-tana world that the writer herself must make as she starts anew as a teacher in Idaho. *Balsamroot*, the sequel to *All But the Waltz*, amplifies Imogene's charm and significance. A kinder, gentler book than the Montana family chronicle, the sequel focuses on the life, dementia, and impending death of "Auntie." While that sounds like grim subject matter, *Balsamroot* conveys a serenity, a comfort with self, that rarely if ever emerges in the earlier book. By focusing on the aunt who lived most of her life on the waters of Puget Sound, Blew allows herself to dwell on the successes much more than on the failures. We also see Blew settling into her new place, finding home through relationships with her older daughter, the daughter's husband, the writer's own male friend, and the Snake River Valley itself. Maybe Blew has beaten the odds: maybe she can break the spell of family fatality that blows through *All But the Waltz*.

Blew's memoirs do not always make easy reading, especially for a male. There's an anger here, a bitterness that at times seems of a piece with her own mother's monologue of rejection and nihilism. There's a strong family resemblance not only in appearance but in tone between mother Doris and her gifted daughter. There are also moments of near cruelty, as in Mary's condescending description of her first husband as "a good fly-fishing Helena boy" (165). In such passages the reader is much like young Mary absorbing Doris's bitter diatribes: Isn't that a bit much? What can motivate such venom? Isn't there something more than a little self-indulgent about these words? But in the next moment it occurs to this reader that these memoirs comprise an "apology" in both senses of that term: both a defense and a confession. Mary rarely spares herself the acerbic glance, acknowledging her own trivial reasons for getting married at eighteen (she wanted to get out of the dorm and find out, finally, what all the fuss over sex was about). She realizes that she must have broken her father's heart by choosing to leave the ranch for good; she knows that she fell hard for the mad cowboy who became her second husband. As I remarked earlier, Blew won't settle for the melodramatic dichotomies, the easy digs, the shopworn tragedy. She forces herself and the reader to confront again and again the scandalous ambiguity of family life and settlement on the plains. There are moments of pure pastoral bliss, punctuated by the horror of an aunt's nearly severed foot and the meaningless death of a gifted grandfather/horseman.

In the end, of course, this is a story about "Leaving Montana" (to quote the title of one of the essays). In that sense *All But the Waltz* can seem another elegy for a dream deprived and depraved. But Blew won't allow us so easy a conclusion. Even as she narrates the search for her missing father, Blew reveals the extended kinship network that encompasses the state like a web. Her competent, caring sister directs the search, showing that at least one Montana girl has managed to hang tough in the place of seemingly dead hope. And after all, Sylva, another cherished aunt, managed to make a kind of home out of a mere shack during the construction of the Fort Peck Dam. If comedy may be too strong a term, a kind of provisional hope glimpses through these tough, bluesy essays: "In the story of how Mary [Welch] scraped and labored and shouldered on, and of the awful price she paid, this remains. She survived, and she handed on the tools for survival to those she could reach" (201).

Rima in the Weeds is quirky, tender, and refreshingly humorous. Deirdre McNamer takes us inside a High Line community in the early 1960s, using the Cuban missile crisis and its attendant military buildup as an effective backdrop for the lives of Margaret Greenfield and Dorrie Vane. Each is a changeling undergoing a transition, Margaret moving into adolescence, Dorrie trying to find a sustainable adult identity. (For this reason, at various moments in her offbeat life, Dorrie might remind us of Ellen Webb.) Through these counterpointed but inter-connected lives, McNamer traces yet another Montana growing-up story, and in the process encompasses many of the issues central to this chapter: the daughter's search for a meaningful identity in a masculin-ist culture; a relationship to place; the need to reconnect with (or even reestablish) a family; and the dread of outsiders, leading to conspiracy theories. *Rima* reminds us of how central coming-of-age stories have been to Montana writers, perhaps because the authors treat their own semiexotic youths, perhaps because characters tend to embody larger trends within the still-young western society.

The most apt term for this at-times-disjointed novel is "provi-sional." The narrative wends its way through sad, lonely lives, showing how Margaret and Dorrie tentatively, awkwardly, painfully advance toward semiformed identities that will allow them to thrive. As with all the stories treated in part III, there's nothing simple or mawkish about this narrative of incomplete if serviceable resolutions. After all, Dorrie's best friend in the small town of Madrid ends up dying pathetically in an alcoholic daze, a victim of desperate loneliness and a sense of inertia, an inability to move on with her life. Rosemary Vane, Dorrie's mother, represents the suppressed creativity and desire of all the female characters in the novel, showing through her eccentric but affecting actions how the stultifying life of High Line Montana could lead a woman to saving madness. Her various attempts at spicing up her life, her momentary outbursts of anger, and her nude romps at the insane asylum all suggest a captive soul, a kind of nuclear missile of desire that seeks its release, its explosive vent. The librarian Holly Harper is forced to flee from Madrid, a victim of Earl Vane's vengeful paranoia and her own inability to sustain a life there. Though the least fully realized of these characters, Holly seems another sign of the suppression and depression that can afflict women in rural western towns.

Add to these complete and partial catastrophes the general obtuseness and sterility of the male characters. Red, husband of the best friend to Margaret's mother, is the classic brutish cowboy, rough around the edges and the heart, crude and mean and indifferent toward his pregnant wife. Steve, Dorrie's short-term boyfriend, is uptight, upright, and judgmental. He seems most at ease when he's beneath the surface, manning the missiles and so operating within the mechanized rules of strategic engagement with the enemy. McNamer characterizes him in almost stereotypical fashion as the handsome but unyielding male who prefers cleaning his gun to carrying on anything like a meaningful conversation with another human being. And last but not least, Earl comes to represent all the paranoid sickness of the radical fringe. Wounded to the core by his wife's psychological defection, he concocts wild theory upon wild theory about the creeping, ubiquitous presence of Communism in small-town Montana. The writer shrewdly hints here that many of the more extremist outbursts in the West emerge from personal hurt and a failure to accept one's own responsibility. It seems far easier for Earl to dwell upon improbably vast machinations than to acknowledge his dehumanizing treatment of his wife. The novel's conclusion does allow for a partial reconstruction of this male character, for we last see Earl preparing a meal and expressing an unexpected contentment upon Rosemary's return from the mental hospital in Warm Springs. Perhaps you can teach an old conspiracy theorist new tricks.

Undergoing their rough transitions in context of these characters and these failings, Dorrie and Margaret must find their way toward endurance and possibly even happiness. Dorrie carries within her the ghosts of her mother's madness, her father's indifference, and her lover's abandonment. Like many Montana kids who journey to the big city to pursue an education or a career, Dorrie at first takes it on the chin in Chicago. She makes a fascinating contrast to Ellen Webb, who flourishes in Minneapolis. But then Ellen had, despite her own doubts, a sustaining, durable set of parents who gave her a confidence, a belief in herself, that Dorrie can only guess at. As a single mother in the hometown that isn't quite sure what to make of her, she must contend with the inner demons, the ballistic missiles of her submerged anger and desire. While Dorrie's violence at the end, especially her shooting of Margaret's horse, can seem too abrupt or insufficiently motivated, McNamer has planted the seeds of despair earlier in the novel. When she breaks her mother's arm and savagely bites a cruelly abusive male, Dorrie shows that a nearly homicidal rage circulates just below the surface. Like her mother, this character demonstrates the price an intelligent, willful woman can pay for taking shelter in a town with few options other than marriage or waitressing. It's a relief for this reader, then, when Dorrie is able to muster the energy to return to the University of Chicago at the conclusion. She has no doubt spared herself the gruesome death of a Gloria or the cycles of insanity of a Rosemary.

Yet, as every reviewer seems to point out, Margaret is the center and key to this fine novel. McNamer shows a sureness of touch with the young adolescent psyche that harks back to Joyce's *Portrait of the Artist as a Young Man*. (I found myself wondering whether Margaret isn't McNamer's self-portrait of her clumsy progress toward her own important career as an artist.) The novel captures the rapid mood swings, hilarious associative leaps, and aching yearning of the girl transforming into a young woman. In this way *Rima* once again recalls *Winter Wheat*, especially that earlier novel's portrayal of Ellen's desperate moodiness following Gil's rejection. But Margaret is a far more humorous character than Ellen. McNamer impressively manages to tease and embrace this character, never condescending to her or converting her into pure comic device. I never sense that the narrator is patronizing Margaret. Margaret just *is*. We watch as her body changes rapidly, her temperament swings from manic joy to depressed moroseness, her fantasy life fluctuates between dread and hope, and her relationship with her parents goes from appreciative to dismissive to perplexed. The daughter's dealings with Roy and MaryEllen provide one of the quieter pleasures of the novel, since the novelist grants these two adults a kind of ambiguous roundness or complexity that seems to be lacking in characters such as Steve and Gloria. McNamer uses a center-of-consciousness point of view to present the parents through the partially blinded eyes of their precocious but hypochondriac daughter. The novel's final scene seems absolutely right, since Margaret returns from her brief journey away from home, ready to rejoin her parents in their collective lives, yet at the same time going through a door that marks her crossing of the liminal space between childhood and adolescence. Margaret does emerge a new and more resilient being at the end of *Rima in the Weeds*. If Dorrie is most like the cat woman of film legend, Margaret is most like the sturdy, playful title character:

> Rima the jungle girl had black hair, long and silky. She ran gracefully through dense foliage and shafts of sunlight, ministering to injured animals who became tame in her presence. At times, she would hear in the distance the faint, plaintive cry of the jungle explorer who loved her and wanted her for his wife. . . . But she didn't answer because she had to be free.[9]

What makes all this possible, in the end, is Margaret's empathy for Dorrie. It's a new and important word for the protagonist, a term signifying her ability to break out of a self-involvement to feel with and through another human being. These tender associations, these generous habits of the heart, are what these woman-centered books are largely about. As Cyra needed her half brothers, as Ellen needed her parents, as Mary needed her grandmother and her aunt Imogene,

Margaret and Dorrie needed each other. This concession to dependence, this recognition of filiation and affection, is one of the abiding lessons of these enduring narratives. Again, let me emphasize that there's nothing sentimental or "emotional" about these books. They are tough, unflinching stories of strained, even broken, lives that can only mend with time and care. They reinforce an important lesson for young Margaret:

> She used to think happiness was like a doorstop she saw once when she was selling the Mary rockets, a doorstop of a little sheltie dog, made out of some kind of heavy plaster or maybe even iron. It was cute, but you couldn't really *like* anything like that, not as a pet. . . . She used to think that happiness, the best kind, was something as immovable as that dog doorstop. Now she thought it was maybe more like a real dog. (265)

Margaret will surely join the company of Cyra McFadden, Hughie Call, Ellen Webb, and Aunt Imogene. Perceptive and articulate, though still growing into her body and her sense of herself, this Montana Rima will find a sustainable belief in herself and the world. Dorrie's story reminds us that traps remain for young women in the rural West. Yet the setting in the early 1960s suggests that McNamer takes a backward glance at a tougher time for talented women. The novel ruthlessly exposes archetypes of male bad behavior, cataloging assumptions of intellectual and physical inferiority in women. In the process, it implies that such boorish behavior often emerges from the insecurities, the self-doubt, of those very males. Astute Margaret has carefully tallied up these insights, openly wondering about the casual cruelty of men, including the adolescent who "rejects" her. It is hard to imagine that she will fall for the romantic allurements of a man like Dorrie's Chicago lover, or the controlling intentions of a Steve, or the punishing self-righteousness of an Earl. She will evade their traps, their inducements to self-doubt. She will take a journey into the world, much like young Antoine in *Wind from an Enemy Sky*, but hers will be a completed pilgrimage, not one truncated by violence and misunderstanding. Margaret provides yet another affecting symbol of western maturation, of finding a way toward canniness and empathy.

All over the West . . . the old story is dying. We find ourselves weathering a rough winter of discontent, snared in the uncertainties of a transitional time and urgently yearning to inhabit a story that might bring sensible order to our lives, even as we know such a story can only evolve through an almost literally infinite series of recognitions of what we hold sacred, individual by individual. If we're lucky, it might be a story that teaches us to abhor our old romance with conquest and progress so that we might revere the particular.

—WILLIAM KITTREDGE,
"New to the Country"

Chapter 9

NEW HOMES
ON THE RANGE

VIOLENT MELODRAMA HAS PROVIDED A COMPELLING VOICE OF WEST-ern masculinity, whether we consider the patently popular Western such as *Riders of the Purple Sage* or the fervid fantasies of fanatics. William Kittredge and Ivan Doig counterbalance the seductive call of this male fantasy with profound rethinking of masculinity in the West. In the process, they self-consciously challenge the catastrophic vision of the West, showing the horrors of domination, the foolish and destructive habits of the imperial heart, but also life beyond the deba-cle, life not "after the fall" but as a compassionate response to tempo-rary failure. *This House of Sky* and *Hole in the Sky,* for instance, provide thoughtful, detailed, exacting first-person narratives about growing up male. These titles reflect their writers' revisionary goals. Doig would take us inside a *house* of sky, showing us domestic relations, strained and loving, within the Big Sky. Kittredge explains early in his fractured, postmodern autobiography that his title plays upon two senses of the image: existentialist despair and a Native American sense of belonging to a sacred order. Doig and Kittredge substitute facticity and a strong sense of place for the melodrama of a whole tradition of masculine self-imagining. In the process, they supply new visions of home on the range, homes anchored in decency toward each other and the place.

William Kittredge has become one of the chief deconstructors of western American mythologies. As a longtime teacher (now retired) in the creative writing program at the University of Montana, he has been central to the region's literature for almost three decades. His nonfictional writings do not so much constitute a program for action as a warning of traps to be evaded. In *Owning It All* and *Hole in the Sky*, Kittredge dismantles fables of identity that have drawn Americans to rural scenes, then betrayed them. While it is not always clear why his troubled autobiography should become a paradigm for all contemporary westerners, Kittredge does capture the peculiar blend of longing and revulsion that circulates around cowboy and agrarian dreams. His mission comes clearest in "Owning It All," the title essay for his haunting collection of personal narratives:

> The teaching mythology we grew up with in the American West is a pastoral story of agricultural ownership. The story begins with a vast innocent continent, natural and almost magically alive, capable of inspiring us to reverence and awe, and yet savage, a wilderness. A good rural people come from the East, and they take the land from its native inhabitants, and tame it for agricultural purposes, bringing civilization: a notion of how to live embodied in law. The story is as old as invading armies, and at heart it is a racist, sexist, imperialist mythology of conquest; a rationale for violence—against other people and against nature.[1]

If Kittredge stopped here, however, he would be no different than many westerners who bemoan our collective past but can do nothing to alleviate the pain or to heal the wounds. Though he works by indirection and innuendo, this writer will occasionally glimpse possibilities for living in even this discredited ranching/farming past. As we read in *Hole in the Sky*, "People stick to [ranching] because they enjoy the feel and smell and sound of things, and because they share those mostly unspoken loves with other people they can trust as being somewhere near to decent."[2] Here Kittredge echoes the insights of Kemmis, the emphasis upon place, people, and community, the essential value of vital practices shared among committed, caring people.

The full-scale autobiography presents Kittredge's deconstructive talents in their rawest, most provocative form. Readers witness a series of failed identities for the young scion of power, the agrarian lord of the manor, the child of rural prosperity and misguided teachings. Underlying the discredited stories of growing up male in the West are the inevitable themes of power, money, and indifference that we saw with McNamer's male characters and Guthrie's Boone. Kittredge shows how the imperialist drive of his grandfather William led to the vast family holdings in southeastern Oregon, but how it led as well to the haunting distances at the heart of the family. When human beings turn land into property, something seems to go dead in the spirit of the conqueror. (This was the same discovery Blew made about her great-grandfather Abraham Hogeland in *All But the Waltz*.) The Kittredges' legacy of conquest included destruction of natural wetlands, of marriages, of father-son love, and of a relationship to the place itself.

Coming of age in the maelstrom of Kittredge manifest destiny, Bill undergoes a series of identities: the fop, the rough, the cowboy, the college boy, the military man, the farm manager, and ultimately, the writer. I stress the passivity of his falling into these roles, since Kittredge shows how the unknowing, uncanny self enters narratives of purpose that are at heart disingenuous, cruelly deceptive, fake. *Hole in the Sky* reads in part like a classic existentialist quest for authenticity, the pursuit of the angst-ridden, preternaturally aware consciousness that would outstrip all the distorting stories handed us by culture. Kittredge is hilariously effective at dismissing these earlier personae, foregrounding the casual cruelty of the inept but eager younger selves.

This forced march through maddeningly inapt identities is punctuated by demonic epiphanies, moments of dread insight into the heart of darkness, the well of loneliness, the abyss of despair. While serving as a damage assessment officer on Guam, for instance, Kittredge encounters an epileptic episode: "A door had opened, and I had been shocked by a sight of what I took to be chaos just at the end of the hallway. That glimpse of what I took to be the unknowability of things cost me some decades—or maybe not. It's hard to figure. Maybe it made me alive. I have no idea what it cost the Guamanian boy" (141). This passage typifies the almost stuttering clarity of Kittredge's prose, its ability to illuminate and retract in the same moment. Even as he proffers a vision of horror, the narrator struggles with the import of that vision, questioning whether the insight led to enervation or reinvigoration. The passage also reminds the reader of Kittredge's nearly solipsistic self-involvement, his focus on the personal to the exclusion of the interpersonal. After all, he does not know what happened to the human being who suffered the seizure.

And that in part is what Kittredge has in mind when he writes of his "two-hearted" existence. The writer ruthlessly exposes the division between the assumed and "real" selves, or between the socialized, adaptive, conformist, seemingly confident exterior self and the terrified, resistant, rebellious, wholly uncertain interior self. Running like a leitmotif through this account of western subjectivity gone wrong is Kittredge's persistent desire to be a writer, to spend time with words, to play upon the piano of language. But the shattered piano that hovers over the first several chapters of the memoir reminds the reader and the narrator of the price to be paid for such effete notions. After all, Kittredge came of age on a combined cattle ranch and farm during the heyday of the film Western; John Wayne must have loomed over all his self-imaginings. Running with hookers and betraying your wife was one thing; but spending time with books and trying to transcribe lived experience in printed texts, that was another. It is no wonder that at one point Kittredge contemplated swallowing a strychnine-laced carrot.

Kittredge's answer to these dilemmas combines the writing life with an almost Thoreauvian romanticism. On the surface, it's difficult to argue with the memoir's claims, since the Missoula-based writer has produced some of the most provocative, challenging prose of the past two decades. And certainly no one would begrudge Kittredge his hard-earned happiness, his sense of contentment after battles with alcoholism, divorce, and mental collapse. But I return to the question: In what sense is Kittredge's pilgrim's progress a paradigm of possibility for other westerners? Surely his call for authenticity, for being true to self and place, surely that gesture rings true and helpful. And many of us do return to American romantics such as Emerson and Whitman for a space of possibility, a home-grown philosophy of living.

Yet Kittredge seems far more convincing on the disease than on the cure. He's more adept at destroying than creating mythologies. My uneasiness rests in part on the stammering, interrogative voice of his prose. I once asked my students to pay attention to the number of times Kittredge uses the phrase "I think" in a given passage; we were all amused and vaguely disturbed by the sheer quantity of qualifying phrases. His style also proceeds by disjointed epigrams, halting and brisk at the same time. Readers do not sense they are in the presence of a complete, coherent vision, but witnesses to a frank if fragmented accounting. The advantage of the approach is clear: a seeming humility that refuses to preach for the masses, to pretend to an ultimate wisdom, a final solution. And surely male readers experience disturbing shocks of recognition as Kittredge tallies the painfully funny maneuvers we go through to put up a good front as capable good ol' boys. But it's difficult to detect a stable perspective, a ground for belief among the flotsam and jetsam he so precisely catalogs.

And so when he promises "Paradise All Around," as he does in his concluding chapter, we should be careful of the claim. He hints that a personal immersion in the wonders of the natural will provide a cure for what ails us out west. Yet Kittredge's solution is potentially of a piece with the solipsism, the selfishness of the epilepsy episode. His stance seems introspective and exclusive. It was Kittredge, after all, who titled the now famous anthology *The Last Best Place*. In that act he reproduced the very vision of a threatened paradise, a world apart, that he has so successfully discredited elsewhere. The writer seems more canny and credible when he reveals, "I was driven to believe in damage control, that we must learn to revere and care for the world and one another if we mean to end up with anything of any value at all" (224). In those words, he echoes the argument of his most important near-contemporary.

Ivan Doig is the region's most prolific contemporary writer, and the result has been an embarrassment of riches. *This House of Sky* remains the very best Montana autobiography, a tough, tender, vital evocation of Bessie Ringer and Charlie Doig and the functional life they made together.[3] *Heart Earth* extends the autobiographical impulse to embrace Ivan's mother, and in the process brings out once again the writer's intense love of place and respect for those who made a go of it here. *Bucking the Sun* is a clever, readable, though somewhat slow-paced fiction focusing on the Fort Peck Dam project. Here the writer's strengths—a dead-on sense of the vernacular, an almost sensual attachment to the landscapes of Montana, and an acute re-creation of memory and its pangs—are suspended in favor of an almost programmatic study of a transformative moment in the state's history.

For my purposes, the Centennial Trilogy, *Dancing at the Rascal Fair, English Creek*, and *Ride with Me, Mariah Montana*, articulates most clearly and persuasively Doig's reading of the Montana destiny. Combined with Guthrie's first three novels of the West and Welch's *Fools Crow*, this trilogy constitutes the nearest thing to an epic of the region we are likely to see. Since most of these novels are set in approximately the same place—the Two Medicine country along the Rocky Mountain front—they provide an unusually thick description of the history and conflicts of a concentrated region in the West. Doig's one-hundred-year chronicle, tracing as it does the unfolding pattern of the McCaskill family history, grants the writer the scope to consider the processes of settlement in the region. The writer has given himself an extended perspective with which to come to terms with the legacy of white conquest. In this way, Doig operates as historian, novelist, and philosopher. He presents an almost dialectical sense of the region's history, showing how forces and counterforces clash to bring us to the centennial of Montana's statehood (1989). It is a mutedly optimistic trilogy as the pain of heartbreak and death culminates in Jick McCaskill's love for Leona and his charismatic daughter. If Hugo often preached risking sentimentality, Doig seems to go all the way, allowing what I call a tough sentimentalism to temper the too-frequent despair in western culture. Doig's vision of pragmatic comedy provides a vital, sustaining counterpoint to the voices of pessimism heard both inside and outside the region.

Dancing at the Rascal Fair is an epic-sized settlement story. Angus McCaskill tells of his migration from Scotland and his first thirty years in Montana, stretching from 1889 to 1920. Doig skillfully weaves a series of sea-changes to the region into this family narrative. He incorporates the mining boom, the open-range era, sheep ranching, the homesteader rush of the early twentieth century, World War I, and the looming depression. In one sense, he reiterates the events narrated so skillfully by the historians Howard and Toole. Yet by making those historical processes human and real, Doig allows us to tally both the hurt and the happiness of these stabs at sticking on the high plains. Above all else, the novel vividly shows that only a minority of homesteaders (of whatever era) manage to hang tough and cling to subsistence: "We went past the empty Duff homestead, and then the empty Erskine place, and what had been Archie Findlater's homestead, and the silent buildings of Allan Frew's."[4] Doig also demonstrates with uncommon clarity, really with a starkness approaching similar moments in Blew's *All But the Waltz*, just how much work it takes to make a go of it in this blustery, unpredictable climate. As Doig has put it bluntly elsewhere, "Montana's basic everyday matters—i.e., work—seem to me to be perpetual fuel for a writer."[5] The McCaskill family motto declares, "*The job was there . . . it was to be done*" (275). In the penultimate sequence of the novel, Angus describes how he, Rob, and Varick will their sleds of poor feed through a bitter winter landscape to save starving sheep. Doig's sense of the harsh conditions, near-death hallucinations, and desperate hanging-on of the three male characters is impeccable. He clearly knows what he writes. Once again, then, a Montana writer employs the vein of georgic discussed in chapter 8. Or as Angus phrases the same idea, "You are permitted to begin in the kind delusion that your utensils of homestead-making at least are the straightforward ones—axe, hammer, adze, pick, shovel, pitchfork. But your true tools are other. The nearest names that can be put to them are hope, muscle and time" (91). But Lucas states the proposition most succinctly, "At least Montana is the prettiest place in the world to work yourself to death, ay?" (95). Kemmis suggests this work ethic can become the basis for community building, a sense of shared hardship and hope. That point is driven home when Isaac Reese, husband of the deceased Anna, offers his horses to Angus so that he can save his winter-blasted sheep. If these rivals in love can overcome their differences to take care of business, anything seems possible.

The novel concludes, however, on an elegiac note with the death of Rob Barclay, a senseless debacle as the bitter, enraged brother-in-law drowns while riding Angus's cherished horse Scorpion. It's a mordant finale to a book full of mixed sorrow and blessings. In his closing words we hear the narrator's longing for dead friends and a lover: Lucas, Rob, and most wrenchingly, Anna Ramsay. Yet Angus proclaims with evident joy upon the return of his son from the war (and their sad separation): "going home, that first day of the year, my son beside me unexpected as a griffin, I would have told you there is as much possibility in life as not" (347). While that's hardly a ringing endorsement of hope, the sometimes dour Angus allows at least a fifty-fifty chance for our most cherished prospects coming to fruition. That same sense of balanced prospects sounds through the novel's refrain:

> Dancing at the rascal fair,
> devils and angels all were there,
> heel and toe, pair by pair,
> dancing at the rascal fair. (12)

My summary so far might suggest an often grim if partly redeeming story. But we should not neglect the remarkable voice of the narrator, for Doig invests so much in that persona, that distinctive self who reaches out to us through the colorful, inflected, ruminative language of the novel. Angus the schoolmaster is, first and foremost, a quoter of poetry. His world is largely defined by the lyrical word, especially the verses of Robert Burns (though Doig confesses in his acknowledgments that he fabricated some of the Burns-like passages). These poetic interludes provide an intimacy with the taleteller, a kind of "you are there" inside look at his thought processes and attitudes. One could quote these passages at length, since they are both amusing and revelatory. To take but one example, Angus pauses to recollect the passage of time in the Two Medicine country, a recollection sparked by the arrival of the dryland farmers en masse: "*The rainbow eyes of memory / that reflect the colors of time*" (249). That's an apt description of the entire novel before us. The poetic voice often shows itself in the narrator's more mundane observations as well, as when Angus describes the lush growing years of the 1910s: "The winters were open and mild. Each spring and summer, rain became grain" (299). We also gain access to the workings of the narrator's rich, involuted memory in italicized scraps of dialogue recalled from years before. In this way, Doig calls upon the technique that serves him so well in *This House of Sky*: reproducing the distinctive language patterns of his beloved grandmother and father. The writer was born with a genius for remembering and reproducing the idiosyncratic voices of the remarkable people who surrounded him. Angus is a kind of spiritual grandfather to the Ivan of the memoir.

This fascinating, involving technique lightens the otherwise heavy burden of the story. There's often a touch of the whimsical and bemused in Angus's storytelling. Except for the absolute darkest moments, as in the influenza-caused deaths of Lucas and Anna, the narrator manages to cover the seemingly tragic with a lilt of lyrical or comical perspective. In the very manner of the telling, then, Angus demonstrates he's a wise pragmatist, a sticker, a survivor. He rarely plunges to an absolute nadir of dread or disappointment. He is far from the confused Archilde, or hopeless Bull, or immature Boone, or homeless Patrick Fitzpatrick. In fact, despite the elegiac mood of the novel's conclusion, there's a sense that Angus has finally, completely come home to Adair and Varick, that he is fully, completely at one with his place, his life's work, his caring family. I'm reminded of a telling moment in the film *Heartland*. Facing financial ruin after a disastrous winter, Clyde Stewart turns inward, blaming himself for the loss of livestock he might have sold the previous autumn. Confronting her demoralized husband, Elinore insists on sticking, reminding him, "I've got a child buried in this land." The fact that she has suffered that loss raises the stakes; the woman homesteader feels an even deeper commitment to toughing it out. The modestly upbeat end of the film suggests that this is precisely what the couple will manage to do.

So also Angus McCaskill and his clan. Doig operates with a sense of history as the gradual working out of a kind of moral and emotional equilibrium. Disaster often leads toward resolution. To take the novel's most dramatic instance, Angus's sorry, ill-requited love for Anna ultimately finds resolution in Varick's marriage to Beth, Anna's lovely daughter. That's a daringly Dickensian touch for a contemporary writer, indulging in the sort of sentimental tying up of loose ends that Victorian readers adored. Yet the plot device works, in large part because the very telling of the wedding carefully avoids the mawkish or the overwrought. When Beth confronts Angus as he stares helplessly at Anna's wedding picture, you feel as though the characters are uncannily aware of their obligations and mistakes. Beth knows what Angus must have meant to her mother, but she by no means either accuses or forgives the father-in-law for his persistent attention to Anna. The characters recognize each other for what they are but do not simply, melodramatically let each other off the hook.

The remaining novels in the trilogy will extend this process of resolution. As Jick puts it in *English Creek*, "I sometimes wonder if life is anything but an averaging out."[6] The love complications that run through the novels will finally find relief in Jick's touching, almost comical "arrangement" with his older brother's femme fatale, Leona Wright. The land-use issues that originate with the arrival of Stanley Meixell and the U.S. Forest Service will find resolution in Jick's decision to donate his family's ranch to the Nature Conservancy. And the vexed parent-child relationships that trouble Angus, Varick, and Jick will culminate in the latter's satisfying rapprochement with his willful daughter Mariah. We're left with a sense of perspective and gratefulness, a tally of terrible losses offset by still more enduring gains. Or as Jick phrases the notion in his centennial speech at Gros Ventre, "what I've come to think is that Montana exists back and forth. . . . That this wide state is a kind of teeter-totter of time. Maybe that expanse, and our born-into-us belief here that life is an up and down proposition, are what give us so much room and inclination to do both our worst and our best."[7]

While most readers I talk to prefer *Dancing at the Rascal Fair* to either *English Creek* or *Ride with Me, Mariah Montana*, I confess to a weakness for the second novel in this list. I suspect that this is so both because Doig narrows the focus of the narrative and because Jick's voice is even more engaging than either Angus's or Jick's own grief-stricken older self's. Doig is at his best when he's sticking to the actual, and the limited scope of Jick's adolescent tale allows a thingliness, an attention to the particular that pulls us into that immediate world. Put differently, in the second novel Doig is not under the obligation to cover immense historical ground (as in *Dancing*) or immense geographic ground (as in *Ride*). Jick's voice is also more relaxed, more colloquial, a bit more hesitant than Angus's. There's a blend of humility and acuteness here. In part that tone results from a clever point of view: while the story is told by the sixty-year-old Jick, it's as though events are filtered through the eyes of his coming-on-fifteen self. And so the reader experiences a combination of mature insight and naive half-glimpses. The fact that Jick is the "off card," the younger, less dramatic brother, contributes to his off-center, earnest, but amusing perspective on events in the McCaskill family.

The novel narrates yet another Montana coming of age, and so our minds rightly hearken back to *Fools Crow, Winter Wheat, Rima in the Weeds,* and *Hole in the Sky.* Passing through his "damned in-between age" (86), Jick struggles to make sense of the adults who surround him, especially the prodigal brother, Alec. This is an intensely masculine book, dominated by male humor, male longings, male initiations. In part One, the most easygoing section of the novel, Jick is initiated into the mysteries of Stanley Meixell, the disgraced but still charismatic ranger who now works as a camptender in the Two country (and beyond). Stanley introduces the distracted but adaptable youth to the pleasures of drinking, memory, and (through his songs) sex. It's as though we've returned to the masculine inflections of Teddy Blue Abbott or Charlie Russell, the western lingo with a sometimes bitter, sometimes sentimental edge. Doig is especially good on the byplay between silence and disclosure at the heart of much masculine conversation. It would seem men don't want to risk giving away too much, putting themselves in jeopardy of ridicule or physical harm, yet the need for human empathy remains. Joking provides a ready means for balancing these needs, a vehicle for revealing and sheltering the self at the very same moment.

For this reason, *English Creek* demonstrates Doig's subtle but significant reimagining of western manhood. He by no means surrenders the love of fishing and hunting, or the bawdy humor, or the fondness for the occasional drink, or the pleasure in just being up and doing in a glorious environment. (In fact, we should concede that Doig is far more successful at recreating the psyches of his male than his female characters. Anna, Adair, Beth, Leona, and Mariah remain externally realized—appealing, intelligent, and independent—but not wholly real.) Jick is at a far remove from the hapless incompetence of B. M. Bower's Manley Fleetwood or the misogynistic cruelty of Guthrie's Boone Caudill. He's observant, a good listener, a young man easily entranced by the past and by the mysteries of concealed personal histories. In an amusing but revealing episode during part Two, while taking a break from digging the family's new outhouse hole, Jick presses his mother about her youth and her engagement to Mac. In the halting give-and-take between mother and son, Doig shows how a maturing male can be both manly and attuned. Jick carefully steps around the mother's past, doing a bit of personal digging, you might say, yet backs off when she seems threatened or uncomfortable. Jick demonstrates that you can be a man and a human being at the same time. Stanley captures that promising combination in his final words to the narrator: "A McCaskill who'll outright say the word sorry. . . . I was more right than I even knew, that time . . . [w]hen I told your folks you looked to me like the jick of the family" (338).

Doig also goes out of his way to characterize the fully established community of Gros Ventre. Angus had a great deal of fun at the expense of this "coming town," suggesting time and again that Lucas's dream of a high plains Athens was misplaced. Yet Jick's sentimental journey through town on the Fourth of July, 1939, suggests that Lucas's hopes were not entirely misguided: "to me the town . . . held a sense of being what it ought to be. Of aptness, maybe is the term. Not fancy, not shacky. Steady" (138). Despite the outmigration of home-steaders, the dust storms, the bank failures, and the unpredictable cattle and sheep prices, Gros Ventre seems sure and steady. The com-munity as a whole appears grounded, organic, interconnected, and substantial: "that day, they seemed to me all distinctly themselves and yet added up together too" (151). Doig reserves some of his best prose for social occasions, including the dances in Angus's narrative, the dawn centennial celebration in *Ride*, and the Fourth of July fandango in *English Creek*: "Didn't I tell you a dance is the McCaskill version of bliss?" (207). These are the oases of pleasure, of sharing and good humor, that punctuate the hard labor of making a go. The Two Medi-cine country has plainly matured over the fifty years stretching from the grandfather's dispiriting arrival. And since the sixty-year-old Jick casts his mind back to that moment of his going-on-fifteen year, we assume that he remains very much at home in a terrain that has not always been kind to his family.

Yet the novel discloses deep rifts within this community as well. In her Fourth of July speech, Jick's mother directly criticizes the land-grabbing tendencies of the Williamson cattle operation. The attack emerges in part from Beth's sincere nostalgia for the families that had been cast out by economic processes beyond their control. But she is also responding to her older son's seduction by the Williamson clan. The tension within the McCaskill family that drives the narrative— the struggle over Alec's immediate future—does double duty as a metaphor for this ongoing conflict within western culture over the fate of the family farm and ranch. Financial necessity seems to dictate incorporation of smaller parcels of land into more efficient ranching outfits, yet the cost seems too high: the loss of good people who could help sustain the community Doig evokes so tenderly. There's nothing

less than the Jeffersonian agrarian dream at stake here, and to give the
writer his due, he doesn't provide a simple resolution to this specific
dilemma. By contrasting the English Creek and Noon Creek settlement patterns, Doig precisely sets before us competing options for
landholding and sustained settlement in the West. Since the Williamsons are treated with a kind of muted scorn throughout the narrative,
the novel seems to fall heavily on the side of the English Creek
arrangement. If Kittredge starkly critiques the agrarian dream, Doig
seems to reinstate it with a heavy dose of sober realism. When in *Ride*
the aging Jick must decide what to do with his place, Pete Reese's
legacy, he describes a nearly ideal small sheep-ranching outfit, a jewel
of agrarian commerce in the shadow of the Rocky Mountains. Since
he has no one to inherit that pastoral parcel, he must weigh his
options: sell out to the "Gobble-Gobble-U" (that is, the Williamsons);
hand over the ranch to the couple who work it for him in his partial
retirement; or donate the land to the Nature Conservancy. Still, the
ideal of the small ranch remains intact in Doig's and the reader's
minds. Despite cynicism about the economic prospects for the "little
guy" expressed by the journalist ex-son-in-law, Jick is able to exercise
reassuring control over his land's fate.

The concluding third of *English Creek* takes us through a moving
series of tragedies and reconciliations. The final effect is reminiscent
of *A River Runs Through It*, another important novel about a Scotch
American family, two brothers, and the search for meaning in separation and death. Paul's murder at the hands of gangsters is echoed in
Alec's death in the African desert during World War II. Both aging
narrators must confront the possibilities of changing those destinies,
the chance that they might have intervened or altered the course of
disaster. But both realize that their brothers' fates were beyond their
reckoning or correction; both must accept that this is what life held for
their siblings, and make the best of that knowledge. The narrator of
River finds solace in the wonder world of Montana, the beauty of fly-
fishing, and the biblical words that sing beneath the flowing waters.
Jick comes to his own complex terms with the seemingly needless
death, in part through respect for his brother's need for independ-

ence, in part through pleasure in his own substantial life, in part through his budding understanding of the messy father-son relationships that have been handed down in the McCaskill clan.

In the end, this is a novel about reconciliations between fathers and sons. Before leaving for the war that will take his life, Alec returns home to achieve a partial understanding with his parents. Mac arrives at his own reconciliation with Stanley, and that coming-together signals yet another closing of the ties that bind. Jick's father "confesses" to his role in the older ranger's firing, and in the process apologizes indirectly for whatever sorrow he brought to Stanley. When he is willing to follow the camp cook's advice in the crucial moment of the raging forest fire, Mac demonstrates that he trusts the seasoned ranger to deliver the goods. In this intensely male world of careful negotiation and half-concealed affection, that trust borders on a warm embrace of the man who cared for him during his separation from Angus. Finally, as if all this were not enough, Jick's father expresses as directly as he is capable his deep, almost desperate love for his younger son. As he prepares to carry out Stanley's plan for controlling the fire, Mac insists that the former ranger and the coming-on-fifteen camp helper head to safer ground. In a phrase freighted with the innuendo of need, the father says simply, "Jick, I can't risk you" (321).

Stanley Meixell turns out to be a second father (or perhaps grandfather) to the narrator as well, not only initiating him into the mysteries of women and drink but giving him the very name that identifies him as uniquely himself. Jick's discovery that Stanley has named him signals the narrator's final embrace of his identity, his true coming of age, his necessary encounter with the drinking man's past and his vital involvement in the adolescent's life. The closing lines of the novel take us back to the nameless narrator's discovery that Yellow Calf is his grandfather in *Winter in the Blood*. If nothing else, Stanley's acknowledgment links Jick to the entire history of the Two Medicine National Forest and the man who knew it better than anyone. It connects him to the collective memory of the place and the wisdom of inhabiting it well, fittingly, with care.

Ride with Me, Mariah Montana begins in elegy and ends in something like contentment. Doig adopts a clever strategy for reviewing the history of Montana in its centennial year: have the recently widowed Jick escort the fiery Mariah and her ex-husband, Riley, around the state as they develop a series of centennial stories for their Missoula-based newspaper, the *Montanian*. What we have is a kind of senior-citizen picaresque. This tactic not only grants the writer the license to travel (quite literally) from epoch-making to epoch-making place, but it provides a comic edge to the whole proceedings. We do delight in the nostalgic father's acerbic interactions with these two grown children, and the two ex-lovers at times generate an amusing byplay between repulsion and desire. Still, Doig seems far more adept at the voice of 1939 than that of 1989. His stabs at purely contemporary dialogue seem a bit forced (in contrast to Welch's dialogue in his novels of contemporary Montana, or McNamer's re-creation of the language of Margaret and Dorrie). This is a minor complaint, one surely overshadowed by the range and cleverness of the novel. And after all, Doig is wrestling with the fate of the state and region for the maturing children of depression-era parents. Coming to terms with the language of a Riley is an inevitable (and necessary) challenge for the novelist.

One immediate payoff from this narrative approach is to grant space for diverse voices of the Montana past and present. Early in the narrative, Jick enters fully into the language of Toussaint Rennie, the Metis witness to the last days of the buffalo, the Blackfeet Starvation Winter of 1883, and the arrival of the sheep and cattle ranches of the Two Medicine country. The ventriloquist Jick replicates the very voice of that witness, forcing the characters and the reader to reconsider again the price of settlement in this region. As Adair mulls out loud to Angus and Rob in *Dancing*, "So much land here, and . . . so empty. It's hard to think of men killing each other over it" (169). While the Scottish immigrant seems to miss the extraordinary beauty and sweep of the place, she does capture that haunting wonderment: What have we (Euramerican culture) wrought here, and can we claim pride in the results? Doig wisely discloses the issue but does not become mired in it. He sidesteps the trap of guilt-ridden contemporaries who become so fully vested in the depredations of the past that we paralyze ourselves, or turn ourselves into extremists every bit as bitter and potentially violent as the Freemen of Montana. Doig seems to say through moments such as Toussaint Rennie's recollections that we must remember, we must bear witness to what has been lost, we must feelingly commemorate the peoples who have come and gone and suffered here, but we must not risk demeaning those who have stuck it out and continue to demonstrate a sustaining connection with the place. We can, of course, also learn from those past mistakes, as a good historian will remind us, and surely that is one reason Jick will finally donate his land to something larger than himself or any given private enterprise. His journey to Moiese and into the buffalo past drives home lessons of the land.

The ghosts of the Montana past continue to plague Jick throughout the first half of the novel: his first (and long former) wife; his dead parents; his dead brother. Most astonishingly (and cleverly), Doig forces Jick to confront the legacy of strained relationships in the McCaskill family at the Montana Historical Society in Helena. Halfheartedly seeking news of his family in the archives, the aging narrator unexpectedly discovers the fully disclosive letters of Isak (Isaac) Riis, letters that show, once and for all, the horse dealer's awareness of Angus's deep and abiding love for Anna. That discovery brings home to the narrator all the collective grief of these twined families, all the miscalculations of heart and word that had riven the bundle of humanity joined by blood and marriage. In a genuinely touching moment, Jick sheds tears at the palpable remnants of desire and loss that sit before him in that year of remembrance, the centennial year of Montana's statehood. As in the earlier novels, that private grief becomes representative of larger woes accessed and scrutinized throughout the novel. At times, *Ride* reads like Jonathan Raban's *Bad Land*, that eloquent testimonial to the decimation of homesteading dreams on the high plains. Whether in the voices of a group of touring senior-citizen used-car delivery men encountered on the road, or in Riley's semicynical accounts of the death of the Jeffersonian vision for rural America, or in Jick's own asperity about Montana "east of Crazy," the novel tallies the repeated collapse of hope in the region. Jick's grief at the Montana Historical Society is as much about the state's bitter past as about his own personal traumas. That's why that mournful moment marks the emotional and political nadir of the novel.

But Doig won't allow that perspective the final word. While Riley will leave the state, following the path of many young Montanans in search of better pay and a larger audience, Mariah will remain a Montanan to the end. While Jick must surrender his beloved sheep ranch on Noon Creek, he will join Leona in the collective enterprise of running a nearly ideal cattle ranch in the shadow of the Crazy Mountains. While Montana has suffered a series of setbacks, it has also survived the shocks to endure and, at times, even flourish. As if these events were not enough, Jick's increasingly comical voice drains away the pressing sadness of people lost, dreams defeated. It's as though he wakes up and starts really paying attention after the return to Gros Ventre midway through the novel, and again when he meets up with Leona after all those years. He can't help ribbing his once-upon-a-time son-in-law or delighting in Leona's teasing humor or even, occasionally, poking fun at his own foibles and crotchets. In Doig country, it's always a good sign when a character can begin to laugh at himself. It's the wild men and women who take themselves too seriously who pose the greatest danger. That's why Stanley Meixell, ever the jester beneath that crusty exterior, stands as a major force and influence throughout the three novels. Unlike the bitter Rob or the petulant Alec, Stanley never quite loses the capacity to rib himself. He's truly a comic pragmatist.

Yet despite its frankness, decency, and humor, Doig's trilogy is not without its controversies. The novelist has, for instance, created a representative Montana family that is distinctly irreligious, bordering at times on antireligious. Doig may have historical support for that move: "The West has long been the least religious section of the United States. . . . Fewer people attend church in the West and fewer people say religion is central to their lives than in other regions."[8] Yet this antitheological streak in the McCaskill clan raises troubling issues about sources of value and grounds for ethical behavior in the American West. We can return once again to that term *pragmatic*, a word that suggests we locate our ethical norms in the pressing needs of the immediate moment, in the imperatives emerging within the specific crisis we encounter. When Jick forgives Leona for her involvement in Alec's troubled final years, he does not do so out of an overarching code or value system. Instead, speaking with the aging woman who was the teen-aged femme fatale, recognizing her losses, recognizing her enduring guilt and sadness, Jick does the decent thing: he literally embraces Leona. You might say he practices the Golden Rule without ever bothering to invoke the biblical injunction.

But while that gesture is moving (and persuasive), we have to consider where such an approach to values might lead. It might, for instance, arrive at the deeply pessimistic existentialist universe of Richard Hugo and Thomas McGuane. If we deplete the universe of a theological agency, if we fall back on a materialist or provisional definition of ethics, we open ourselves to the possibility that finally, ultimately, there is nothing to supply meaning to our lives. Yet an even more frightening prospect looms: the extreme religious positions of the most radical movements in the region. Having stripped away (or never imported) established religious traditions, westerners grant space to alternatives such as the Christian Identity movement. For westerners with a lingering need for spiritual solace and an explanation for their sometimes difficult lives, the white-supremacist nonsense concerning the true children of Israel could start to make sense.

Doig might respond quite reasonably that he has sketched in grounds for value, grounds that would defeat the sad maunderings of the Freemen and Militia of Montana: history, people, and place put ethical demands upon us. We must act as though we are part of a larger scheme of human action; we must recognize our necessary interaction with diverse peoples and respect their needs as well as ours; we must treat the earth as a living being deserving of the same respect we accord the people of the region. But even these claims carry their own seeds of controversy, especially the argument about our relationship with the land. Doig has gone out of his way to instill in the McCaskill clan a rapport with the Forest Service and the Nature Conservancy. From Angus's first welcome of Stanley Meixell to Jick's final decision about his ranch, the McCaskills have embraced a vision of the land as part of a public trust, a commonwealth. That vision, however, runs directly counter to the alternative western view of land as private property, a value that takes on near-theological status in many western homes. The infamous "War on the West" battle of the mid-1990s reflected this intense clash in the region. When Secretary of the Interior Bruce Babbitt proposed raising grazing fees on Bureau of Land Management lands, all hell broke loose. It is in such moments that we realize just how closely mainstream western culture can approach that of our more wild-eyed citizens. I seriously wondered if Babbitt would face physical harm during his trips west to explain his proposal. Many ranchers in the region believe they have been squeezed and squeezed and squeezed by the economy. They believe that Washington is a distant, overbearing, even authoritarian force. They believe that few folks outside the ranching community can begin to understand the pressures of relying on volatile markets from year to year. And in the year I write, with cattle prices at low ebb and ranchers facing terrible choices about whether to sell their livestock, I have to empathize.

So when Doig evokes a vision of the land as part of a commonwealth, he touches upon a central faith and fear of western farmers and ranchers: the land belongs to the families that will care for it best because it is, after all, in their best interest to care for it well. Ranchers will also tell you that they love the place as much as anybody and have no vested interest in overgrazing range or despoiling water supplies by overfertilizing their crops. As the example of the "War on the West" shows, however, we need to slow down and listen to each other better on these crucial questions. Since ranchers and farmers have been my neighbors, and I have taught their children, and my economic well-being once depended directly on the health of the agricultural community, I have learned to take the time to understand their needs, their desires, and their fears. At the same time, we all have to tone down our rhetoric of disrespect and even abuse. It does no one good to characterize a secretary of the interior who grew up on a ranch as a kind of Gestapo agent in a business suit. Language so harmful hurts at the deepest levels, it warps public discourse, it makes the search for decent, reasonable negotiation difficult, if not impossible. Whatever readers finally make of Jick's decision to donate his place to the Nature Conservancy, we have to concede this much: he took his time, he weighed his options, he considered the needs of those around him, he considered what was best for the land and the region, and he made his decision without fanfare or superheated rhetoric. He did what he saw as the right thing, and he did so with dignity.

Jick embodies a new possibility for western masculinity, one with increasing appeal in contemporary culture. In contrast to the deranged militancy of Owl Child or the land-grabbing blindness of Abraham Hogeland or the technological arrogance of the Kittredges, Jick puts his will to power in check. Despite his own sad memories and bitter disappointments, he does not lash out in the simple, adolescent fashion. His verbal jousts with Riley yield an unexpected benefit: Jick is compelled to clarify his values for himself and others. He must determine his foundations of belief, what ultimately matters. The result is an embrace of two women and the place he loves. Jick remains the irascible, sometimes suspicious man to the end, but he has come full circle to the wisdom of Stanley Meixell. In this sense, he is at a far remove from the melodramatic sensibilities of the Militia of Montana and the Unabomber.

Conclusion

SETTLING DOWN IN MONTANA

I TOOK A DRIVE UP TO YELLOWSTONE KELLY'S GRAVE ONE AUTUMN day. The monument rests on a rise of ground atop the rimrocks that define the cityscape. You get a fine panorama of the Yellowstone River valley, the mountains to the south, and Billings itself. It's a place of vistas and vision. But Kelly would have mixed feelings about the prospect. He would be struck by the loveliness of this fall in south-central Montana: the vivid orange-gold of cottonwoods, elms, and aspens; the alluring blue of the Bighorn, Pryor, and Beartooth Mountains; the sandstone-tan of rimrock in the fading light. But he would also be struck by the white-on-black industrial development of east and south Billings, including oil refineries, the Montana Power complex, and a sugar-beet processing plant. Off to the west, beyond the familiar American downtown, the hospitals, colleges, and schools rise up out of the residential landscape. Those neighborhoods are expanding at a constant rate, making some citizens worry about their community's sprawl, its hunger.

As geologic formations stand forth throughout this region, the layers of history and settlement are distinctly visible in this late October light. Casting our minds back, we can think of the native peoples who crisscrossed this terrain, and the cattle ranchers, homesteaders, sugarbeet workers, miners, bankers, lawyers, and teachers who came and often stayed. We can think of the difficult economic times—replayed in the current agricultural struggles—and the intense political debates, and the hard choices made about land use. We can remember the temptations of despair and the more promising voices of possibility. What strikes me most about this place is that it is, after all, a place. It has a definition, a clarity, a history. People have settled down here in the Yellowstone Valley. While they can be complacent about serious problems, especially the air pollution produced by those inescapable industries, they have shown a capacity to challenge the more vicious angels of our nature.

That's why the extremists of the recent past must be seen as distant, distorted images of ourselves. We share with them a lurking anxiety, a suspicion of large-scale corporate and federal structures, and a concern about our isolation and powerlessness. But the militants remain locked in a childlike melodramatic sensibility that converts real-world issues into cartoons. That sensibility flattens, distorts, and exaggerates the agents of ill that challenge Montanans. As this study has shown, a sophisticated literary tradition offers a needed alternative to a simplistic, sophomoric world view. That tradition provides a complex, emotionally rich, politically astute conception of our history and needs. Early narratives register loss and survival as parallel possibilities. Catastrophic tragedies lend dignity to the awful and wracking transformations to characters and places. Pragmatic comedies incorporate tragic elements but mainly encourage endurance and adaptation.

To take a telling example, the narratives of Black Elk, D'Arcy McNickle, and James Welch all treat Indian catastrophes. They can be read as a kind of triptych, a three-paneled painting in which each section provides a necessary element of a single experience. Black

Elk discloses the holocaust of the Indian Wars and the Ghost Dance massacre. His haunting story shows how his people have been driven from the red road—the road of life—to the black road of death. His representation of his pain, his longing, his failed efforts to relieve this people's suffering lingers as the necessary historical ground for all subsequent Native American narratives.

McNickle extends that dire story by focusing on the reservation experience of northwestern Montana. Readers are taken inside the tensions and negotiations of native peoples living in the constricted space allotted them by the American solution to "the Indian problem." Characters such as Archilde and Antoine combine firsthand knowledge of white culture with lessons in the old ways. The result is characters caught at the crossroads, that legendary tragic setting, where many options and opportunities converge, but where disaster lurks. McNickle writes in the tragic mode of the impossibility of choice, the failure of hope, the loss of innocence. Worlds fall apart for these vital protagonists not only because of their own cognitive dissonance but because of the diverse, often well-meaning, but ultimately patronizing agents that intervene in their lives: the priests, BIA agents, industrialists, and even kin who place unbearable responsibility and demands upon them.

Welch revises these two tragic accounts by looking backward and forward from the climactic moments in Black Elk and McNickle's narratives. *Fools Crow* predates the Indian Wars of the 1870s and the Ghost Dance nightmare of the '80s and '90s. Welch recreates the lived experience of one tribe at the moment before its cultural collapse. In the process, this Montana writer helps the contemporary reader reinhabit a meaningful, sustaining tradition, providing us with a bridge to a past that had seemed vaporized. In that sense, this epic narrative resurrects a way of being in Montana that had seemed lost forever. *Winter in the Blood* goes even farther down the path of recovery, for this near-contemporary fiction, set after the reservation debacles represented so fully in *The Surrounded* and *Wind from an Enemy Sky*, takes us to the nadir of native despair, showing how the nameless narrator lacerates himself with guilt and memory. For most of the novel, hope is not just elusive but impossible. But Welch grants this despairing character a resurrection related to that in *Fools Crow*: Yellow Calf, a Blackfeet warrior of real courage and resilience, reveals himself as grandfather to the storyteller. Once again, a process of recovery provides a possibility of home, of belonging, of salvation from the sickness of the soul. While Welch carefully modulates the novel's optimism, perhaps to avoid an overly sentimental, even mawkish, tone, he does allow the narrator a hope well-nigh unthinkable at the start of the story. The narrator can rightly claim his status as heir to Fools Crow.

This study has traced out similarly complementary responses in texts focused on ranchers and farmers. Teddy Blue Abbott's memoir, Hugo's poetry, and Doig's Montana trilogy can be seen as another triptych, this one dedicated to the legacy of the cowboy life in Montana. While Abbott's account is predominantly elegiac, recalling for the reader a lost world of the open range, he also demonstrates a pragmatic spirit of adaptation and adjustment. Hugo's unforgettable poems, especially lyrics such as "Montana Ranch Abandoned," amplify the tragic dimension of the cowboy experience. By contrast, Doig provides a complex, often sad, but cautiously upbeat interpretation of ranching culture. Similarly, Percy Wollaston's *Homesteading*, Howard's *Montana: High, Wide, and Handsome*, and Mildred Walker's *Winter Wheat* evoke interrelated interpretations of farming in the state.

Reading this full array of representations allows contemporary Montanans a balance and perspective especially needed during this perplexing transitional time in both the nation and the state. Where do we find sustenance and significance in a postmodern economy? How do we establish and sustain meaningful communities in a world dominated by multinational corporations? Are we fated to repeat patterns of misfortune familiar to residents of the state? While Montanans negotiate the answers to these dilemmas in their communities and region, they have access to a vital archive of insight in their sophisticated literary tradition. That rich heritage comprises the most significant and usable wealth of the Treasure State.

Notes

INTRODUCTION

1. Catherine McNicol Stock, *Rural Radicals: Righteous Rage in the American Grain* (Ithaca, N.Y.: Cornell University Press, 1996), 7.

2. John McCormick and Bill Turque, "America's Outback," *Newsweek*, 9 October 1989: 76.

3. For an informative, provocative account of rural radicalism in our own time, see Joel Dyer, *Harvest of Rage: Why Oklahoma City Is Only the Beginning* (Boulder: Westview, 1997). Dyer emphasizes rural citizens' despair at losing control of their lives in a time of vertical and horizontal integration of the agricultural market. In "The Current Weirdness in the West," *Western Historical Quarterly* 28 (spring 1997): 5–16, Richard White traces the history of western antipathy toward the federal government's involvement in land issues. He notes the irony of this distrust: the government has poured more largesse into western states than into any other region. Yet this "conservative West . . . sees its genealogy not in the history of federal development in the region but instead in terms of a set of archetypes: the isolate, armed male, the courageous homesteading family, the poor but industrious immigrant. It is no wonder that the regional icon is John Wayne" (9). Finally, for an account of the Christian Identity theology that underlies many protest movements, see Michael Barkun, *Religion and the Racist Right: The Origins of the Christian Identity Movement*, rev. ed. (Chapel Hill: University of North Carolina Press, 1997).

4. For the definitive treatment of Montana history, see Michael P. Malone, Richard B. Roeder, and William L. Lang, *Montana: A History of Two Centuries*, rev. ed. (Seattle: University of Washington Press, 1991). To observe how Montana conforms to regional patterns of economic, political, and cultural change, see Michael P. Malone and Richard W. Etulain, *The American West: A Twentieth-Century History* (Lincoln: University of Nebraska Press, 1989). For a magisterial history of the entire region from first encounters between Europeans and natives down to the present day, see Richard White, *"It's Your Misfortune and None of My Own": A History of the American West* (Norman: University of Oklahoma Press, 1991).

5. I deploy the phrase *catastrophic tragedy* with apologies to Norman Maclean, who carefully distinguishes between "catastrophe" (pointless, patternless suffer-

ing) and "tragedy" (suffering with a *telos*, a purpose, a meaning). Most Montana writers in the tragic mode have not shared Maclean's faith in a higher purpose for the dire form. They have, instead, highlighted an almost inexplicable trauma. For Maclean's sustained reflections on tragedy, see *Young Men and Fire: A True Story of the Mann Gulch Fire* (Chicago: University of Chicago Press, 1992).

6. My reflections on tragedy and comedy are partly indebted to Northrop Frye's *Anatomy of Criticism: Four Essays* (Princeton, N.J.: Princeton University Press, 1957).

PART I. WORLDS TRANSFORMED: 1862–1940

1. For a brilliant fictional treatment of Butte's mining past, its labor radicalism, and its own catastrophic story, see Myron Brinig, *Wide Open Town* (1931; reprint, with an introduction by Earl Ganz, Helena: Montana Magazine and American & Geographic Publishing, 1993). For an account of Butte's resurgence as a paradigm of possibility in Montana, see William Kittredge, *Who Owns the West?* (San Francisco: Mercury House, 1996), 125–28.

2. William E. Farr, "Troubled Bundles, Troubled Blackfeet: The Travail of Cultural and Religious Renewal," *Montana: The Magazine of Western History* 43 (autumn 1993): 8.

CHAPTER I. VANISHING AMERICANS

1. E. C. Abbott ("Teddy Blue") and Helena Huntington Smith, *We Pointed Them North: Recollections of a Cowpuncher* (1939; reprint, Norman: University of Oklahoma Press, 1955), 145. All further references will be cited in the text.

2. Here I invoke the title and argument of Patricia Nelson Limerick's *The Legacy of Conquest: The Unbroken Past of the American West* (New York: Norton, 1987).

3. Luther S. Kelly, *"Yellowstone Kelly": The Memoirs of Luther S. Kelly*, ed. M. M. Quaife (1926; reprint, Lincoln: University of Nebraska Press, 1973), xi. All further references will be cited in the text.

4. As Michael Kimmel observes of this masculine code, "At the turn of the nineteenth century, American manhood was rooted in landownership (the Genteel Patriarch) or in the self-possession of the independent artisan, shopkeeper, or farmer (the Heroic Artisan). In the first few decades of the nineteenth century, though, the Industrial Revolution had a critical effect on those earlier definitions. American men began to link their sense of themselves as men to their position in the volatile marketplace, to their economic success—a far less stable yet far more exciting and potentially rewarding peg upon which to hang one's identity. The Self-Made Man of American mythology was born anxious and insecure, uncou-

pled from the more stable anchors of landownership or workplace autonomy. Now manhood had to be proved." Kimmel, *Manhood in America: A Cultural History* (New York: Free Press, 1996), 9.

5. For a helpful discussion of Bennett Stein's handling of Garcia's manuscript, see William W. Bevis, *Ten Tough Trips: Montana Writers and the West* (Seattle: University of Washington Press, 1990), 36–37.

6. Andrew Garcia, *Tough Trip through Paradise, 1878–1879,* ed. Bennett H. Stein (San Francisco: Comstock, 1967), 17. All further references will be cited in the text.

7. Rosemary Jackson, *Fantasy: The Literature of Subversion* (London: Methuen, 1981), 4.

8. Peter Nabokov, *Two Leggings: The Making of a Crow Warrior* (Lincoln: University of Nebraska Press, 1967), 103. All further references will be cited in the text.

9. Black Elk, *Black Elk Speaks: Being the Life of a Holy Man of the Oglala Sioux,* ed. John G. Neihardt (1932; reprint, with a preface by John G. Neihardt, New York: Washington Square, 1972), 2. All further references will be cited in the text.

10. Kenneth Lincoln, *Native American Renaissance* (Berkeley: University of California Press, 1983), 89 and 92.

11. Frank B. Linderman, *Pretty-shield: Medicine Woman of the Crows* (1932; reprint, Lincoln: University of Nebraska Press, 1972), 54–64, 183–95. All further references will be cited in the text.

12. Frank B. Linderman, *Plenty-coups: Chief of the Crows* (1930; reprint, Lincoln: University of Nebraska Press, 1962), 265. All further references will be cited in the text.

13. For an intelligent overview of McWhorter's collaboration with Mourning Dove, see Susan K. Bernadin, "Mixed Messages: Authority and Authorship in Mourning Dove's *Cogewea, The Half-Blood: A Depiction of the Great Montana Cattle Range,*" *American Literature* 67 (1995): 487–509.

14. For clear evidence that Mourning Dove consciously critiqued popular fictions about the West, see Peter G. Beidler, "Literary Criticism in *Cogewea*: Mourning Dove's Protagonist Reads *The Brand,*" *American Indian Culture and Research Journal* 19, no. 2 (1995): 45–65. Beidler concludes that "the object of Mourning Dove's literary criticism is to encourage readers of all cultures to read more closely both their own fiction and that of other cultures, and to appreciate more fully the relevance of narrative to their own lives" (62).

15. Mourning Dove, *Cogewea, The Half-Blood: A Depiction of the Great Montana Cattle Range* (1927; reprint, with an introduction by Dexter Fisher, Lincoln: University of Nebraska Press, 1981), 142.

16. Louis Owens, *Other Destinies: Understanding the American Indian Novel* (Norman: University of Oklahoma Press, 1992), 48.

17. Mourning Dove, *Mourning Dove: A Salishan Autobiography*, ed. Jay Miller (Lincoln: University of Nebraska Press, 1990), 3.

18. Owens, *Other Destinies*, 48.

CHAPTER 2. DON'T FENCE ME IN

1. Jim Robbins, *Last Refuge: The Environmental Showdown in Yellowstone and the American West* (New York: William Morrow, 1993), 92.

2. Ivan Doig interview, in *Talking Up a Storm: Voices of the New West*, ed. Gregory L. Morris (Lincoln: University of Nebraska Press, 1994), 69.

3. Richard Maxwell Brown, "Violence," in *The Oxford History of the American West*, ed. Clyde A. Milner II, Carol A. O'Connor, and Martha A. Sandweiss (New York: Oxford University Press, 1994), 402.

4. Ibid., 393. Although skeptical about the interpretive value of these categories, Richard White pointedly observes that many westerners have adopted the roles defined by Brown: "The national media does not so much provide news or analysis as a series of representations that organize current events into conventional categories. For politics in the West the categories are: populism or Populism, individualism, frontier, pioneers, vigilantism, and the homestead. To say that these representations simply mask what is going on is to misunderstand them. They are like the Lone Ranger's mask: they are worn quite willingly by some of the maskees; they are *part* of their persona." White, "Current Weirdness in the West," 6.

5. Brown, "Violence," 394.

6. Julia Watson, "Engendering Montana Lives: Women's Autobiographical Writing," in *Writing Montana: Literature under the Big Sky*, ed. Rick Newby and Suzanne Hunger (Helena: Montana Center for the Book, 1996), 122–23.

7. Nannie Alderson, *A Bride Goes West*, with Helena Huntington Smith (1942; reprint, Lincoln: University of Nebraska Press, 1969), 55. All further references will be cited in the text.

8. Mary Clearman Blew, *All But the Waltz: A Memoir of Five Generations in the Life of a Montana Family* (New York: Penguin, 1991), 187.

9. Gwendolen Haste, "The Ranch in the Coulee," in *The Last Best Place: A Montana Anthology*, ed. William Kittredge and Annick Smith (Helena: Montana Historical Society Press, 1988), 695. As a final instance of this trauma for homesteading women, consider the fate of Old Jules's second wife in that most detailed and daunting of all settlement narratives: "For Henriette, taken to the asylum at Norfolk, and for many others, [the rain] came too late." Mari Sandoz, *Old Jules* (1935; reprint, with an afterword by Helen Winter Stauffer, Lincoln: University of Nebraska Press, 1985), 215.

10. B. M. Bower, *Lonesome Land* (1912; reprint, with an introduction by Pam

Houston, Lincoln: University of Nebraska Press, 1997), 64–65. All further references will be cited in the text.

11. Joan Acocella, "Cather and the Academy," *New Yorker,* November 27, 1995: 59.

CHAPTER 3. A HANDFUL OF DUST

1. Malone, Roeder, and Lang, *Montana: A History of Two Centuries,* 283.

2. For an excellent overview of the Poppers' buffalo commons concept and its reception in the West, see Anne Matthews, *Where the Buffalo Roam* (New York: Grove Weidenfeld, 1992).

3. For a strangely comical account of homesteading failure, see D'Arcy McNickle's short story "The Hawk Is Hungry" in *The Hawk Is Hungry and Other Stories,* ed. Birgit Hans (Tucson: University of Arizona Press, 1992), 55–64. McNickle tells of two New England sisters who transplant themselves in the ungenerous soil of the agrarian West. The result is harsh disappointment, blended with a stubborn refusal to return to their Connecticut roots. In this way, "The Hawk Is Hungry" constitutes one of the most devastating critiques of the agrarian myth handed down from Montana writers. See also Dan Cushman's *Plenty of Room and Air* (Great Falls, Mont.: Stay Away, Joe Publishers, 1975) for an often comical account of the homestead boom on the High Line. Cushman is especially telling on the paranoid fantasies surrounding Catholics, Wobblies, and Germans in the rural Montana of the 1910s.

4. Pearl Price Robertson, "Homestead Days in Montana" (1933), reprinted in *Last Best Place,* ed. Kittredge and Smith, 537–38. All further references will be cited in the text.

5. Percy Wollaston, *Homesteading* (New York: Lyons Press, 1997), 48. All further references will be cited in the text.

6. Relying on first-person accounts by homesteading women, Laurie K. Mercier has evoked their sense of pleasure, even joy: "Despite a life of hard work, few of the women interviewed expressed bitterness about their past, insisting that agricultural life had advantages. . . . They remembered fondly the more pleasant aspects of rural life: picnics, fishing and berry-picking trips, visits with neighbors, dances, and Home Demonstration, community club, farm organization and church meetings." Mercier, "Women's Role in Montana Agriculture: 'You Had to Make Every Minute Count,'" in *The Montana Heritage: An Anthology of Historical Essays,* ed. Robert R. Swartout Jr. and Harry W. Fritz (Helena: Montana Historical Society Press, 1992), 147.

7. Richard Roeder, "Country, Town, and Reservation," in *Last Best Place,* ed. Kittredge and Smith, 522.

8. Malone, Roeder, and Lang, *Montana: A History of Two Centuries,* 267.

9. Dyer, *Harvest of Rage*, 143.

10. Rex C. Myers, "Homestead on the Range: The Emergence of Community in Eastern Montana, 1900–1925," *Great Plains Quarterly* 10 (fall 1990): 218.

11. Dale Eunson, *Up on the Rim* (New York: Farrar, Straus, and Giroux, 1970), Foreword.

PART II. THE TRAGIC SENSIBILITY: 1940–PRESENT

1. For an excellent analysis of New Deal programs in the West, see Malone and Etulain, *American West*, 94–107.

2. Thomas McGuane, *Nobody's Angel* (New York: Random House, 1981), 48. All further references will be cited in the text.

3. Dan Cushman, *Stay Away, Joe* (1953; reprint, Great Falls, Mont.: Stay Away, Joe Publishers, n.d.), 218.

CHAPTER 4. A TALE OF TWO NOVELISTS

1. All biographical information on McNickle is drawn from Dorothy R. Parker's excellent *Singing an Indian Song: A Biography of D'Arcy McNickle* (Lincoln: University of Nebraska Press, 1992).

2. D'Arcy McNickle, *Wind from an Enemy Sky* (Albuquerque: University of New Mexico Press, 1978), 256. All further references will be cited in the text.

3. D'Arcy McNickle, *The Surrounded* (1936; reprint, with an afterword by Lawrence W. Towner, Albuquerque: University of New Mexico Press, 1978), 108. All further references will be cited in the text.

4. Owens has observed, "Like other products of American naturalism, McNickle's Indians are caught in the grip of forces they can neither comprehend nor escape. And those forces—the operatives of the white world surrounding the Salish people—fail to understand their roles in the historic tragedy. The destruction for Archilde's people moves toward its conclusion amidst misunderstanding, mistrust, fear, and accident, and Archilde, caught in the middle, is destroyed." Louis Owens, "The 'Map of the Mind': D'Arcy McNickle and the American Indian Novel," *Western American Literature* 19 (1985): 279.

5. Owens, *Other Destinies*, 89. Jay Hansford C. Vest has highlighted Antoine's role as a survivor and future "hero": "just as Coyote transcends death in a new day's adventure, Bull's teachings and the Little Elk traditions transcend his death through Antoine's cultural empowerment. . . . The youth in this context has the revivifying role of the Fox and it is the tradition (Coyote) which lives on; long may it be so." Vest, "Feather Boy's Promise: Sacred Geography and Environmental Ethics in D'Arcy McNickle's *Wind from an Enemy Sky*," *American Indian Quarterly* 17 (winter 1993): 61.

6. Owens, *Other Destinies*, 89.

7. See William W. Bevis, "McNickle: Homing In," chap. 6 in Bevis, *Ten Tough Trips*, 92–116.

8. John Lloyd Purdy asserts about the conclusion of the novel, "Ironically, [Archilde] is, in a way, matching the movements of his hands and heart to those of his people, who have long been the prisoners of the newcomers yet have maintained their own freedom of character. Although shackled and with his bodily movements restricted, Archilde is still freer than he was in Portland under the restrictions and constrictions of his host society." Purdy, *Word Ways: The Novels of D'Arcy McNickle* (Tucson: University of Arizona Press, 1990), 77.

9. Parker, *Singing an Indian Song*, 54.

10. Ibid., 51–52.

11. Ibid., 47.

12. Elliott West, "Stories: A Narrative History of the West," *Montana: The Magazine of Western History* 45 (summer 1995): 76. See also Robert G. Athearn, *The Mythic West in Twentieth-Century America* (Lawrence: University Press of Kansas, 1986), esp. chap. 8, "The Fictional West," 160–89.

13. Quoted in Purdy, *Word Ways*, 80–81.

14. Thomas W. Ford, "A. B. Guthrie's *Fair Land, Fair Land*: A Requiem," *Western American Literature* 23 (1988): 18.

15. A. B. Guthrie Jr., *The Blue Hen's Chick* (New York: McGraw-Hill, 1965), 200.

16. Ibid., 52.

17. Mary Clearman Blew, "Dreamers of Horses," in *Stories from an Open Country: Essays on the Yellowstone River Valley*, ed. William L. Lang (Billings: Western Heritage Center, 1995), 85–86.

18. Guthrie, *Blue Hen's Chick*, 186.

19. A. B. Guthrie Jr., *The Big Sky* (New York: Bantam, 1952), 142. All further references will be cited in the text.

20. See William W. Bevis, "Guthrie's Big Sky," chap. 1 in *Ten Tough Trips*, 3–19. For a helpful overview of the mythology of Edenic wilderness and the pitfalls of that ideology, see William Cronon, "The Trouble with Wilderness; or, Getting Back to the Wrong Nature," in *Uncommon Ground: Toward Reinventing Nature*, ed. William Cronon (New York: Norton, 1995), 69–90.

21. Annette Kolodny, *The Lay of the Land: Metaphor as Experience and History in American Life and Letters* (Chapel Hill: University of North Carolina Press, 1975).

22. Fred Erisman, "Coming of Age in Montana: The Legacy of A. B. Guthrie Jr.," *Montana: The Magazine of Western History* 43 (summer 1993): 72.

23. Thomas W. Ford, *A. B. Guthrie Jr.* (Boston: Twayne, 1981), 22.

CHAPTER 5. MOONS FOR THE MISBEGOTTEN

1. Richard Hugo, "Writing Off the Subject," in *The Triggering Town: Lectures and Essays on Poetry and Writing* (New York: Norton, 1979), 6.

2. Richard Hugo, *The Real West Marginal Way: A Poet's Autobiography* (New York: Norton, 1986), 194.

3. Bevis, *Ten Tough Trips*, 146.

4. Richard Hugo, *Making Certain It Goes On: The Collected Poems of Richard Hugo* (New York: Norton, 1984), 319. All further references will be cited in the text.

5. In an eloquent testimonial to Hugo's compassion, Michael Allen has asserted, "To Hugo, the American dream is not the unlimited possibilities of expansion but the ache of need. His landscape, vast and rugged as it still is, is a place where a man's possibilities are limited by that ruggedness and its associated weather and winds that beat against human enterprise and make . . . connections between people that much more important." Allen, "'Only the Eternal Nothing of Space': Richard Hugo's West," *Western American Literature* 15 (spring 1980): 26.

6. Wallace McRae, "Applied Genesis," in *Cowboy Curmudgeon and Other Poems* (Salt Lake City: Peregrine Smith Books, 1992), 81.

7. Paul Zarzyski, "Silos," in *Last Best Place*, ed. Kittredge and Smith, 1142.

8. Sandra Alcosser, "Fox Fire," ibid., 1068.

9. Jim Harrison, *Legends of the Fall* (New York: Delta/Seymour Lawrence, 1978), 209. All further references will be cited in the text.

10. Richard Ford, "Sweethearts," in *Rock Springs and Other Stories* (New York: Vintage, 1988), 56. All further references will be cited in the text.

11. Richard Ford, "Good Raymond," *New Yorker*, October 5, 1998: 75.

12. Hugo, *Real West Marginal Way*, 110.

13. Mary Clearman Blew interview, in *Talking Up a Storm*, ed. Morris, 29.

14. James Welch, *Winter in the Blood* (1974; reprint, New York: Penguin, 1986), 2.

CHAPTER 6. JEREMIADS

1. To take but one example of this concern, see Wilbur Wood, "The First Next Place: Conversations about *The Last Best Place*," in *Writing Montana*, ed. Newby and Hunger, 204. In fairness to the editors of the anthology, they do include an excerpt from *Montana: High, Wide, and Handsome*.

2. For an excellent, concise account of Howard's work with the Montana Study, see Richard Roeder, "The Genesis of *Montana Margins*," in *Writing Montana*, ed. Newby and Hunger, 220–28. In "Joseph Kinsey Howard and His Vision of the West," *Montana: The Magazine of Western History* 30 (winter 1980), Roeder concludes about Howard's overall career: "Much of Howard's writing is a litany of

social failure, of how greed and stupidity made riches for a few on the frontier but left no real legacy for those who settled permanently in the West. But his writings also embody his vision of possible future greatness, a hope that we could learn from the past and not repeat mistakes" (8).

3. Harry W. Fritz completed a follow-up poll in 2001. In this more recent survey, Howard's text came in second to Ivan Doig's *This House of Sky,* while Toole's history landed in the seventh slot. Fritz presented these results at the Montana History Conference in Helena on October 27, 2001. He will provide a fuller treatment of the poll in a forthcoming issue of *Montana: The Magazine of Western History.*

4. See Sacvan Bercovitch, *The American Jeremiad* (Madison: University of Wisconsin Press, 1978), for the definitive scholarly account of this tradition.

5. Joseph Kinsey Howard, *Montana: High, Wide, and Handsome* (1943; reprint, with a preface by A. B. Guthrie Jr., Lincoln: University of Nebraska Press, 1983), 138. All further references will be cited in the text.

6. This site has since disappeared from the Web (although "Billings or Beijing?" can still be found online by using a search engine). It was but one of many websites dedicated to explaining and defending the Freemen's position. In fact, the Internet is the true home of militant theorizing and proselytizing. To indulge my own paranoid metaphor briefly, the Internet comprises a shadow reality that offers instant access to anyone with a computer and a modem.

7. Judith Heffernan, "Our Daily Bread: The Business of Rural America," *Sojourners* (September/October 1995): 17–18. This magazine is self-described as a progressive Christian publication.

8. Roeder, "Genesis," 224–25.

9. Joseph Kinsey Howard, "Introduction," in *Montana Margins: A State Anthology,* ed. Howard (New Haven: Yale University Press, 1946), ix.

10. Merrill G. Burlingame, "K. Ross Toole: A Memorial," *Montana: The Magazine of Western History* 31 (October 1981): 58.

11. K. Ross Toole, *Montana: An Uncommon Land* (Norman: University of Oklahoma Press, 1959), 5. All further references will be cited in the text.

12. In *Montana: A History of Two Centuries,* Malone, Roeder, and Lang assert: "The Confederate sympathizers never came near gaining a majority of the Montana vote, but they sometimes raised enough hell to give observers that impression" (98).

13. In his historical text, McNickle does observe, "The Flathead Tribe of Montana borrowed $65,000 to finance individual farm plans. The amount has been repaid in full and the tribe is now operating a credit program out of income derived from the use of tribally owned land and other resources, and in addition has invested heavily in other land and livestock." D'Arcy McNickle, *They Came Here First: The Epic of the American Indian* (Philadelphia: Lippincott, 1949), 297.

PART III. PROVISIONAL HOPES: 1940–PRESENT

1. Wallace Stegner, *Where the Bluebird Sings to the Lemonade Springs: Living and Writing in the West* (New York: Penguin, 1992), xv.

2. Bill Borneman, "A Philosophy of the Open Air," in *Writing Montana*, ed. Newby and Hunger, 119.

3. See Albert Borgmann, *Technology and the Character of Contemporary Life: A Philosophical Inquiry* (Chicago: University of Chicago Press, 1984) and *Crossing the Postmodern Divide* (Chicago: University of Chicago Press, 1993); Daniel Kemmis, *Community and the Politics of Place* (Norman: University of Oklahoma Press, 1990) and *The Good City and the Good Life: Renewing the American Community* (Boston: Houghton Mifflin, 1995); and David Strong, *Crazy Mountains: Learning from Wilderness to Weigh Technology* (Albany: State University of New York Press, 1995).

4. Kemmis, *Community*, 79.

5. Stegner, *Where the Bluebird Sings*, 199.

6. William G. Robbins, "Creating a 'New West': Big Money Returns to the Hinterland," *Montana: The Magazine of Western History* 46 (summer 1996): 72.

7. Kemmis, *Community*, 103.

8. James Welch, *Fools Crow* (New York: Penguin, 1986), 390. All further references will be cited in the text.

CHAPTER 7. THE RETURN OF THE NATIVE

1. James Welch, *Killing Custer: The Battle of the Little Bighorn and the Fate of the Plains Indians* (New York: Norton, 1994), 286. All further references will be cited in the text. For an excellent analysis of this text, and more specifically Welch's involvement in the narrative, see O. Alan Weltzien, "George Custer, Norman Maclean, and James Welch: Personal History and the Redemption of Defeat," *Arizona Quarterly* 52 (winter 1996): 115–33. Weltzien is especially compelling on Welch's strategies for connecting collective history with personal history, his people's past with his own present. By these means, Welch authenticates his role as a remembrancer or memorialist for the Blackfeet.

2. In a useful overview of Welch's fictions and criticism about those texts, Ron McFarland asserts that the novelist intended promising conclusions to his narratives. Yet "[i]nto each of his endings Welch injects a molecule of uncertainty" (326). See McFarland, "'The End' in James Welch's Novels," *American Indian Quarterly* 17 (summer 1993): 319–27.

3. Owens, *Other Destinies*, 165–66.

4. William Bevis, "Wylie Tales: An Interview with James Welch," *Weber Studies* 12 (fall 1995): 25.

5. Dorothy M. Johnson, *Buffalo Woman* (New York: Dodd, Meade, 1977), 30. All further references will be cited in the text.

6. The definition of an image is Ezra Pound's, as quoted in William Pratt, "Introduction," in *The Imagist Poem: Modern Poetry in Miniature*, ed. Pratt (New York: E. P. Dutton, 1963), 18.

7. James Welch, "Long Time Ago," in *Last Best Place*, ed. Kittredge and Smith, 8.

8. Cushman, *Stay Away, Joe*, 151.

9. Welch, *Winter in the Blood*, 98. All further references will be cited in the text.

CHAPTER 8. EVEN COWGIRLS GET OVER THE BLUES

1. Cyra McFadden, *Rain or Shine* (New York: Vintage, 1987), 3. All further references will be cited in the text.

2. Hughie Call, *Golden Fleece* (Boston: Houghton Mifflin, 1942), 23.

3. Watson, "Engendering Montana Lives," 122–23. For Watson's astute commentaries on *All But the Waltz* and *Rain or Shine*, see ibid., 146–53. Katherine G. Morrissey makes an important related argument when she asserts, "In popular culture as well as scholarship the American West is most often associated with masculine images. . . . Imbued with these masculine images, the ideology of the West celebrates a particular, and gendered, form of American identity." Morrissey, "Engendering the West," in *Under an Open Sky: Rethinking America's Western Past*, ed. William Cronon, George Miles, and Jay Gitlin (New York: Norton, 1992), 133.

4. I could of course cite many other examples of compelling writing by contemporary western women, including Marilynne Robinson's *Housekeeping*, Louise Erdrich's *Love Medicine*, and Kathleen Norris's *Dakota*. Since these important narratives are set outside Montana's borders, I have chosen not to consider them here.

5. Mildred Walker, *Winter Wheat* (1944; reprint, with an introduction by James Welch, Lincoln: University of Nebraska Press, 1992), 3. All further references will be cited in the text.

6. Maile Meloy, "Landscape with Figures: The Georgic in Montana Literature," in *Writing Montana*, ed. Newby and Hunger, 250.

7. Blew interview, 26.

8. Blew, *All But the Waltz*, 17, italics in the original. All further references will be cited in the text.

9. Deirdre McNamer, *Rima in the Weeds* (New York: HarperPerennial, 1991), 39–40. All further references will be cited in the text.

CHAPTER 9. NEW HOMES ON THE RANGE

1. William Kittredge, *Owning It All: Essays* (St. Paul: Graywolf, 1987), 62–63.

2. William Kittredge, *Hole in the Sky: A Memoir* (New York: Vintage, 1992), 172. All further references will be cited in the text.

3. For a telling discussion of Doig's masterpiece, see William W. Bevis, "Doig's House of Sky," chap. 10 in Bevis, *Ten Tough Trips*, 161–70. I am especially taken with Bevis's insight that "the lone rogue male of nineteenth-century myth is finally gone. Everywhere is family, tied up in a web of style that mirrors the intricacy and mystery of relationship. And relations lie at the heart of this book" (165).

4. Ivan Doig, *Dancing at the Rascal Fair* (New York: Harper and Row, 1987), 384. All further references will be cited in the text.

5. Ivan Doig, "You Can't *Not* Go Home Again," *Montana: The Magazine of Western History* 35 (winter 1985): 12.

6. Ivan Doig, *English Creek* (New York: Penguin, 1984), 130. All further references will be cited in the text.

7. Ivan Doig, *Ride with Me, Mariah Montana* (New York: Penguin, 1990), 317.

8. White, "Current Weirdness in the West," 7. But for an important counterview, see Lawrence F. Small, ed., *Religion in Montana: Pathways to the Present*, 2 vols. (Billings: Rocky Mountain College, 1993–95). Small and his contributors argue that religious conviction has been at the core of Montana history and culture. Michael D. Quinn also asserts that a "century of urbanization and secularization has not ended efforts to maintain some form of religious communalism in the West. Why did the ideal of a 'city on a hill' die in the East with the Puritans and transcendentalists, whereas the ideal of a 'commune in a valley' lives on in the West?" Quinn, "Religion in the American West," in *Under an Open Sky*, ed. Cronon, Miles, and Gitlin, 166.

Bibliography

Abbott, E. C. ("Teddy Blue"), and Helena Huntington Smith. *We Pointed Them North: Recollections of a Cowpuncher.* 1939. Reprint, Norman: University of Oklahoma Press, 1955.

Acocella, Joan. "Cather and the Academy." *New Yorker,* November 27, 1995: 56–71.

Alcosser, Sandra. "Fox Fire." In *The Last Best Place: A Montana Anthology.* Ed. William Kittredge and Annick Smith, 1067–68. Helena: Montana Historical Society Press, 1988.

Alderson, Nannie, with Helena Huntington Smith. *A Bride Goes West.* 1942. Reprint, Lincoln: University of Nebraska Press, 1969.

Allen, Michael. "'Only the Eternal Nothing of Space': Richard Hugo's West." *Western American Literature* 15 (spring 1980): 25–35.

Athearn, Robert G. *The Mythic West in Twentieth-Century America.* Lawrence: University Press of Kansas, 1986.

Barkun, Michael. *Religion and the Racist Right: The Origins of the Christian Identity Movement.* Rev. ed. Chapel Hill: University of North Carolina Press, 1997.

Beidler, Peter G. "Literary Criticism in *Cogewea:* Mourning Dove's Protagonist Reads *The Brand.*" *American Indian Culture and Research Journal* 19, no. 2 (1995): 45–65.

Bercovitch, Sacvan. *The American Jeremiad.* Madison: University of Wisconsin Press, 1978.

Bernadin, Susan K. "Mixed Messages: Authority and Authorship in Mourning Dove's *Cogewea, the Half-Blood: A Depiction of the Great Montana Cattle Range.*" *American Literature* 67 (1995): 487–509.

Bevis, William W. *Ten Tough Trips: Montana Writers and the American West.* Seattle: University of Washington Press, 1990.

———. "Wylie Tales: An Interview with James Welch." *Weber Studies* 12 (fall 1995): 15–31.

Black Elk. *Black Elk Speaks: Being the Life of a Holy Man of the Oglala Sioux.* Ed. John G. Neihardt. 1932. Reprint, with a preface by John G. Neihardt, New York: Washington Square, 1972.

Blew, Mary Clearman. *All But the Waltz: A Memoir of Five Generations in the Life of a Montana Family.* New York: Penguin, 1991.

———. *Balsamroot: A Memoir.* New York: Viking, 1994.

———. "Dreamers of Horses." In *Stories from an Open Country: Essays on the Yellowstone River Valley.* Ed. William L. Lang, 79–91. Billings: Western Heritage Center, 1995.

———. Interview. In *Talking Up a Storm: Voices of the New West.* Ed. Gregory L. Morris, 24–32. Lincoln: University of Nebraska Press, 1994.

Bogart, Barbara Allen. "Knowing Our Place: Memory, History, and Story in the Yellowstone Valley." In *Stories from an Open Country: Essays on the Yellowstone River Valley.* Ed. William L. Lang, 65–78. Billings: Western Heritage Center, 1995.

Borgmann, Albert. *Crossing the Postmodern Divide.* Chicago: University of Chicago Press, 1993.

———. *Technology and the Character of Contemporary Life: A Philosophical Inquiry.* Chicago: University of Chicago Press, 1984.

Borneman, Bill. "A Philosophy of the Open Air." In *Writing Montana: Literature under the Big Sky.* Ed. Rick Newby and Suzanne Hunger, 108–20. Helena: Montana Center for the Book, 1996.

Bower, B. M. *Lonesome Land.* 1912. Reprint, with an introduction by Pam Houston, Lincoln: University of Nebraska Press, 1997.

Brinig, Myron. *Wide Open Town.* 1931. Reprint, with an introduction by Earl Ganz, Helena: Montana Magazine and American & Geographic Publishing, 1993.

Brown, Richard Maxwell. "Violence." Chapter 11 in *The Oxford History of the American West.* Ed. Clyde A. Milner II, Carol A. O'Connor, and Martha A. Sandweiss. New York: Oxford University Press, 1994.

Burlingame, Merrill G. "K. Ross Toole: A Memorial." *Montana: The Magazine of Western History* 31, 4 (October 1981): 57, 58–59.

Call, Hughie. *Golden Fleece.* Boston: Houghton Mifflin, 1942.

Cronon, William. "The Trouble with Wilderness; or, Getting Back to the Wrong Nature." In *Uncommon Ground: Toward Reinventing Nature.* Ed. William Cronon, 69–90. New York: Norton, 1995.

Cronon, William, George Miles, and Jay Gitlin, eds. *Under an Open Sky: Rethinking America's Western Past.* New York: Norton, 1992.

Cushman, Dan. *Plenty of Room and Air.* Great Falls, Mont.: Stay Away, Joe Publishers, 1975.

———. *Stay Away, Joe.* 1953. Reprint, Great Falls, Mont.: Stay Away, Joe Publishers, n.d.

Doig, Ivan. *Dancing at the Rascal Fair.* New York: Harper and Row, 1987.

———. *English Creek.* New York: Penguin, 1984.

———. Interview. In *Talking Up a Storm: Voices of the New West.* Ed. Gregory L. Morris, 66–80. Lincoln: University of Nebraska Press, 1994.

———. *Ride with Me, Mariah Montana.* New York: Penguin, 1990.

———. "You Can't *Not* Go Home Again." *Montana: The Magazine of Western History* 35 (winter 1985): 2–15.

Dyer, Joel. *Harvest of Rage: Why Oklahoma City Is Only the Beginning.* Boulder: Westview, 1997.

Erisman, Fred. "Coming of Age in Montana: The Legacy of A. B. Guthrie Jr." *Montana: The Magazine of Western History* 43 (summer 1993): 69–74.

Eunson, Dale. *Up on the Rim.* New York: Farrar, Straus, Giroux, 1970.

Farr, William E. "Troubled Bundles, Troubled Blackfeet: The Travail of Cultural and Religious Renewal." *Montana: The Magazine of Western History* 43 (autumn 1993): 2–17.

Ford, Richard. "Good Raymond." *New Yorker,* October 5, 1998: 70–79.

———. *Rock Springs and Other Stories.* New York: Vintage, 1988.

Ford, Thomas W. "A. B. Guthrie's *Fair Land, Fair Land*: A Requiem." *Western American Literature* 23 (1988): 17–30.

———. *A. B. Guthrie Jr.* Boston: Twayne, 1981.

Fritz, Harry W. "The Five Best Books about Montana." Montana History Conference, Helena, October 27, 2001.

Fromm, Pete. *Indian Creek Chronicles.* New York: St. Martin's Press, 1993.

Frye, Northrop. *Anatomy of Criticism: Four Essays.* Princeton: Princeton University Press, 1957.

Garcia, Andrew. *Tough Trip through Paradise, 1878–1879.* Ed. Bennett H. Stein. San Francisco: Comstock, 1967.

Guthrie, A. B., Jr. *The Big Sky.* New York: Bantam, 1952.

———. *The Blue Hen's Chick.* New York: McGraw-Hill, 1965.

Harrison, Jim. *Legends of the Fall.* New York: Delta/Seymour Lawrence, 1978.

Hart, Sue. "'Eyes to See': The Writers of Eastern Montana." In *Writing Montana: Literature under the Big Sky.* Ed. Rick Newby and Suzanne Hunger, 38–60. Helena: Montana Center for the Book, 1996.

Haste, Gwendolen. "The Ranch in the Coulee." In *The Last Best Place: A Montana Anthology.* Ed. William Kittredge and Annick Smith, 695. Helena: Montana Historical Society Press, 1988.

Heffernan, Judith. "Our Daily Bread: The Business of Rural America." *Sojourners* September/October 1995: 16–19.

Howard, Joseph Kinsey. "Introduction." In *Montana Margins: A State Anthology.* Ed. Joseph Kinsey Howard, vii–xiii. New Haven: Yale University Press, 1946.

———. *Montana: High, Wide, and Handsome.* 1943. Reprint, with a preface by A. B. Guthrie Jr., Lincoln: University of Nebraska Press, 1983.

Hugo, Richard. *Making Certain It Goes On: The Collected Poems of Richard Hugo.* New York: Norton, 1984.

———. *The Real West Marginal Way: A Poet's Autobiography.* New York: Norton, 1986.

———. *The Triggering Town: Lectures and Essays on Poetry and Writing.* New York: Norton, 1979.

Jackson, Rosemary. *Fantasy: The Literature of Subversion.* London: Methuen, 1981.

Johnson, Dorothy M. *Buffalo Woman.* New York: Dodd, Meade, 1977.

Kelly, Luther S. *"Yellowstone Kelly": The Memoirs of Luther S. Kelly.* Ed. M. M. Quaife. 1926. Reprint, Lincoln: University of Nebraska Press, 1973.

Kemmis, Daniel. *Community and the Politics of Place.* Norman: University of Oklahoma Press, 1990.

———. *The Good City and the Good Life: Renewing the American Community.* Boston: Houghton Mifflin, 1995.

Kerouac, Jack. "On the Road Again." *New Yorker,* June 22 and 29, 1998: 46–59.

Kimmel, Michael. *Manhood in America: A Cultural History.* New York: Free Press, 1996.

Kittredge, William. *Hole in the Sky: A Memoir.* New York: Vintage, 1992.

———. "New to the Country." In *The Montana Heritage: An Anthology of Historical Essays.* Ed. Robert R. Swartout Jr. and Harry W. Fritz, 1–12. Helena: Montana Historical Society Press, 1992.

———. *Owning It All: Essays.* St. Paul: Graywolf, 1987.

———. *Who Owns the West?* San Francisco: Mercury House, 1996.

Kittredge, William, and Annick Smith, eds. *The Last Best Place: A Montana Anthology.* Helena: Montana State Historical Society, 1988.

Kolodny, Annette. *The Lay of the Land: Metaphor as Experience and History in American Life and Letters.* Chapel Hill: University of North Carolina Press, 1975.

Limerick, Patricia Nelson. *The Legacy of Conquest: The Unbroken Past of the American West.* New York: Norton, 1987.

Lincoln, Kenneth. *Native American Renaissance.* Berkeley: University of California Press, 1983.

Linderman, Frank B. *Plenty-coups: Chief of the Crows.* 1930. Reprint, Lincoln: University of Nebraska Press, 1962.

———. *Pretty-shield: Medicine Woman of the Crows.* 1932. Reprint, Lincoln: University of Nebraska Press, 1972.

McCormick, John, and Bill Turque. "America's Outback." *Newsweek,* October 9, 1989: 76–80.

McFadden, Cyra. *Rain or Shine.* New York: Vintage, 1987.

McFarland, Ron. "'The End' in James Welch's Novels." *American Indian Quarterly* 17 (summer 1993): 319–27.

McGuane, Thomas. *Nobody's Angel.* New York: Random House, 1981.

Maclean, Norman. *A River Runs Through It and Other Stories.* Chicago: University of Chicago Press, 1976.

———. *Young Men and Fire: A True Story of the Mann Gulch Fire.* Chicago: University of Chicago Press, 1992.

McNamer, Deirdre. *Rima in the Weeds.* New York: HarperPerennial, 1991.

McNickle, D'Arcy. "The Hawk Is Hungry." In *The Hawk Is Hungry and Other Stories.* Ed. Birgit Hans, 55–64. Tucson: University of Arizona Press, 1995.

———. *The Surrounded.* 1936. Reprint, with an afterword by Lawrence W. Towner, Albuquerque: University of New Mexico Press, 1978.

———. *They Came Here First: The Epic of the American Indian*. Philadelphia: Lippincott, 1949.

———. *Wind from an Enemy Sky*. Albuquerque: University of New Mexico Press, 1978.

McRae, Wallace. *Cowboy Curmudgeon and Other Poems*. Salt Lake City: Peregrine Smith Books, 1992.

Malone, Michael P., and Richard W. Etulain. *The American West: A Twentieth-Century History*. Lincoln: University of Nebraska Press, 1989.

Malone, Michael P., Richard B. Roeder, and William L. Lang. *Montana: A History of Two Centuries*. Rev. ed. Seattle: University of Washington Press, 1991.

Matthews, Anne. *Where the Buffalo Roam*. New York: Grove Weidenfeld, 1992.

Meloy, Maile. "Landscape with Figures: The Georgic in Montana Literature." In *Writing Montana: Literature under the Big Sky*. Ed. Rick Newby and Suzanne Hunger, 249–72. Helena: Montana Center for the Book, 1996.

Mercier, Laurie K. "Women's Role in Montana Agriculture: 'You Had to Make Every Minute Count.'" In *The Montana Heritage: An Anthology of Historical Essays*. Ed. Robert R. Swartout Jr. and Harry W. Fritz, 131–47. Helena: Montana Historical Society Press, 1992.

Morris, Gregory L., ed. *Talking Up a Storm: Voices of the New West*. Lincoln: University of Nebraska Press, 1994.

Morrissey, Katherine G. "Engendering the West." In *Under an Open Sky: Rethinking America's Western Past*. Ed. William Cronon, George Miles, and Jay Gitlin, 132–44. New York: Norton, 1992.

Mourning Dove. *Cogewea, The Half-Blood: A Depiction of the Great Montana Cattle Range*. 1927. Reprint, with an introduction by Dexter Fisher, Lincoln: University of Nebraska Press, 1981.

———. *Mourning Dove: A Salishan Autobiography*. Ed. Jay Miller. Lincoln: University of Nebraska Press, 1990.

Myers, Rex C. "Homestead on the Range: The Emergence of Community in Eastern Montana, 1900–1925." *Great Plains Quarterly* 10 (fall 1990): 218–27.

Nabokov, Peter. *Two Leggings: The Making of a Crow Warrior*. Lincoln: University of Nebraska Press, 1967.

Newby, Rick, and Suzanne Hunger, eds. *Writing Montana: Literature under the Big Sky*. Helena: Montana Center for the Book, 1996.

Owens, Louis. "The 'Map of the Mind': D'Arcy McNickle and the American Indian Novel." *Western American Literature* 19 (1985): 275–83.

———. *Other Destinies: Understanding the American Indian Novel*. Norman: University of Oklahoma Press, 1992.

Parker, Dorothy R. *Singing an Indian Song: A Biography of D'Arcy McNickle*. Lincoln: University of Nebraska Press, 1992.

Pratt, William, ed. "Introduction." *The Imagist Poem: Modern Poetry in Miniature*. New York: E. P. Dutton, 1963. 11–39.

Purdy, John Lloyd. *Word Ways: The Novels of D'Arcy McNickle.* Tucson: University of Arizona Press, 1990.

Quinn, Michael D. "Religion in the American West." In *Under an Open Sky: Rethinking America's Western Past.* Ed. William Cronon, George Miles, and Jay Gitlin, 145–66. New York: Norton, 1992.

Raban, Jonathan. *Bad Land: An American Romance.* New York: Pantheon, 1996.

Robbins, Jim. *Last Refuge: The Environmental Showdown in Yellowstone and the American West.* New York: William Morrow, 1993.

Robbins, William G. "Creating a 'New West': Big Money Returns to the Hinterland." *Montana: The Magazine of Western History* 46 (summer 1996): 66–72.

Robertson, Pearl Price. "Homestead Days in Montana." 1933. Reprint in *The Last Best Place: A Montana Anthology.* Ed. William Kittredge and Annick Smith, 532–43. Helena: Montana Historical Society Press, 1988.

Roeder, Richard B. "Country, Town, and Reservation." In *The Last Best Place: A Montana Anthology.* Ed. William Kittredge and Annick Smith, 518–23. Helena: Montana Historical Society Press, 1988.

———. "The Genesis of *Montana Margins.*" In *Writing Montana: Literature under the Big Sky.* Ed. Rick Newby and Suzanne Hunger, 220–28. Helena: Montana Center for the Book, 1996.

———. "Joseph Kinsey Howard and His Vision of the West." *Montana: The Magazine of Western History* 30 (winter 1980): 2–11.

Sandoz, Mari. *Old Jules.* 1935. Reprint, with an afterword by Helen Winter Stauffer, Lincoln: University of Nebraska Press, 1985.

Small, Lawrence F., ed. *Religion in Montana: Pathways to the Present.* 2 vols. Billings: Rocky Mountain College, 1993–95.

Stegner, Wallace. *Where the Bluebird Sings to the Lemonade Springs: Living and Writing in the West.* New York: Penguin, 1992.

Stock, Catherine McNicol. *Rural Radicals: Righteous Rage in the American Grain.* Ithaca: Cornell University Press, 1996.

Strong, David. *Crazy Mountains: Learning from Wilderness to Weigh Technology.* Albany: State University of New York Press, 1995.

Toole, K. Ross. *Montana: An Uncommon Land.* Norman: University of Oklahoma Press, 1959.

Van Cleve, Spike. *40 Years' Gatherin's.* Kansas City, Mo.: Lowell, 1977.

Vest, Jay Hansford C. "Feather Boy's Promise: Sacred Geography and Environmental Ethics in D'Arcy McNickle's *Wind from an Enemy Sky.*" *American Indian Quarterly* 17 (winter 1993): 45–67.

Walker, Mildred. *Winter Wheat.* 1944. Reprint, with an introduction by James Welch, Lincoln: University of Nebraska Press, 1992.

Watson, Julia. "Engendering Montana Lives: Women's Autobiographical Writing." In *Writing Montana: Literature under the Big Sky.* Ed. Rick Newby and

Suzanne Hunger, 121–62. Helena: Montana Center for the Book, 1996.

Welch, James. *Fools Crow*. New York: Penguin, 1986.

———. *Killing Custer: The Battle of the Little Bighorn and the Fate of the Plains Indians*. New York: Norton, 1994.

———. "Long Time Ago." In *The Last Best Place: A Montana Anthology*. Ed. William Kittredge and Annick Smith, 2–8. Helena: Montana Historical Society Press, 1988.

———. *Winter in the Blood*. 1974. Reprint, New York: Penguin, 1986.

Weltzien, O. Alan. "George Custer, Norman Maclean, and James Welch: Personal History and the Redemption of Defeat." *Arizona Quarterly* 52 (winter 1996): 115–33.

West, Elliott. "Stories: A Narrative History of the West." *Montana: The Magazine of Western History* 45 (summer 1995): 64–76.

White, Richard. "The Current Weirdness in the West." *Western Historical Quarterly* 28 (spring 1997): 5–16.

———. *"It's Your Misfortune and None of My Own": A History of the American West*. Norman: University of Oklahoma Press, 1991.

Wollaston, Percy. *Homesteading*. New York: Lyons Press, 1997.

Wood, Wilbur. "The First Next Place: Conversations about *The Last Best Place*." In *Writing Montana: Literature under the Big Sky*. Ed. Rick Newby and Suzanne Hunger, 198–205. Helena: Montana Center for the Book, 1996.

Zarzyski, Paul. "Silos." In *The Last Best Place: A Montana Anthology*. Ed. William Kittredge and Annick Smith, 1142–43. Helena: Montana Historical Society Press, 1988.

Index